The Modern Family in Japan

JAPANESE SOCIETY SERIES
General Editor: Yoshio Sugimoto

Lives of Young Koreans in Japan
Yasunori Fukuoka

Globalization and Social Change in Contemporary Japan
J.S. Eades, Tom Gill and Harumi Befu

Coming Out in Japan: The Story of Satoru and Ryuta
Satoru Ito and Ryuta Yanase

Japan and Its Others:
Globalization, Difference and the Critique of Modernity
John Clammer

Hegemony of Homogeneity:
An Anthropological Analysis of Nihonjinron
Harumi Befu

Foreign Migrants in Contemporary Japan
Hiroshi Komai

A Social History of Science and Technology in
Contemporary Japan, Volume 1
Shigeru Nakayama

Farewell to Nippon: Japanese Lifestyle Migrants in Australia
Machiko Sato

The Peripheral Centre:
Essays on Japanese History and Civilization
Johann P. Arnason

A Genealogy of 'Japanese' Self-images
Eiji Oguma

Class Structure in Contemporary Japan
Kenji Hashimoto

An Ecological View of History
Tadao Umesao

Nationalism and Gender
Chizuko Ueno

Native Anthropology: The Japanese Challenge
to Western Academic Hegemony
Takami Kuwayama

Youth Deviance in Japan: Class Reproduction of Non-Conformity
Robert Stuart Yoder

Japanese Companies: Theories and Realities
Masami Nomura and Yoshihiko Kamii

From Salvation to Spirituality:
Popular Religious Movements in Modern Japan
Susumu Shimazono

The 'Big Bang' in Japanese Higher Education:
The 2004 Reforms and the Dynamics of Change
J.S. Eades, Roger Goodman and Yumiko Hada

Japanese Politics: An Introduction
Takashi Inoguchi

A Social History of Science and Technology in
Contemporary Japan, Volume 2
Shigeru Nakayama

Social Stratification and Inequality Series

Advanced Social Research Series

A Sociology of Happiness
Kenji Kosaka

Frontiers of Social Research: Japan and Beyond
Akira Furukawa

A Quest for Alternative Sociology
Kenji Kosaka and Masahiro Ogino

MODERNITY AND IDENTITY IN ASIA SERIES

Globalization, Culture and Inequality in Asia
Timothy S. Scrase, Todd Miles Joseph Holden and Scott Baum

Looking for Money:
Capitalism and Modernity in an Orang Asli Village
Alberto Gomes

Governance and Democracy in Asia
Takashi Inoguchi and Matthew Carlson

The Modern Family in Japan

Its Rise and Fall

by

Chizuko Ueno

Trans Pacific Press

Melbourne

First published in Japanese in 1994 by Iwanami Shoten as *Kindai kazoku no seiritsu to shūen.*
First published in 2008 by
Trans Pacific Press, PO Box 164, Balwyn North, Victoria 3104, Australia
Telephone: +61 (0)3 9859 1112 Fax: +61 (0)3 9859 4110
Email: tpp.mail@gmail.com
Web: http://www.transpacificpress.com

Copyright © Trans Pacific Press 2008

Designed and set by digital environs, Melbourne, Australia. www.digitalenvirons.com

Distributors

Australia and New Zealand
UNIREPS
University of New South Wales
Sydney, NSW 2052
Australia
Telephone: +61(0)2-9664-0999
Fax: +61(0)2-9664-5420
Email: info.press@unsw.edu.au
Web: http://www.unireps.com.au

USA and Canada
International Specialized Book
Services (ISBS)
920 NE 58th Avenue, Suite 300
Portland, Oregon 97213-3786
USA
Telephone: (800) 944-6190
Fax: (503) 280-8832
Email: orders@isbs.com
Web: http://www.isbs.com

Asia and the Pacific
Kinokuniya Company Ltd.

Head office:
3-7-10 Shimomeguro
Meguro-ku
Tokyo 153-8504
Japan
Telephone: +81(0)3-6910-0531
Fax: +81(0)3-6420-1362
Email: bkimp@kinokuniya.co.jp
Web: www.kinokuniya.co.jp

Asia-Pacific office:
Kinokuniya Book Stores of Singapore Pte., Ltd.
391B Orchard Road #13-06/07/08
Ngee Ann City Tower B
Singapore 238874
Telephone: +65 6276 5558
Fax: +65 6276 5570
Email: SSO@kinokuniya.co.jp

ISSN   1443–9670 (Japanese Society Series)

ISBN   978–1–876843–56–4 (Hardcover)
ISBN   978–1–876843–62–5 (Paperback)

Cover illustration: A pair of dolls displayed for the *hinamatsuri* festival held on 3 March, at which families with girl children pray for their well-being.

Contents

Figures

Tables

Foreword

Ayako Kano

Chizuko Ueno is Japan's foremost feminist scholar, and her name has become virtually synonymous with Japanese feminism as a form of intellectual martial arts. Her prominence can be glimpsed from the titles of books such as *Can Chizuko Ueno Save Women?*, *Who's Afraid of Chizuko Ueno?*, and *Learning How to Fight from Chizuko Ueno*.[1] Born in Toyama Prefecture and trained in sociology at Kyoto University, Ueno has traveled far and often, seemingly untouched by fear or fatigue. Venturing beyond her academic home base, she has reached out to the provinces of historians, marketing specialists, literary scholars, political scientists, architects, and experts in aging and care work. After teaching for ten years at Heian Women's Junior College and for four years at Kyoto Seika University, she was recruited in 1993 to join the faculty at the University of Tokyo, Japan's most prestigious institution of higher education. Over the past thirty-odd years, Ueno has published twenty-seven single-authored books, eighteen co-authored books, five edited books, sixty-four co-edited books, and at least one volume of *haiku* poetry. In order to introduce *The Modern Family in Japan* translated here, it may be useful to begin by sketching an outline of Ueno's academic trajectory.

Ueno's earliest published scholarship explored the intersection of sociology and structuralist anthropology; indeed, one of her first academic publications was a 1975 paper on the epistemological model of structuralism in Claude Lévi-Strauss.[2] But she soon became famous as a prolific writer who published two types of books: academic investigations of Japanese society, mainly from a Marxist feminist perspective,[3] and clever musings on topics ranging from sexy advertising to the history of underwear.[4] Playfully referencing the Japanese obsession with the blood-type theory of personality, Ueno has labeled the former her serious 'blood type A' books, and the latter her tongue-in-cheek 'blood type B' books, which together constitute her own rare 'blood type AB.'[5] These two aspects of her work have also invited comparison to a kind of bilingualism: Ueno has commanded attention as a fluent user of the languages of scholarship and of journalism, the vocabularies of men and of women, the styles of rigorous logic and of almost flippant rhetoric.[6] Wielding these conceptual and linguistic tools, Ueno had penned more than a dozen books in rapid succession before the 1994 publication of *Kindai kazoku no seiritsu to shūen*, the volume translated here as *The Modern Family in Japan*.

English-language readers may already be familiar with some of the central aspects of Ueno's work. Sandra Buckley's 1997 introduction and interview sets Ueno's early work in the context of the various strands of Japanese feminist debates in the 1980s and early 1990s.[7] Ueno's own somewhat condensed summary of Japanese feminist thought is translated in Buckley's volume as 'Are the Japanese feminine? Some problems of Japanese feminism in its cultural context.' Two more essays by Ueno are included in a volume on contemporary Japanese thought edited by Richard F. Calichman, with a cogent introduction by the editor.[8] *Nationalism and Gender*, Ueno's important monograph exploring the entanglement of women and gender in nationalism and militarism, was translated by Beverley Yamamoto and published in 2004 by Trans Pacific Press.[9] Together, these introductions and translations reflect Ueno's contributions to three areas of inquiry: feminist thought, modern Japanese history, and Japanese literary criticism. The last of these areas, while only suggested by references to literary texts in the article 'Collapse of "Japanese Mothers"' in the Calichman volume, may have particular resonance for potential readers of *The Modern Family in Japan*. In a groundbreaking series of discussions with psychologist Chikako Ogura and novelist Taeko Tomioka published in 1992, Ueno lambasted canonical male writers of modern Japanese literature and exposed the masculinist bias of the literary establishment.[10] Ueno went on to publish a collection of essays on literature in 2000, including some of her most trenchant feminist critiques of Japanese literary discourse, along with analyses of the increasing prominence of literature about aging.[11] The interest in the topic of aging and care work, already hinted at in Chapter 11 of *The Modern Family in Japan,* would emerge fully as a central concern for Ueno in more recent years. In 2007, the year she turned sixty, she published a how-to guide for living as a single – or 'single again' – woman in old age. It became a social sensation, sold over 750,000 copies, and was ranked number eight on the non-fiction best seller list in 2008.[12]

Ueno's feminism has always been connected to action, if not always to organized feminist activism. The impact of her presence as a teacher, interlocutor, and role-model for a generation of young scholars probably goes without saying,[13] but some of her most important actions have also come in the form of raising awareness about, and creating grievance procedures against, sexual harassment and other forms of power harassment in academia.[14] She has promoted the idea that policy addressing the needs of those in positions of social vulnerability, such as women, children, the aged, and the disabled, should give primary consideration to the agency of 'those who are concerned' (*tōjisha*).[15] On the other hand, Ueno is deeply aware of the ways in which women have been recruited to participate in the operations of the nation-state – the target of her investigation and critique in *Nationalism and Gender*. She has kept a distance from the mechanisms of 'state feminism,' which have gained prominence since the mid-1990s through the government's overt program to establish a 'gender equal society.'[16] In maintaining this stance, Ueno presents an interesting contrast to another University of Tokyo professor and feminist, Mari Ōsawa, who as a member of the government's Council on Gender Equality played a major role in formulating state gender policy in the 1990s. Nevertheless, as evidenced in the discussion between Ueno and Ōsawa, Ueno has a deeply pragmatic understanding of the policy-making process.[17] While she has written often of the 'failure' of feminist activists to make the 1985 Equal Employment Opportunity Law truly progressive, and while this may partially account for her skepticism towards the state feminist enterprise in the 1990s, Ueno is well aware of her own visibility and of the symbolic power that it confers. In recent years, Ueno has spoken out strongly and publicly against the nationalistic backlash directed at feminism in its various manifestations.[18]

Having seen a quick overview of Ueno's varied and extensive oeuvre, let us now approach the area explored in *The Modern Family in Japan*. The core of Ueno's early academic work was in Marxist feminist analysis, culminating in *Patriarchy and Capitalism: The Horizon of Marxist Feminism* published in 1990 (not yet available in English). It is this monograph that solidified Ueno's reputation as a serious scholar. Ueno argues here that patriarchy and capitalism are dual systems that work sometimes in tandem, sometimes in opposition to each other. Distinguishing herself from orthodox Marxists who see capitalism as the source of women's oppression, and from radical feminists who see patriarchy as the culprit, Ueno proposes a more complex and flexible model based on the conjunction of the two systems. At the same time, in insisting that patriarchy constitutes in itself a *material* base, rather than being merely a superstructure perched on top of the capitalist base, Ueno is led to analyze the family as the locus of reproductive politics. The impact of this Marxist feminist framework is felt in *The Modern Family in Japan* as well.

The Modern Family in Japan belongs to the 'blood type A' category of academic books, but is different from *Patriarchy and Capitalism* in several important ways. First, it is a collection of essays and articles originally written for various venues and thus presents variations on the theme of 'modernity and family in Japan,' rather than one sustained and coherent argument. Second, it reflects Ueno's commitment to describe and analyze social phenomena as they really exist, rather than as they are logically derived from a Marxist feminist perspective. This is what makes Ueno's work so resilient yet also often controversial: as the situation of women and families kept changing in the 1970s, 1980s, and 1990s, Ueno's mind kept shifting with the changes. Nothing is farther from her stance than that of the disappointed intellectual, chastising the public for its failure to live up to the ideals of a utopian society. Ueno celebrates the positive feminist potential in the bubble-driven consumerism of the 1980s at the same time as she warns against the potentially negative consequences of the Equal Employment Opportunity Law of 1985. In what may be the most provocative aspects of this book, she confronts the paradox of the 'happy housewife' in modern Japan: the woman who is the most financially dependent on the husband appears to be most independent of the labor market, the most endowed with money, time, and energy, and overall the most content with her lot in life. Ueno refuses to chastise these housewives as trapped in 'false consciousness,' but she also remembers to point out that the structural conjunctions that made the happy housewife possible are historically contingent and are changing rapidly. This historical awareness, indicated in the original Japanese book title by the phrase *seiritsu to shūen* (rise and fall) of the modern family, runs through all the chapters.

Part I, The Ambiguous Transformation of the Modern Family, consists of two chapters that trace recent changes in Japanese family life. Chapter 1, 'Exploring Family Identity,' came out of a collaborative research project conducted in 1990.[19] The research method, of first conducting 'simulations' or thought experiments about possible patterns of unconventional families and then trying to find people to match these patterns, may strike some readers as unorthodox. In this case, the research is secondary to Ueno's polemic, which highlights the diversity in the shapes of Japanese families as they currently exist. This aspect may turn out to be what is most valuable to readers of the English version of this chapter: the great heterogeneity in the forms and mentalities of families represented, and the glaring discrepancy between the picture of the ideal family in modern Japan and what the family looks like from the perspective of individual family members. The conclusion Ueno draws from the data is that the Japanese family is transforming, giving rise to new forms of identities and illusions.

Chapter 2, 'Women's Transformation and the Family,' was written in 1991 as part of a book on the transformation of Japanese society since 1970.[20] It thus provides an overview of the changes in women's roles during the 1970s and 1980s. Ueno shows that what may appear to be a diversification of women's lifestyle choices is in fact illusory, and that options for women are still limited: the majority of women engage in low-wage, part-time labor on top of being responsible for most of the housework, resulting in an exhausting double-shift. Being a full-time housewife is only affordable for the economically advantaged, and is thus a status symbol for young women.

Part II, Modernity and Women, comprises the core of the book, with three chapters focusing on history, modernity, and the family in Japan. Chapter 3, 'Formation of the Japanese Model of Modern Family,' argues that the *ie*, the patrilineal Japanese family system long regarded as a feudal remnant, is in fact a modern 'invented tradition.'[21] The implications of this claim are many. The positing of *ie* has been a central feature of the discourse of Japanese uniqueness that accompanied the economic boom of the 1980s, and Ueno seeks to debunk the notion of *ie* as a marker of Japanese tradition by showing how the Meiji government sought to promote it as a model of 'modern' family, suited to the building of the modern nation-state. The chapter concludes with a discussion on patriarchy, which links the present volume back to Ueno's Marxist feminist concerns.

Chapter 4, 'Modernity for the Family,' was written as part of a commentary on the multi-volume compendium of primary documents of modern Japanese intellectual history.[22] According to Ueno, this was the first project in which she read and interpreted primary documents from the Meiji period. Having been trained as a sociologist, Ueno increasingly appropriated the historian's tools. She describes a growing interest in locating the beginnings of that which appears to us as given in society, so that we may then glimpse its ending as well. This chapter, along with Chapter 3, delineates the rise of the modern family, while many of the other chapters in this volume suggest its demise.

Chapter 5, 'Women's History and Modernity,' presents a concise and useful summary of the various Japanese feminist debates on modernity since the 1970s.[23] It shows how modernity was first seen as liberating for women, and then as oppressive for women. Ueno's own debate with Yayoi Aoki, discussed in some detail in Sandra Buckley's aforementioned volume, is summarized here as consisting of Aoki's ecologically driven critique of modernity, and of Ueno's warning that such a critique could lead to a reactionary celebration of premodern patriarchy. To see modernity as ambivalent for women leads also to the view of women's history as ambivalent: a history of women as oppressors, as well as of women as the oppressed. The ambivalence does not end there – the chapter touches on the debate between materialist feminists, such as Ueno herself, and postmodern cultural feminists, an important feature of the discursive space of 1980s and early 1990s feminism.

Part III, The Development of Home Science, considers the intersection of the history of the family and the history of technology, specifically through the figure of the housewife engaged in domestic labor.

Chapter 6, 'The Evolution of Umesao's Home Science,' was initially a commentary attached to the collected works of anthropologist Tadao Umesao, and has some of the qualities of a eulogy.[24] This commentary links the present volume to Ueno's earlier two-volume collection documenting the 'housewife debates' in the period from the 1950s to the 1970s.[25] Umesao, an unwitting participant in these debates, was ahead of his time in declaring the demise of the housewife role: the electric rice cooker would come to replace the housewife as expert rice cooker.

Chapter 7, 'Technological Innovation and Domestic Labor,' further traces the development of home technology and argues that the work performed by the housewife is a historically contingent phenomenon.[26] Written for a series on the changing family, the essay serves as a practical application of the kind of 'home science' advocated by Tadao Umesao.

Part IV, 'Postwar Economic Growth and the Family,' depicts the family as a troubled entity in postwar Japan. This is the negative counterpart of the family often celebrated as a highly functioning component of the economic growth of the same period.

Written at the invitation of Jun Etō as an afterword to a new edition of his book *Maturity and Loss*, Chapter 8, 'A Postwar History of the Mother,' is a far-reaching meditation on the maternal figure in postwar Japanese intellectual and literary discourse.[27] Analyzing fiction and literary criticism by postwar writers and intellectuals, Ueno paints a devastating picture of the unhappy Japanese family: it consists of the miserable father (who has lost prestige due to the war), the frustrated mother (who is nonetheless dependent on the father), the incompetent son (who despises the father but sees himself as growing up to be like him), and the irritating daughter (who is sullen because she sees no option but to grow up to be like her mother). However, unlike conservative social critics who advocate the recovery of patriarchal tradition to solve all manner of social ills, Ueno simply notes that the modern family is broken and that it cannot be fixed by wishing back a strong father or a self-sacrificing mother.

Chapter 9, 'Wives at "Midlife Crisis" Stage,' continues the theme of the unhappy housewife, but takes Shigeo Saitō's journalistic portrayal of such women as the starting point.[28] It was initially written at the invitation of Saitō as an afterword to his 1982 reportage, and thus begins by noting how extraordinary it was for a journalist at the time to describe the lives of ordinary women as newsworthy. Ueno ends the chapter by noting that the 'housewives' midlife crisis' might be a temporary phenomenon: the younger generation of women is better at letting off steam and having fun. While readers might find that the negative consequences of the troubled family and of the frustrated mother may well have become more visible in the ensuing decades, Ueno's purpose in this chapter is to ask the sociological question, 'If only a minority of housewives is visibly unhappy, how is the majority staying happy?' The paradox of the happy housewife is the thread that connects this chapter to other works that Ueno published in the 1980s and early 1990s, which seemed to celebrate certain aspects of consumerist society while remaining cynical about it as well.

Part V, The Paradox of Sexism, collects a number of essays that deal with the varied interactions of sexism, family-ism, ageism, and nationalism.

Chapter 10, 'The Trap of Separate Surnames for Married Couples,' takes up an issue that became the target of heated debate in the early 1990s. The increasing presence of women in the professions meant that more and more women were facing the inconvenience of having to change their surnames upon marriage. The law required (and still requires, as of the end of 2008) a married couple to choose either the husband's or the wife's surname as their joint surname. The persistent mentality of the *ie* system dictates that in 97% of the cases the husband's surname is chosen, and the law leaves no possibility for the woman to officially retain her maiden name if her husband does not consent to change his surname. The debate pitted feminist advocates of a legal change that would allow couples to retain their separate surnames against conservatives who argued that this would lead to the collapse of family identity. Ueno's article was first published in a psychology journal's special issue on this debate, and questions the fundamental belief that members of a family ought to have the same surname.[29] The real target for Ueno's critique, however, is the valorization of legally sanctioned marriage. When feminists advocate separate surnames for married couples, the 'trap' is that this advocacy can lead to the privileging of legal marriages at the expense of other forms of social life.

Chapter 11, 'Old Age as Lived Experience,' is one of Ueno's early forays into a topic that was to become a major theme of her later work. Originally published in 1986 as part of a prescient multi-volume series on aging, it touches on a number of themes that would emerge more clearly in later books.[30] Ueno urges us to reorient the discussion away from old people as social problems to be managed, towards the negotiation of old age by individuals exercising their agency.

The original title of Chapter 12, 'The Possibility of Female Bonds,' was *'Eraberu en, erabenai en'* or 'bonds that can be chosen, bonds that cannot be chosen.'[31] The focus on choice is crucial, since in this essay Ueno focuses on the selective bonds that married women opt to forge with each other, distinct from family bonds, local community bonds, and company bonds. Because they are freely chosen and can also be abandoned, these female bonds have attractive characteristics not found in other kinds of bonds. It is in this article that Ueno seems to come closest to celebrating the lifestyles of the 'happy housewife.'

Chapter 13, 'Paradox of Sexism: Cross-cultural Adaptation and Gender Difference,' was originally published in a volume discussing the meaning of foreign culture for contemporary Japanese society, as part of a project initiated by the National Museum of Ethnology.[32] The essay begins by noting that gender difference has not been sufficiently investigated in studies of cross-cultural adaptation. The paradox of sexism manifests itself in the fact that women generally adapt faster than men when placed in liminal situations, such as living in a foreign country. The exception is to be found in wives of Japanese expatriate businessmen, and here the factor of 'family' enters into the equation: confined within the home and a social network consisting only of other Japanese corporate wives, the wife of an expatriate businessman has less access to the local culture and adapts less easily than other members of her family. This is in contrast to women venturing abroad as students, who generally adapt more quickly than male students. The essay concludes with the insight that it is the socially gendered individual, not the family, that constitutes the unit of cross-cultural adaptation, and that cross-cultural adaptation raises the question of hierarchies between cultures. To readers of the English version, this essay may serve as a fascinating introduction to what is happening to the Japanese family in an era of increasing internationalization. The picture is not a pretty one – the wife lonely and depressed, the husband indifferent to the family's troubles, the son sent back to rejoin the elitist Japanese rat-race, the daughter winding up an exotic bilingual gal or *bilingal* who is sometimes celebrated but only as an outsider of Japanese society.

If one were to summarize Ueno's insights in this book as a series of statements about the family and women's status in modern Japan, it might look something like this: the family is transforming and thus becoming hard to define beyond the members' own sense of family identity, yet this does not mean that the family is disappearing; it is merely changing shape (Chapter 1). Despite the appearance that more women are employed outside the home, the expectation that women bear most of the burden of housework has not changed, and the full-time housewife, who does not have to do a double-shift with wage labor, is a status symbol (Chapter 2). The history of the modern family in Japan is traced to the policies (Chapter 3) and media discourse (Chapter 4) of the Meiji period, and the history of recent feminist evaluations of modernity are traced through a series of debates (Chapter 5). Ueno follows in the footsteps of scholars (Chapter 6) who have focused on the history of technological change in order to elucidate the transitional roles of housewives (Chapter 7). She also sheds light on the quiet despair of wives, mothers, and daughters within the seeming economic success of the postwar family, as portrayed in literature (Chapter 8) and journalism (Chapter 9). Finally, she turns to the varied and sometimes paradoxical manifestations of sexism in phenomena such as the debate over surnames for married couples (Chapter 10), gendered expectations for aging (Chapter 11), group bonds among housewives (Chapter 12), and cross-cultural adaptation (Chapter 13).

In the twenty-first century, more than ten years after this book was first published, the options for women in Japan still remain circumscribed. Although everyone acknowledges that exceptions exist, 'family' and 'work' continue to be seen as the respective primary domains of women and men. Despite the government's efforts to promote a balance between the dual roles of wage-earner and mother, women continue to 'exit' the workplace rather than try to change its family-unfriendly culture: two-thirds of employed women quit their jobs by the time they give birth to their first child. When they return to the labor market, they do so as low-paid, part-time laborers, another reality that has not changed since 1994. Within the global trends of neoliberal economic restructuring, in a process that Maria Mies has called the 'housewifization of labor,' unstable and disposable forms of employment have become increasingly common for men, as well as for women. Thus the happy full-time housewife – with money to spend on luxury goods, energy to spare for hobbies and activism, and time to lavish on elaborate meal preparation for her family – is increasingly a mirage. And yet, the figure continues to exert a curiously strong ideological power, as evidenced by the recent backlash against state feminism and the attending celebration of the full-time housewife as 'Japanese tradition.' As Chizuko Ueno herself might put it, the era of the modern family may have reached its demise, but the specter of the modern family still haunts us today.

Department of East Asian Languages and Civilizations
University of Pennsylvania
January 2009

Preface to the English Translation

The original title of the Japanese publication of this book is *Kindai kazoku no seiritsu to shūen*, literally *The Rise and Fall of the Modern Family*. When this book was published in 1994, some said that it was too early to talk about the fall, as the modern family had not yet been established in Japan. However, with various symptoms in demographic changes and social phenomena, it seemed clear to me that the modern family had already started to disintegrate.

The modern family is not a normative concept but a descriptive one, and is a historical construct that family historians found though the process of modernization. In this respect, Japan is not an exception, and this book challenges an Orientalist view that sees the Japanese family system as somewhat particular and exceptional.

The book was awarded the Suntory Academic Prize in the year of publication. I am pleased that it has since become a milestone for the study of family history in Japan. It has caused controversy over whether Japan's *ie* system established in the Meiji period represents a continuation from its premodern antecedents or a departure from them. In retrospect, more than ten years since then, I have nothing to change in my view on this point.

However, let me briefly add some observations about the changes that have taken place in the decade since the publication of this book. The decade of the 1990s is now called 'the lost ten years,' when Japan suffered a long-lasting economic recession. The so-called Japanese-style management, which provided employees with job security and shared prosperity, belongs to the past, as does the disintegration of the family. Job security went hand in hand with marriage stability as long as the economic growth continued, but Japanese companies can no longer afford job security. Diversification in women, which had already started in the early 1990s when I wrote this book, has progressed to the extent that non-regular workers constituted 52% of all female employees in 2006. In the entire workforce, including both females and males, one in every three workers is a non-regular worker engaged in a dispatch, contract, temporary or part-time job. Of male workers, 17% are now non-regular, which proves that 'housewifization of labor,' which I discuss in this book, is taking place both in men and in women. One might point out that the so-called working poor, or those non-regular workers who earn a wage below the survival level, have become a social problem only when this issue is de-gendered.

On the family front, two demographic indices of the disintegration of the modern family are discernible in most advanced societies; one is an increase in divorce rates, and the other an increase in extramarital births. The former is the index of marriage instability, and the latter that of extramarital sexual relationships. Both indicate the weakening of the connection between marriage and sex, which in turn serves as a sign of the disintegration of the modern family, based on conjugal ties. While most advanced societies in the West show similar demographic trends in both indices, Japan shows a relatively smaller divorce rate and almost negligible cases of extramarital births. Conservatives take this as a sign of particular stability of the Japanese family system, which differs from those of other developed societies. On the contrary, however, Japan has two other demographic indices, which may look strange but are functionally equivalent. They are, one, an increase in unmarried singles, both men and women, and, the other, an extreme decrease in fertility. The former is equivalent to the divorce rate, as Japanese women would not enter the marital relationship and then break it. The latter is equivalent to extramarital birth, but it is interrupted by abortion in most cases in Japan where it is accessible safely and inexpensively. Both result in extreme low fertility with a rapidly aging population.

Whether we call our time postmodern or late modern, I would again argue the modern family is over. However, it does not mean the end of the family itself. What we witness is the change of formation and perception of the family, but no one can predict what will come next. A sense of anxiety at a critical moment of history may cause reactionary and anachronistic responses among people, as observed in a slogan, 'defend the family value.' However, what is necessary at the present historical turn is that we face reality as it is so that we can adjust our system to the newly created circumstances. In this respect, I find myself consistent in my thinking.

Finally, I would like to express my gratitude to various parties involved in this translation project. This is the second of my books to be translated into English, following *Nationalism and Gender*, published in 2004 by the same publisher, Trans Pacific Press. I am deeply grateful to Professor Yoshio Sugimoto at La Trobe University and Publisher at Trans Pacific Press, who made this translation project possible. For their painstaking and outstanding work, I owe much to the three translators, who are modest enough to prefer to remain anonymous since they believe they have done the job simply as professional translators. Thanks are also due to two text editors at Trans Pacific Press, Cathy Edmonds and Miriam Riley, for their exceptional care and invaluable suggestions. In particular, I am extremely pleased that Dr. Ayako Kano, Associate Professor in the Department of East Asian Languages and Civilizations at the University of Pennsylvania, an expert in comparative literature, theater arts and cultural history, has contributed a foreword to this English translation. I highly value the insight and sharp analysis that characterize the work of Dr. Kano, who, in my view, is the best scholar to introduce my work to the English-speaking audience. Her foreword is well balanced and focused, and locates this book in the intertextual context of my other works – and with a witty style.

Numerous scholars and editors have helped me to form the ideas that this book expresses and provided me with opportunities for presentations, commentaries, contributions and academic exchanges. They include Tamito Yoshida, Nagao Nishikawa, Shinzō Ogi, Tadao Umesao, Shunsuke Tsurumi, Shigeo Saitō, Jun Etō, Sōichi Endō, Atsushi Naoi, Kōji Takamura, and many other individuals whose names I cannot mention here.

I would like to thank JSPS (Japan Society for the Promotion of Science) for financial support under the Grant-in-Aid for Publication of Science Research Result scheme, without which this translation project would not have been possible.

Chizuko Ueno
January 2009

Part I

The Ambiguous Transformation of the Modern Family

1 Exploring Family Identity[1]

Discourses on a potential crisis

Historical turning points are often accompanied by similar phenomena. Today, at the end of the twentieth century, there have been loud concerns about a potential 'crisis in the family.' Similar concerns were raised at the end of the nineteenth century. In reality, the family did not disintegrate. What happened instead was that, both in Western countries and in Japan, the family simply changed its form and function.

Although there is no doubt that the family is undergoing transformation, this does not mean that it is facing a potential disintegration. However, many people see a crisis in the family at the very sight of its transformation into something unknown to them. These people simply do not know or cannot imagine any other form of family than the existing one. This situation is similar to that which surrounded the changes in the family at the end of the previous century, which also horrified conservative people. 'Protect the family tradition' is a conservative discourse that has always been heard in times of change to represent a reactionary view. It did not take long before this discourse was replaced by the ideal of the *modern family*. People are frightened by the very fact that they do not know what may be waiting for them after the change. Where did the family come from, and where is it going? Attempts are now needed to answer this question.

Family identity

What makes a family a family? To answer this question, cultural anthropologists have attempted to formulate a cross-cultural definition of family, but have long abandoned the endeavour due to the diversity of cultures. Blood relationship cannot be included in the definition of family because some cultures have an adoption system. In an African culture where ghost marriage (marriage between a living bride and a deceased groom) is practiced, even the deceased are members of the family. In order to define family in an operational manner, the minimum definition of family at which cultural anthropologists arrived was a community 'sharing fire (kitchen),' or sharing meals. Accordingly, setting a 'separate fire' is regarded as a separation of the household (and often of the family members).

Similarly, the Japanese national census relies on the principle of 'one kitchen in one household.' Since it started in 1920, the census has been based solely on current address because surveys based on family registers or certificates of residence have become unreliable due to the increased flux of family in legal and institutional terms. However, what is intentionally covered by the census is the concept of *household* only; the concept of family is carefully avoided. The concept of household is based on the 'sharing of residence.' However, some families do not share a residence if one parent lives away from the family because of work or for other reasons. Thus, the concepts of household and family do not completely overlap one another. The minimum definition created by cultural anthropologists applies to *household* but not to *family*.

A family exists both in reality and in the members' perception. For instance, two people who regard each other as total strangers might actually belong to the same family as blood-related members. However, as long as both remain totally unaware of their relationship, there is no chance that they can form part of the same family in reality. As is the case with Japanese war orphans who were left in China during the Second World War and are now searching for relatives who are willing to sponsor them to live in Japan, a family is formed only when its members confirm their family identity and perceive each other as part of the same family. Yet one member's perception of himself or herself as part of the family may be denied by the other members. This means that the existence of a family is based more on its members' perception than on reality.

Let us here refer to such family members' perception that underlies their existence as a family as *family identity*, or FI. As the term literally suggests, family identity is a concept intended to identify what a family is by defining the boundary between what is and what is not a family. The psychological term *identity*, which was first used by Erik H. Erikson in personal contexts, later came to be used in various group contexts. Examples of such uses include *corporate identity* (CI) and *national identity*. However, even though a corporation is conceptualized as an entity independent of its individual members, its CI must rely on its individual members' perception. Group identity has been an issue in groups that are artificially formed and are thus fragile. Hence, it has never particularly been an issue in groups that have been regarded as naturally occurring, such as primary groups including families and communities.[2]

Despite these circumstances, I choose to use the term FI here for the following three reasons.

First, the family has come to be regarded as a somewhat artificial construct rather than a natural entity. Second, a disparity has emerged between what has traditionally been regarded as the *substance* of a family and FI. Third, while FI must rely on individual family members for its existence, the concept of FI can be used to describe the gaps between different family members by focusing on different aspects of those members on which FI's existence relies. When analyzing families in this time of change, FI is a useful concept to describe the gap between perception and reality and the gap between different family members.

From conventional to unconventional family models

Let us apply the concept of FI to the conventional Japanese family. For example, the conventional Japanese *ie* (household) was regarded as an entity independent of its individual members, but it would have collapsed as soon as its members ceased to perceive themselves as part of it. However, just as personal identity is physically based on the person's body, the conventional household as an extended family had its physical foundations: shared family business, shared family name, shared family house, shared family property and shared family finances.

The family members' perception of themselves as part of the same household as *ie* continued only because it had a sufficient physical foundation. Even if the former Japanese Civil Code guaranteed the headship of a household in legal terms, it would have been difficult for the household members to maintain their FI as part of the same household if they had needed to rely solely on symbolic foundations (such as family name), without physical foundations (such as family business or family property). Today's FI is increasingly based on more limited physical foundations, such as a shared family house or shared family finances. Yet even these foundations have been shaken by the splitting of households and the increasing number of double-income households.

What, then, is the minimum foundation on which FI can be maintained?

The concept of family as used in anthropology incorporates the undifferentiated concepts of household and descent. The principle of household is *shared residence* (or *shared hearth* in a cultural anthropological term), while that of descent is *shared blood lineage*. Each of the two concepts has three patterns: paternal (patrilineal/patrilocal), maternal (matrilineal/matrilocal) and bilateral (bilineal/bilocal or neolocal). There is not necessarily a concurrence between the residence and descent patterns (Figure 1.1).[3]

Assuming that *shared residence* and *shared blood lineage* are independent concepts, we can construct a diagram as shown in Figure 1.2. Quadrant I contains conventional families where there is a concurrence between residence and blood lineage. Quadrant II contains families where there is shared blood lineage, but there has been a separation of households, such as in the case of marital separation or where one parent lives away from his or her family because of work. Quadrant IV contains cases of co-residence of people who do not share a blood lineage, such as in the case of a married couple without children or a household with adopted children. Quadrant III includes entities that meet neither of the two minimum requirements for being a family (i.e. shared residence and shared blood lineage). Should they then be denied as being families? Then some novel phenomena are encountered. Our research (described later) has found numerous reports of cases where people share an FI despite their lack of both shared residence and shared blood lineage. One example is a common-law couple in which the husband lives overseas and separately from his wife. They do not share name, family finances or even sexual relations, but still feel that they are part of the same family. Another example is a man who became a foster parent of a child living on Negros Island in the Philippines. Although he did not meet the child until some time later, he felt that the child was part of his family.

Even if neither of the two minimum requirements – shared residence and shared blood lineage – is met, FI can still exist. More precisely, the FI that is currently undergoing change has presented diverse aspects that cannot be understood based solely on the conventional requirements for being a family, or the principles of residence and blood lineage. In order for the project to pick up changes occurring in the family, the original static diagram shown in Figure 1.2 had to be abandoned and a new dynamic one created to include more diverse variables. Changes in the family occur both in the members' perception and in the family's form. The 'family yet to be seen' will be totally different from that which has been

Figure 1.1: Residence and descent patterns

	Descent	
Residence	*Paternal*	*Maternal*
Paternal	Patrilineal and patrilocal	(Matrilineal and patrilocal)
Maternal	Patrilineal and matrilocal	Matrilineal and matrilocal

Figure 1.2: Shared blood lineage and shared residence

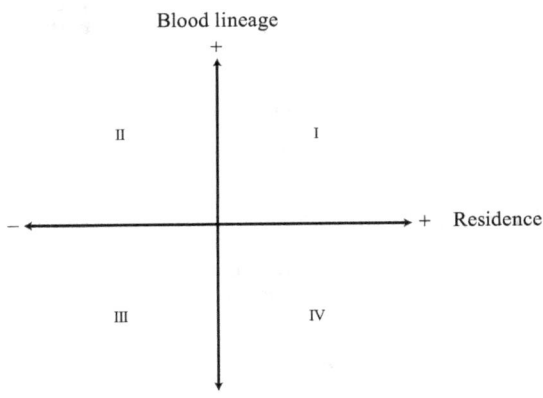

Blood lineage
+

II   I

−   +   Residence

III   IV

−

known to us. In the process of change to a new family model, gaps will occur between the change in the family members' perception and that in the family's form. Specifically, the transition period sees families whose form has long been changed but whose members maintain the conventional perception or, conversely, those whose form remains conventional but whose members have a totally unconventional perception. In order to conceptualize both changes, a working hypothesis is shown in Figure 1.3. Quadrant I includes families that are conventional in both the members' perception and the family's form. In contrast, quadrant III includes families that are unconventional in both the members' perception and the family's form. Quadrant II includes families with conventional perception and unconventional form, while quadrant IV includes those with conventional form and unconventional perception. The directions of change are as shown in Figure 1.4.

Since the intention of our research was to explore the directions of change in the family, we conducted simulations and listed as

Figure 1.3: Family members' perception and family form

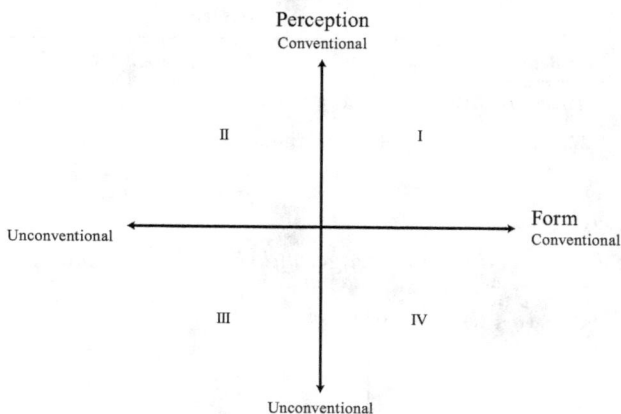

Perception
Conventional

II   I

Unconventional ←——————————————→ Form
                                                    Conventional

III   IV

Unconventional

Figure 1.4: Changes of conventional and unconventional types

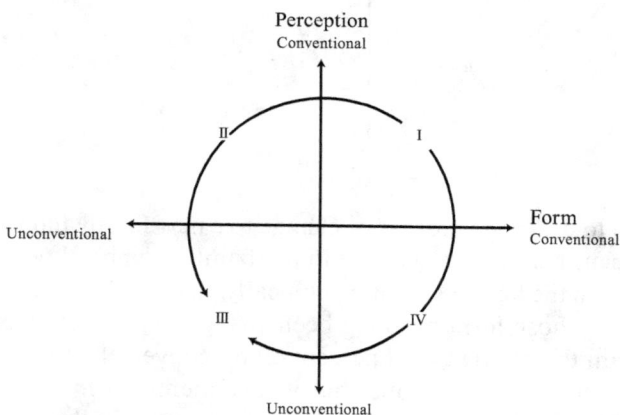

Perception
Conventional

II   I

Unconventional ←——————————————→ Form
                                                    Conventional

III   IV

Unconventional

many unconventional family models as we could think of (in both perception and form) for the three quadrants other than quadrant I. Then we searched for empirical cases to fit these models. In cases where we had access to the family, we conducted interviews. In other cases (i.e. cases that do exist but where we had difficulty accessing the family due to privacy issues or for other reasons, such as in the case of a woman married to an imprisoned criminal) we relied on secondary materials, such as reportage, newspaper articles or memoirs. Being an epoch of 'family experiment,' the past dozen years have seen the publication of countless numbers of nonfiction works describing unconventional families. What we did not have was conceptual apparatus to analyse the changes occurring during this period.

Our simulations resulted in approximately fifty models of unconventional family. We sampled thirty-nine families that fitted these models and conducted interviews with them. As basic data, we collected information on family structure, the extent of co-residence and family history.

If the sampled families are mapped on Figure 1.4, the mapped figure will look as follows: quadrant II will contain families whose members have conventional perception but whose form has become unconventional as a result of a failure to maintain a form corresponding to the members' perception. More precisely, families falling under this model have chosen to separate one or more members from the main household in order to defend their conventional perception of family. Family members who have been separated from the main household are usually elderly people, husbands and/or children. Elderly people tend to be institutionalized once they become bedridden or senile. Children with disabilities or behavioral problems are sometimes institutionalized or sent to rural schools for a 'change of air.' The institutionalization of these elderly people or children is also generally recommended by caseworkers. As for husbands, the most likely cause of separation from the family is a transfer (unaccompanied by family) to a new post. These families tend to choose to separate affected members from the main household rather than to unite against a crisis. In a way, they could be likened to abandoners of old parents, children or husbands. To this extent we can say that the contemporary family is very vulnerable.

In contrast, quadrant IV contains families whose form is conventional but whose members have unconventional perception. Some are three-generation families, but not all of them are conventional patrilocal ones; an increasing number become matrilocal or bilocal. Others are typical core families, but are different from baby-boomer families whose husband and wife were called 'friend-like couples' but actually ended up being another old-fashioned gender role model. These quadrant IV families with unconventional perception include couples who share hobbies and interests and can 'play together;' DINK (double income, no kids) families without children; and 'twin-like couples' who started out as two of a kind and married when they found that they happened to be a man and a woman. While these families are based on friendship, other quadrant IV families include those that have broken down in reality, such as in the case of 'in-house separation' where a couple separate but continue to live in the same home.

There is an intermediate model of family between the conventional perception/unconventional form model and the unconventional perception/conventional form model. The intermediate model includes families that have non-blood-related members but have made various attempts to maintain a conventional form of a family, such as families with adopted children or those of remarried couples. They could be called *reconstructed families*.

Finally, quadrant III contains families that are unconventional in both perception and form. Neither their form nor perception looks like that of a family at all from a conventional point of view, but the members believe that they do constitute a family in their own view. These families include collectives and various communal groups; lesbian or gay couples; and families including deceased members and non-human members (i.e. pet animals). At the far north end of this quadrant are ideological single people who choose not to have a family. However, even if you choose to avoid having your own family of procreation, you cannot escape from being part of your own family of orientation to which you were born. Therefore, a grown-up child and his or her old parents still remain as a family.

Our interview consisted of very simple questions. Our first question was, 'What is the extent of people (or things, animals and so on) whom you consider to be part of your family?' This question was intended to clarify the interviewee's definition of the boundary between family and the outside world based on his or her FI. Then we asked the interviewee to use his or her own categorization to describe the minimum requirements for identification as a family member.

We employed an interview method for the following reasons. In this time of rapidly changing families, any a priori definition of family is of no use, and a quantitative survey with predetermined categories would not produce meaningful results. Therefore, we must focus on a qualitative survey, but in doing so we should use the *native* category of interviewees wherever possible, instead of a deductive category. If the family has a complex structure, we should conduct interviews with two or more members to check whether there is any discrepancy between different members in their definitions of the boundary between their family and the outside world based on their FI. We expected that if FI is still maintained in unconventional families, new images of family would emerge by using the *native* categories.

Families with conventional perception and unconventional form

Quadrant II of Figures 1.3 and 1.4 includes families that are conventional in perception and unconventional in form. They include families whose members maintain conventional FI but have been forced to separate one or more members from the main household due to outside pressure or compelling reasons.

A typical example of this is a husband living away from his family because of work.

The case of Ms A., a company employee aged thirty-nine

Ms A. has two children with her husband, who was a friend from high school. She is an experienced office clerk and has worked for an airline company for twenty years. Believing that a woman should have a job just like a man does, she did not rely on her husband during her hardest time with child care. Last summer her husband was transferred to a post in Kyūshū. She felt no hesitation letting him live away from the rest of her family so that he could take the new post. Her life and her children's lives have not changed very much. About the only change is that her husband now pays less of the family expenses, which have been shared between herself and her husband. As both have always worked, her husband can take care of himself. He seems to do his laundry and cleaning somehow and seems to be eating out most of the time.

Most husbands who choose to relocate to a new post unaccompanied by their families do so for the sake of their children's education and/ or wives' work. The latter reason has become increasingly common. There are even cases where a wife without a job has created a local network of friends and refuses to accompany her husband under the pretext of their children's education. Other reasons for not accompanying relocating husbands include maintenance of the family house and caring for old parents. In the case of Ms A., her family had substantially been fatherless since before her husband's assignment to Kyūshū and there has virtually been no change in her and her children's lifestyles since he began living away from the rest of the family. In fact, his absence has made Ms A. and her children an even more relaxed fatherless family and they do not welcome his infrequent visits. Here we can see a contrast between the husband who chose work over family and the wife who chose children over husband. Ms A.'s husband seems to be working hard at the new office, while he creates quasi-families based on business relationships or on drinking together.

What is intriguing is that there is a disparity between Ms A. and her husband in FI (Figure 1.5). Ms A.'s FI covers her two children only and does not extend to her husband. Her husband's FI includes all four members, and corresponds with the children's FI, which includes their father. If Ms A. and her husband were to divorce, the figure depicting their FI would immediately shift to the one shown in Figure 1.6. Specifically, the figure shows that while the children's perception of their parents would not change, Ms A. is already so distant from her husband that her FI would not change before or after their imaginary divorce. The husband is not always the first member to cause a separation of the household. Elderly members or children of the family can also do the same.

The case of Ms B., a housewife aged forty-five

Ms B.'s husband is the second son of his family. His mother lived alone in the country for a long time. Ms B.'s understanding was that if something happened to her mother-in-law, the family's eldest son would take care of her. However, when she did fall ill and required nursing at home, the eldest son refused to take the responsibility. A family meeting was held, at which the eldest daughter also refused to look after her mother, partly because her child was preparing for entrance exams to schools; it was eventually decided that the second son, Ms B.'s husband, would look after his mother. Ms B.'s family bought a house for this purpose. Just when they finally started a new life, the mother-in-law began to show signs of dementia. Ms B. struggled with her mother-in-law's dementia for a year, but it grew progressively worse and the mother-in-law was institutionalized. Ms B. was finally 'free.' Her husband visits his mother once a month. Ms B. and her child have seldom visited her mother-in-law, partly because she does not recognize Ms B. or her child. It seems to Ms B. that someone who had not been part of her family suddenly came and then left, so she does not miss her mother-in-law or feel guilty or otherwise about her.

There is a disparity between Ms B.'s FI and her husband's, as shown Figure 1.7. As seen in Ms B.'s case, today it is not always the eldest son's obligation to form a patrilocal family. In addition, as was the case with Ms B.'s family, an overwhelming proportion of patrilocal

Figure 1.5: Current FI of Ms A.

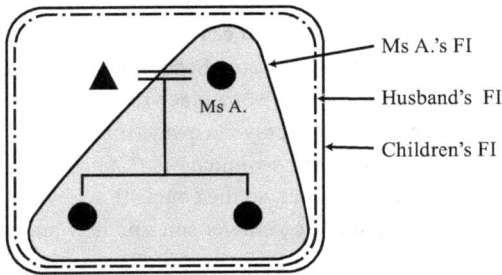

The gray area indicates the extent of co-residence.

Figure 1.6: FI of Ms A. after possible divorce

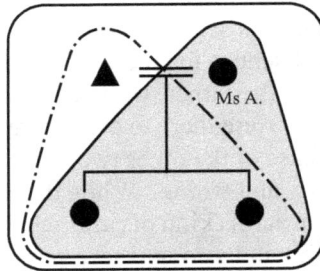

The gray area indicates the extent of co-residence.

families start to live together only some time after the son's marriage. Even after they start to live together, the old parent will usually be institutionalized once dementia sets in. The expensive admission fee is, in a sense, a fee for discarding the parent. Faced with the reality of elderly care, which may ruin the entire family, the family chooses to protect itself by institutionalizing the elderly parent. The institutionalized parent will have access only to his or her son's generation, and will not be able to enjoy exchanges with grandchildren with whom he or she is not familiar. There are also cases of children being discarded.

The case of Ms C., a housewife in her forties

Ms C. married a man with three children (one daughter and two sons). She first had trouble with the daughter, but they gradually understood and respected each other. However, she had difficulty coping with the two sons, who had poor academic abilities, told lies, and were lazy and susceptible to temptation. Their father would say, 'We have no choice but to send them to the Totsuka Yacht School (a school known for its Spartan method of education) or someplace like that.' After the sons entered junior high, they repeatedly ran away from home and engaged in delinquent acts. No matter how much Ms C. and her husband told them to stop, they did not listen, so the couple thought about sending the sons to a rural school. The younger son said he wanted to go, but the older son said, 'No.' They were eventually convinced by Ms C. and their father and his parents to go. The decision was not made upon the children's request, the tuition was expensive, and they could not always expect good results, but Ms C. had no other choice as the situation was beyond her capability.

Yasaka Village in Nagano Prefecture had accepted six children from outside the village into its school as of 1990. These children had been sent to the rural school for the following reasons: one child had been discarded by the father, who had remarried; one was an extramarital child; two were there to prepare for entrance exams to schools; and, in the case of the other two, their parents wanted the children to be 'healthy and strong.' While the original justification for educating children at this kind of rural school was to help urban children grow healthy and strong, these schools are also used as temporary care centers for children who are not welcomed by their parents, as resting places for children who have difficulty adapting to school and need a rest, and as shelters for children who do not get

Figure 1.7: FI of Ms B.

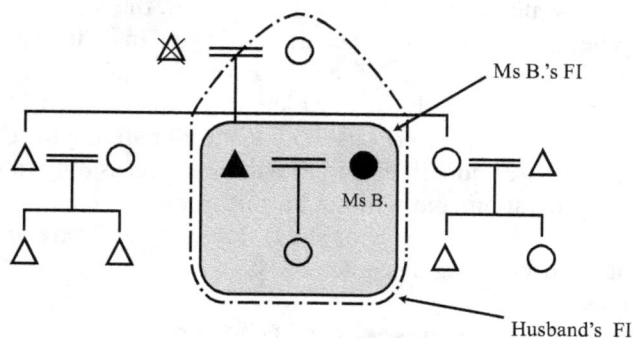

The gray area indicates the extent of co-residence.

along well with their family members. Here we can see the egoism of parents who want peace of mind so as to protect their families by discarding these children in exchange for expensive tuition fees. Conversely, children who voluntarily choose to go to one of these rural schools may have the hidden intention of discarding their parents as part of their motivation.

A family's decision to separate the household is often associated with discarding the husband, parent(s) or child(ren). The main household members' FI does not very often cover the member(s) who have been separated. The family members' FI covers only the members who get along with the rest of the family. Once a certain member of the family is found unfavorable by the other members, he or she will be discarded in order to protect the rest of the family. This is most obviously seen in the case of people with acquired disabilities.

The case of Mr D., a newly blind man aged fifty-two

Mr D. was a public employee. He suffered a sudden retinal detachment due to overworking and eventually lost his sight. He made three unsuccessful suicide attempts and was hospitalized seven times. He is aware that he has caused much trouble to his wife, so he says 'thank you' to her each time she does something for him. Although he is careful not to offend her, he is not comfortable with her. She has refused to go out with him, saying that she will be embarrassed. As a result, Mr D. was confined to home for two years after he lost his sight, but he is now able to go out with the help of volunteers. He is aware that his wife does not divorce him only because he has money.

A family member is regarded as such by the rest of the family as long as his or her presence is favorable to them. As soon as he or she is found unfavorable, they will discard him or her. This is a fact sensationally demonstrated by a judgment on the 'Alzheimer divorce case,' which was passed in Nagano Prefecture in September 1990.[4] This judgment granted a divorce to a husband from his wife, who had Alzheimer's disease. The judgment completely overturned the view that family serves as security against personal crisis. In reality, however, whether or not the law permits it, families facing crises have defended themselves by discarding members with problems. The contemporary family is extremely vulnerable to crises. The image of a family fighting as one against a crisis of external origin, as seen in Laura Ingalls Wilder's family in *Little house on the prairie*, belongs to a myth. The contemporary family is more likely to fail to endure

Figure 1.8: FI of a husband and wife and their daughter

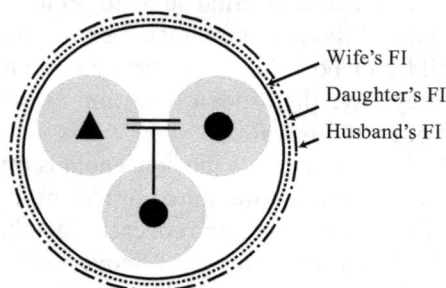

The gray area indicates the extent of co-residence.

a crisis and to collapse rather than to unite to fight it.[5] The fact that a family does not serve as security against its members' crises reflects the reduced strength of the physical foundation of a family. Belief in blood ties are not enough to support FI.

Conversely, a family may choose to separate the household for positive reasons. For example, in one family of three, the husband has left for Germany to take up his new post, the wife works in Tokyo, and their only daughter goes to a boarding school in Summer Hill, England. This family has thus separated into three households. In this case, however, the family members maintain their FI despite the long distances between the three households (Figure 1.8). In this family, priority has been given to individual members' personal interests over the family's co-residence. However, this family's FI is supported by its economic strength that allows the maintenance of the three households and by the shared blood lineage. Although the family members have chosen to live away from each other, they regard this choice as temporary and inevitable to respect the parents' respective careers and the daughter's personality. Even though this family takes an extremely unusual form, its perception of family is conventional. The members intend to restore the family from the separation of the household in time and to match their form with their perception.

Families with conventional form and unconventional perception

In contrast to the type of family described above, quadrant IV of Figures 1.3 and 1.4 covers all the families whose form remains conventional but whose members' perception has totally changed.

One example is a new urban type of three-generation family. Although this type of family appears to be based on a conventional family system, there has been a tendency towards a shift from patrilocal to matrilocal residence (Figure 1.9).[6] There has also been an increasing number of cases of selective shared residence, in which the parents and the family of one of their children (not necessarily the eldest son or daughter) live together by mutual choice (Figure 1.10). The most unconventional three-generation family would be one that practices bilocal residence.

The case of Ms E., a public employee aged thirty-nine

Ms E. has one daughter (in grade one) with her husband whom she became acquainted with when she was a student. After marriage, the couple first lived in public housing and later bought a condominium.

Figure 1.9: Distribution of patrilocal and matrilocal residences

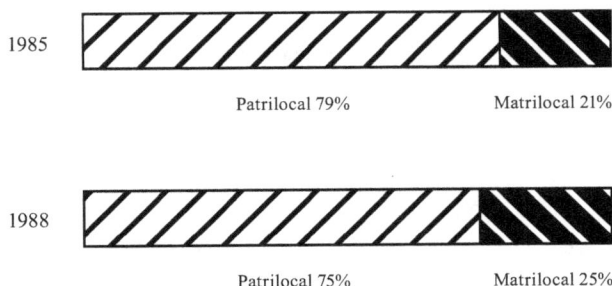

1985

Patrilocal 79%   Matrilocal 21%

1988

Patrilocal 75%   Matrilocal 25%

Source: The number of purchasers of Asahi Kasei's two-family houses, 1990.

Figure 1.10: Distribution of selective residence types

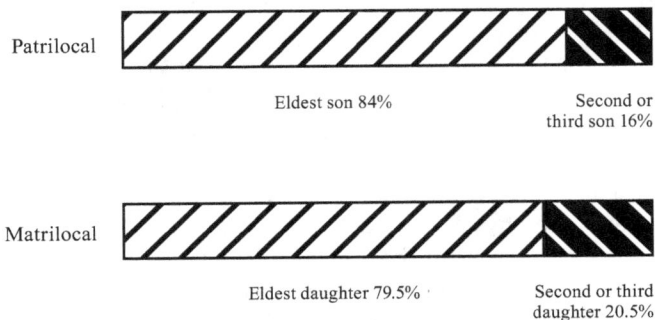

Patrilocal

Eldest son 84%   Second or third son 16%

Matrilocal

Eldest daughter 79.5%   Second or third daughter 20.5%

Source: Same as Figure 1.9.

Figure 1.11: FI of Ms E.

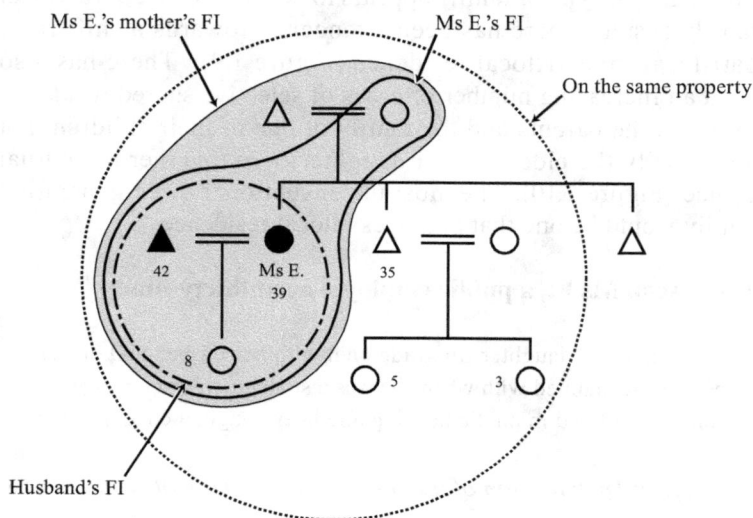

The gray area indicates the extent of co-residence.

After they had a child, both Ms E. and her husband became increasingly busier with their work. Consequently, the couple, joined by Ms E.'s younger brother and his wife, approached Ms E.'s parents with a proposal to rebuild the parents' house so they could live together. All expenses of reconstruction were paid by Ms E. and her husband. Ms E.'s family and her parents live in a two-family house. Ms E.'s younger brother has built another house on the same property. Ms E. does minimum housework and entrusts the care of her child almost entirely to her mother.

Ms E.'s family members' FI is shown in Figure 1.11. While Ms E.'s FI covers her mother, Ms E.'s husband's FI covers his nuclear family only (i.e. his wife and child).

The phenomenon seen in this family is that the principle of uni-lineality fails to apply to the sharing of residence and, instead, both the daughter's and the son's households eventually choose to live with their own parents, who own real property against the backdrop of rising land prices in the urban areas. This case shows that family property as the physical foundation of a family is a more powerful determinant of the form of residence than the family ideology of unilineality and that family property has become a foundation that unites generations in new urban-type families. It also shows that in many cases it is the working daughter's family that takes the initiative in the decision to take this form of residence. There is also evidence that in both patrilocal and matrilocal families, full-time working wives with children under six years of age are more likely to live in a three-generation family than are non-working wives under conditions that are otherwise the same. Behind the seemingly conventional form of these three-generation families, we can see working mothers' needs. These mothers have also caused the increased rate of matrilocal residence. This type of family can be likened to an old wineskin containing new wine.

In contrast to the case of one parent living away from his or her family because of work, *kateinai rikon* (in-house divorce) is a situation where the family continues to share a residence but has collapsed in substance. This situation has suddenly entered the limelight as a result of Iku Hayashi's work that used this term as its title (Hayashi 1985). Although the number of families in this situation cannot be known from statistical data, there seems to be a large number of them.

The case of Ms F., a housewife aged sixty-two

Ms F. and her husband are an ordinary couple in their sixties. They have been married for forty years. Ms F. now says, 'It is irritating to share the same dining table with my husband.' The reason why she still stays with him is that she would not be able to make a decent living if she divorced him and he would not be able to pay her a divorce settlement. She would lose out if she divorced him. Ms F. also thinks that she is now too old to have sufficient vigor and desire to undergo divorce proceedings. Still, she never eats with her own husband, even though she does prepare his meals. She absolutely does not want to be consigned to her husband's tomb. She plans to ask her daughters to ensure that she will be entombed according to her own wishes.

Figure 1.12 shows Ms F.'s family's FI. Although the husband and the wife live together, their FI does not cover each other. However, both firmly believe that their married daughters and their grandchildren are part of their family. Their daughters' views are unknown.

According to Iku Hayashi's *Kateinai rikon*, the main reason why a husband and wife who have mentally divorced do not take the decision to separate or formally divorce is that they share a house, or property. They continue to live apart under the same roof.[7] In the cases reported by Hayashi, the wives unanimously say reflectively that they were able to continue to live with their

Figure 1.12: FI of Ms F.

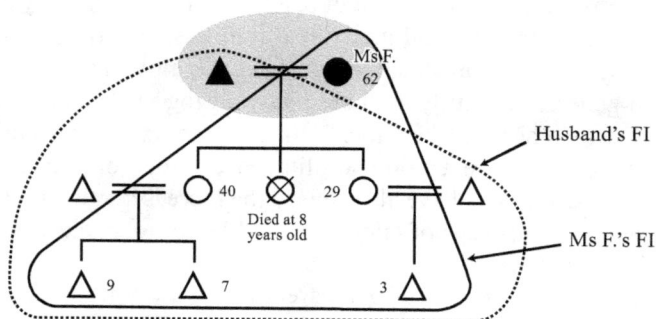

The gray area indicates the extent of co-residence.

husbands separately under the same roof only because they had no sex with their husbands. This suggests that even though they share residence, these couples no longer share sexual relationships.

Adoption, a product of the conventional family system, is another factor undergoing change. Conventionally, a family without a male heir arranged an adoption in order to obtain one. In contrast, today it is reported that more than 80% of adoptive parents wish to adopt a girl between zero and three years of age. This indicates that these parents give priority to the selfless joy of child rearing over a desire to obtain an heir. Viewed from another angle, in light of the fact that child rearing is in a way the 'price for security for old age,' we could also understand that these adoptive parents may have higher expectations that an adopted daughter will take care of them in their old age, against the backdrop of the fact that care for the elderly is more costly in terms of labor than in terms of money.

One contemporary form of adoption is a foster parent system on a voluntary basis.

The case of Mr G., a public servant aged forty-two

Mr G. has a family of five, including his wife, who was his colleague, two children (a junior high school student and a senior high school student) and Mr G.'s mother. Through his business he became acquainted with a woman from the Philippines, and he became a foster parent to a girl living on Negros Island. For three years Mr G. has sponsored the girl, now eleven years old, which costs him 10,000 yen

Figure 1.13: FI of Mr G.

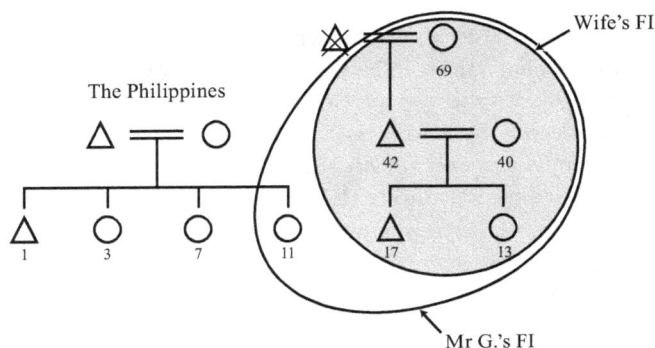

The gray area indicates the extent of co-residence.

per year for school education. Mr G.'s wife is quite indifferent to her husband's foster child. She thinks that the couple's two children are hers and the foster child is her husband's. Mr G. writes to his foster child once every two months, to which the girl never fails to reply. This summer he went to Negros Island to see her.

Mr G.'s foster family is like a family game that he enjoys with his pocket money. This Japanese version of the *Daddy-long-legs* story, which has been made possible by the increased value of yen, requires only a small amount of resources and a little bit of volunteer spirit. Figure 1.13 shows Mr G.'s family's FI. Mr G.'s foster family may seem to represent his effort to create his own quasi-family as a man who has been excluded from the close relationship between his wife and children.

Ms H.'s case is an extreme example where a seemingly old wineskin now contains totally new wine.

The case of Ms H., a writer aged fifty-one

Ms H. divorced her husband when she was forty-seven. After divorce, she came to live with her former father-in-law, yielding to his words, 'I don't want to be away from you.' Because her former husband's family was of ancient extraction and was surrounded by a large group of relatives in the old town, when she lived with him as his daughter-in-law their relationship was that of a lord and his servant. Many times she had wished he would die soon, never even imagining that she would end up living with him even after she divorced her husband. Thus, as soon as Ms H. started to live with her former father-in-law, she told him that he now must take care of himself. She taught him housework, scolding him without hesitation and mercy. That way, she thought, he would give up and run away to live with his own son. Contrary to her expectations, however, he quickly learned housework skills and has reached a point where he says he enjoys housework. Before she was aware, her former father-in-law became indispensable to her. He helps Ms H. greatly with housework and also acts as her secretary by answering telephone calls for her during the day. Ms H.'s two children have grown up and each lives in a separate house, leaving only Ms H. to live with her former father-in-law.

In families of the war dead, it was not uncommon for a widow to continue to live with her parents-in-law and her children (Figure 1.14). If a widow had no children she was usually sent to her parents' home, but if she had children, it was often the case that she stayed with her deceased husband's family as a person responsible for raising the family's heir.[8]

In the case of Ms H., her family's structure looks very similar to that of conventional families seen in the days after Japan's defeat in the Second World War. It is difficult to distinguish Ms H.'s family from the conventional stem family (with missing members) based solely on the statistical data on her family's structure. However, Ms H.'s family differs greatly from the conventional model in that she divorced her husband instead of losing him and that it was of her own accord that she came to live with her former father-in-law. In Ms H.'s case, she and her former father-in-law were unrelated to each other but happened to be part of the same family. (Ms H. and her former father-in-law have no blood relationship [Figure 1.15]. Moreover, his reason for asking her to stay with him was not that he did not want to be away from his grandchildren who were related to him by blood.) They chose to live together, which created a family that is similar in form to the conventional model of family.

A typical example of a family whose form is conventional but whose members have unconventional perception is a de facto couple. This applies to most couples who have chosen not to register their marriages so that both the parties can keep their surnames. However, while most de facto couples are DINKs and refrain from registering their marriages only until the first child is born, Ms I., who formally registered her child by her husband as an extramarital child, ideologically maintains her de facto marriage.

Figure 1.14: Living together with a parent of the deceased husband

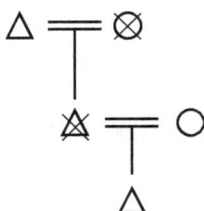

Figure 1.15: FI of Ms H.

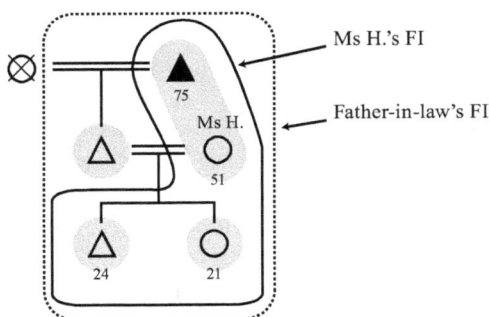

Ms H.'s FI

Father-in-law's FI

The gray area indicates the extent of co-residence.

The case of Ms I., a university lecturer aged forty-six

Ms I. currently lives with her husband, who is thirteen years younger, and their seven-year-old daughter. The couple has chosen not to register their marriage. Ms I. has not let her husband acknowledge their child as his, based on her belief that Japan's patrilineality is associated with discrimination against women and that the society would function better under a matrilineal system. There is always tension between her and her husband. If she feels any discrepancy between her husband and herself, she may warn him by such means as refusing to share a bed with him. Since she and her husband are both aware that they can choose to separate at any time, the couple will collapse if they fail to always care for each other. To prevent this from happening, Ms I. values conversation with her husband and makes it a policy to discuss everything with him as much as possible. She also talks about everything with her daughter and brings her to rallies and meetings, as she

Figure 1.16: FI of Ms I.

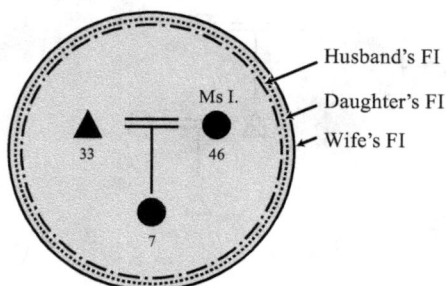

Husband's FI
Daughter's FI
Wife's FI

Ms I.

33   46

7

The gray area indicates the extent of co-residence.

wants her daughter to know the way the couple has chosen to live their lives and to be aware of what is happening in the community.

Ms I.'s husband is actively involved in child rearing. Although he and his daughter have no legal relation as parent and child, their bond as de facto parent and child is stronger than between an ordinary father and his child. While de facto couples are currently subject to various disadvantages from a legal viewpoint, if de facto marriage is entitled to legal protection equal to that of legal marriage (and if discrimination against extramarital children is removed), Ms I.'s family will be no different from an ordinary nuclear family. Technically, both Ms I. and her husband are unmarried. However, on a strict 'current address basis' as in the case of the Japanese national census (which defines marriage strictly on a de facto basis – i.e. 'if a man and woman with no blood relation live together'), Ms I.'s family is categorized in the same category as other nuclear families. Ms I.'s family members' FI is in perfect accordance with the extent of co-residence, with no disparity in FI between family members (Figure 1.16).

What is intriguing is that, whether or not the husband and wife live together, de facto couples who deny legal marriage have a tendency to emphasize their substance as a family as if to declare, 'We *are* a true family.' Paradoxically, the ideology of the modern family represented by the image of 'the husband and wife loving each other and the parents and children sharing a strong bond of love' (Ochiai, 1989) seems to be embodied by de facto couples in a more purified form. These couples are more puritanical in that they attempt to achieve correspondence between what family should be and what family really is. If 'what it should be' (i.e. the legal system) catches up with 'what it really is,' nothing will distinguish de facto marriage from legal marriage. In fact, de facto couples' demands – such as the enactment of legislation allowing married couples to keep separate surnames, removal of the discrimination against extramarital children and abolition of the family registration system – will, if satisfied, dissolve the foundation on which they are categorized as an unconventional model in terms of their perception. If these demands are satisfied, will de facto couples return to quadrant I, where families are conventional in both perception and form?

The case of Ms J., a company employee aged thirty-one

Ms J. met a man with a wife and children when she was twenty-four years old. She had children by him at the ages of twenty-five and twenty-eight. Her partner readily accepted her decision to have his children, assuming that she would have and raise them on her own. He visits her on one or two weekdays a week. He pays child support to her when he earns money from his business, about once every few months. She works full-time while her children are looked after at day care. Having to do everything on her own is tiring. Ms J. does not think she wants to marry her partner, but does hope that he will be more involved in child rearing. His wife says that she is determined to protect her own family, even if only for form's sake. He has no intention to divorce his wife either, and properly plays his role as a husband in ceremonies, the New Year, the Bon Festival and family functions.

What is it like if a couple that denies legal marriage lives separately and if either lives in de facto bigamy?

Ms J.'s situation, despite her progressive perception that she voluntarily chose to be there, is no different from that of a man living in bigamy with a mistress or concubine. Although Ms J. thinks that she is 'sharing' the man with his family, his involvement in child rearing is poor, with which she is dissatisfied. The difference of her family from the conventional model is that she does not place an economic burden on her partner because she is both economically and mentally independent, and she does not destroy his 'family.' Based on her opposition to the marriage system, Ms J. does not admit that she is having an 'affair' with him but places him within the scope of her FI. In contrast, to her partner his family means that of his married wife and her children (Figure 1.17). In the de facto fatherless family, Ms J. bears a heavy burden in child rearing,

Figure 1.17: FI of Ms J.

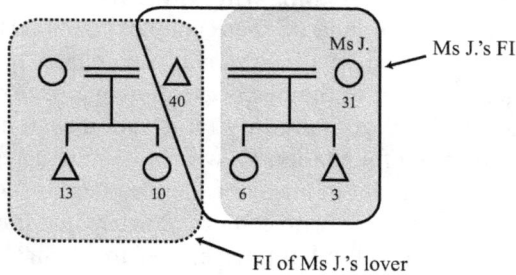

The gray area indicates the extent of co-residence.

while the man does nothing more than occasionally 'play house.' The case of Ms J. is a contemporary version of concubine. However, compared to former days when keeping a concubine used to cost the man her upkeep, the improved independence of modern women has ironically resulted in the increased tolerance for men's lack of dependability.

When a bigamous marriage consists of a de facto marriage and a legal marriage, the latter is always favorable. In the case of another woman who is in a similar situation to Ms J., when she demanded her partner's acknowledgment of their child after her birth, the man's wife countered with a demand for compensation for the infringement of her rights as a wife. The rights as a wife are as strong as ever.

It is difficult to predict whether Ms J.'s belief in de facto marriage will ideologically develop into a belief in monogamy or in bigamy. If only the legal obstacle is cleared, will she hope that her partner will dissolve his legal marriage and start to live with her? In this case, the extent of co-residence will completely overlap with that of FI. Alternatively, will she continue to live separately from her partner and maintain her single-mother household? In this case, will she live separately from her partner in monogamy, or will it be possible that she may live in a bigamous situation in which either party has more than one partner at a time? This certainly includes the possibility of her own bigamous marriage. Based on the sexual double standard, isn't it likely that her partner will not accept her bigamous marriage, despite his own? Various questions arise.

If Ms J.'s choice is de facto monogamy, it represents a modern ideology of family similar to Ms I.'s. In this case, Ms J.'s current situation only represents a transitional form of family that is forced to be that way by the legal restrictions. If so, Ms J.'s situation is nothing novel in terms of her perception either. It is true that Ms J. is wavering, and it is also true that her partner has taken advantage of her incomplete 'novelty.'

There is a tendency for more and more stepfamilies to be formed as a result of remarriages. In particular, if both the remarried partners bring their own children from their previous marriages, the creation of the stepfamily represents an encounter of two different cultures. The novelty found here in both form and perception is that women bring their children from their previous marriages to their remarriages. First, in the traditional patrilineal stem family system, divorce meant a women had to leave her children with her former husband's family. It has been only a few decades since mothers began to obtain custody more often than fathers after divorce in Japan, where joint custody is still not allowed by law. Second, divorced women with children seldom used to remarry and, when they did, most did so without bringing their children from their previous marriages. It is a relatively new phenomenon that a man accepts his wife's children from her previous marriage. If, in a case of such remarriage, the man is getting married for the first time, he is often younger than his wife.

The case of Ms K., a pharmacist aged fifty

Ms K.'s husband died of illness soon after she had a baby. She remarried later and brought her three-year-old daughter to her new family. Her new husband had a son from his previous marriage. Soon after remarriage, her husband came home drunk and hit Ms K.'s daughter. Ms K. thought that her new marriage would not work with her daughter, and had her adopted by her grandmother (Ms K.'s mother). Subsequently, she focused on the education of her husband's son. However, around grade five the boy began to fall behind in his grades and proved contrary to her expectations. As a result, she terminated her custody of the boy. He is currently employed and lives on his own. Ms K. is on good terms with her daughter, as a result of sharing the same 'mother.' However, her daughter is in some ways distant from her. Ms K. thinks she cannot help it, as she has no right to say anything to her own daughter.

If both the husband and wife bring children from their previous marriages, the family will have complex personal relationships – the

Figure 1.18: FI of Ms K.

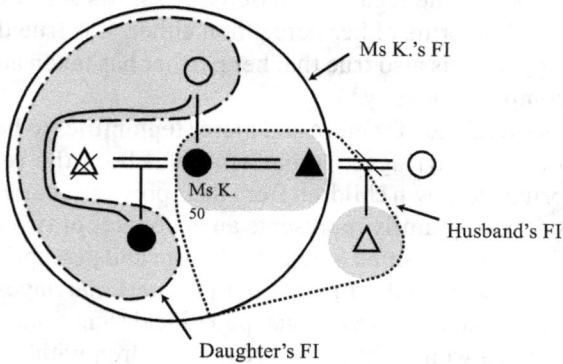

The gray area indicates the extent of co-residence.

relationships between each of the parents and each of the children, in addition to the relationship between the husband and wife. Ms K. gave priority to her relationship with her husband over her relationship with her child, and even chose to get rid of her own child whom she had found obstructive to her new life. Ms K. first entered into an adoption arrangement with her husband's son,[9] but later terminated her custody when her stepchild proved to be poor at school. She regards both husband–wife relationship and parent–child relationship as something that can be entered into or canceled by agreement. As a result, however, she has to endure being discarded by her own child, to whom she has denied the priority of blood relationship (Figure 1.18).

The case of Ms K. may seem to fall under a conventional model in that she discarded her own child to remarry and devoted herself to rearing her new husband's child. However, she is consciously rational and practical in her choice of giving priority to the husband–wife relationship and getting rid of obstacles to save the relationship amid the complicated situation in the family. There certainly are many cases of stepfamilies with children from previous marriages that are doing well, unlike the case of Ms K. Still, it is not easy to run a stepfamily due to the complex personal relationships involved, as seen in cases in America with such problems as sexual abuse of the wife's children by the husband, discord among stepbrothers and stepsisters, and intervention by non-resident parents of the children. Maintaining FI where there is no illusory belief in blood relationship requires greater efforts by the family members involved.

Families with unconventional perception and unconventional form

Quadrant III of Figures 1.3 and 1.4 contains unconventional families in both perception and form, which include families described below. First, one indicator that can be mentioned in the context of deviation from the norms of family in form is inconsistency between blood relationship and residence. A first type of this form of family is co-residence of people not related by blood. The second type is non-co-residence of people related by blood, which has resulted in the reduction of family size to the minimum level (i.e. a single-person household).

Speaking of co-residence of people not related by blood, a husband and wife are originally one such form. A husband and wife are a starting point to make two originally unrelated people into a family. As seen in cases of in house divorce, sharing a sexual relationship is not an essential requirement for a husband–wife relationship. Sharing a sexual relationship is something that is simply confirmed by its results (i.e. the generation of a blood relationship represented by children). Sexually inactive young couples (such as sexless couples seen recently), couples who marry during old age and do not necessarily attach importance to having sex, and couples who chose not to have children (such as DINKs) or who are unable to have children would not constitute a family by the conventional definition of family. When the 'generation of blood relationship' has been excluded from the purpose of sharing a sexual relationship and when, further, the sharing of a sexual relationship is no longer an essential requirement, you could live with a partner of the same sex and could also have more than one partner. If the parties involved share the same FI, any group can constitute a family. This type of family can be found in groups that have been known as collectives or communes.

The case of Ms L., a partner of a printing house aged thirty-five

Ms L. currently lives with two other women. They jointly run a small printing business. They have run the business for eight years, with changes in the members and fluctuations in their number. They met through women's liberation activities, and their motive for starting to live together was to create a workplace for themselves and to try a new way of living with members without blood relationship and without the involvement of men. It was also more economical to live together. At first they had quarrels almost every day. Even though they thought they shared the same ideals, their ways of daily living differed from each other. Sometimes Ms L. found some of the others untidy, and at other times too strict, and all these often made her tired. After 'natural selection,' the current members who live together are 'birds of a feather.' They have seldom had quarrels and have efficiently allocated both business tasks and housework. There were some love affairs with men along the way, but Ms L. eventually reached a conclusion that it is easier to live with women only.

There are senior versions of collectives. Kiyoko Yoshihiro's *Sukuranburu kazoku* (Scrambled families) (1989) mentions an example of a collective consisting of retired nurses.

The case of Ms M., a retired nurse of the Japan Red Cross aged sixty-five

Four women worked as nurses at the Japan Red Cross Hospital throughout the turbulent period spanning before and after the Second World War. They built four independent houses in a row and currently live in a community together under the policy that 'the most important is the four members' and enjoy their senior lives to the full. Each lives in a two-storied house with a front garden on a plot of approximately 300 square meters. The four houses are connected via intercom, an alarm and a garden that provides free access to all members. The houses' respective living rooms also serve as a connecting corridor. All four members have meals together and two at a time take a bath together. Other than that, all or some of them get together for occasional tea and for a walk every morning. Each has her own hobby or subject of research that she pursues day and night. They say, 'We are a family of kindred spirits and an unorthodox community whose members are bound together more closely and strongly than sisters.'

There are various cases of collectives, with some consisting of the same gender, while others consist of both genders, and with some allowing sexual relationships, while others do not. The point in common found for the time being in relatively stable groups is that they consist only of women sharing no sexual relationship. Historically, there certainly were dormitories and armies where groups of men shared residence, but these men did not call such groups *family* but regarded them as a transit point that they were being forced to go through at the moment. Recent research of ours has failed to find a single case where a group of men has voluntarily formed FI associated with co-residence. Cases reported in other documents include ecologically oriented communities, such as Kainow-juku and Milky Way. These communities consist of both genders, with some containing husband–wife and/or parent–child relationships. Although they certainly fall under an unconventional model of family, they are closer to 'blood-related family with some unrelated members' or an extended family in a broad sense. In addition, as these extended families are also business associations, they share physical foundations such as a farm. The fact that we found no examples of men-only collectives may represent a limitation of the gender socialization; that is, a male group may tend to be instrumental in nature and may have difficulty relying solely on a self-sufficient, emotional feeling of community.

Instead of these collectives, men create pseudo-families sharing drinking together.

The case of Olive, a bar in Minami, Osaka

Olive is a bar located in Minami, Osaka. It has counter seats only and accommodates a maximum of about ten customers. The bar proprietress (who is called *Mama* according to a Japanese custom in this trade) is in her late forties and has a big sisterly air about her. Her customers are company employees, most of whom are regular patrons. The bar thrives every night, with customers singing songs in karaoke and chatting with and around Mama. She prepares gifts for her customers not only for Valentine's Day but also for each customer's birthday, when all other customers sing *Happy birthday* for the birthday customer. Sometimes after they drink, they go out together with Mama as a leader and 'eat out' and then come back home. They also share sushi, cakes or other refreshments provided by customers. They take a hot spring trip once a year, the cost for which is shared equally by the bar and the customers.

The existence of the woman called Mama, and the sharing of food and drink and Mama, create brother-like relationships among the customers (Figure 1.19). The bar offers a family ritual or birthday parties that have been forgotten by the real families of the customers. They also have an annual family trip. However, this quasi-family

Figure 1.19: Pseudo-family under the mistress of a bar

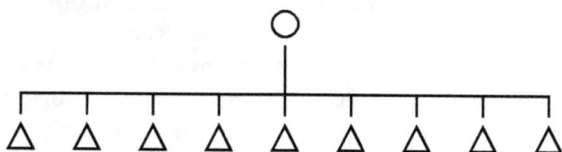

Figure 1.20: Four types of partner relationship

Sharing of sexual relationship

	Yes	No
Both sexes	Husband and wife	Divorce in the family Sexless couple
Same sex	Lesbian or gay couple	Collective Senior house

gives way to the customers' real families when true family rituals take place, such as the New Year or the Bon Festival. The customers pay for a brief, 'make-believe game of family' in which they play the parts of carefree children without being required to fulfill their responsibility as fathers.

If two people of the same gender share sexual relationships, they form a lesbian or gay couple. According to the conventional usage of the term *married couple*, a married couple must (i) share sexual relationships and (ii) consist of both genders. If these two factors are treated separately from each other, with each being expressed by a binary variable (share/not share sexual relationships; consisting of both genders/the same gender), various forms of partnership are possible, as shown in Figure 1.20. Certainly, there have long been women-only households whose members live together 'like sisters.' In the meantime, amid the gay and lesbian liberation movement influenced by feminism, demands for official recognition and for legal guarantee of the relationships between lesbian/gay partners began to be made openly. In California homosexual couples are entitled to legal marriage. No blood relationship will arise from this marriage, but a parent–child relationship can be generated by adoption arrangements or artificial reproduction. However, as shown in *American couples* by Schwartz and Blumstein (1985), while male homosexuals have a strong tendency for polygamous relationship, lesbians show a marked tendency for monogamous relationship. Specifically, lesbians tend to create relatively long, stable relationships with the same partner and are strongly family-oriented. The following is an example of a lesbian couple.

The case of Ms N., a company employee aged forty

Ms N. got married at nineteen when she was a student. Her husband, a faithful man, is one year older. They bought a family home and have children aged eighteen and fourteen. Now Ms N. has separated from her husband and lives with a twenty-seven-year-old woman. Ms N. tried to communicate with her husband for twenty years, but they failed to understand each other. He was a good man in some respects, including that he was not repressive as a man. However, Ms N. was unable to get along well with him because of a gap between them in sensitivity and an awareness that they failed to fill despite much discussion. Ms N. believes that she should basically be able to live on her own, but does admit that it is also important to help each other. It is comfortable for her to live with her current partner, who says that her involvement with Ms N. made her believe in her relationships with other people. Ms N. is considering entering into an adoption arrangement with her partner in the near future.

When non-blood-related people live together, metaphors implying blood relationship are often used, such as 'like sisters,' 'closer than sisters' or 'like parent and child.' When a relationship has no substantial foundations, the members are inclined to reinforce their relationship in kinship terms (Figure 1.21).

In contrast, an intention to open up one's family in an un-conventional direction is expressed in non-kinship terms to represent the family, such as metaphors like 'friend-like couple' or 'friend-like parent and child.' Friend-like couples typified by married couples in the new family generation originally had a vision that breaks down the conventional perception of what family is. While 'friend-like couples' in the baby-boomer generation are said to have been a mere slogan and have actually ended up creating old-fashioned families

Figure 1.21: FI of Ms N.

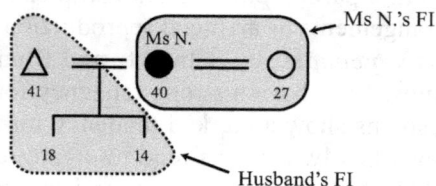

The gray area indicates the extent of co-residence.

with traditional gender role assignment in substance, this trend has been taken over by 'club-mate couples' found in the so-called *shinjinrui* (new breed) of Japanese. These couples are characterized by the same age, the sharing of hobbies and activities, and immaturity, which often involves refusal to have children. In these couples, the husband and wife are not complementary to each other as assumed in the background assumption of the Altman system, a computerized matchmaking data system that originated in postwar Germany and was introduced into Japan in the 1970s; instead, they are two of a kind. DINK couples are one version of this friend-like couple. They not only dislike restrictions that prevent their club-mate activities but also fear that the birth of a child will inevitably start the division of labor between father and mother and will ruin their friend-like relationship.

The case of Ms O., a dancer aged thirty-seven

Ms O. married her husband, a company employee, at the age of twenty. She decided not to have children when she was twenty-one or twenty-two because it seems to her that having children will make her way of thinking conservative. Without children, Ms O. thinks, her husband and she can live freely. Being free is extremely important to her. She also says she cannot stand her relationship with her husband being interrupted by children. She dislikes a relationship that focuses on children in everything and where the husband and wife call each other mom and dad. However, her husband wishes to have children. He is just being patient out of respect for his wife's way of life. Ms O. takes the contraceptive pill. When her husband sometimes mutters, 'With no children, we're not a family,' she feels uneasy and is afraid that this marriage may collapse.

The ideal model of the club-mate couple is often portrayed in girls' comics as a 'twin-like couple.'[10] While a set of twins fatefully forms a pair, each is also a sibling to the other and they are prohibited from sharing sexual relationships. Club-mate couples welcome the introduction of sexually neutral metaphors, such as 'like a brother and sister,' to their husband–wife relationship. Their motives for this attitude are (i) an intention to minimize sexual elements in the relationship between the two, and (ii) an intention to ensure, by achieving the first intention, openness (which is club-like in the literal sense of the word) of the two-party relationship to invite third and fourth parties to it. In fact, as seen in many club-mate couples who, after marriage, continue to spend leisure time with other couples, this type of couple tends to avoid exclusive activities.

A set of twins is a fateful pair, and they are prohibited from having sex with each other. We cannot hastily conclude whether these twin-like couples represent an attempt to dissolve or open up family by minimizing the exclusive sharing of sexual relationships, or the other way around (for the time being, this minimizing of sexual relationships is developing in a direction towards 'absence of sex' instead of 'liberation of sex,' unlike in former days). The use of kinship terms, such as 'mother–son' and 'brother–sister,' to describe a husband–wife relationship is a routine method to provide a foundation for quasi-stability to the partners, who originally have no blood or family relation to each other. At this time, when families have weaker foundations, an illusion of twins might provide a stronger psychological stability than that of husband and wife. After all, a husband and wife are originally unrelated, while a set of twins inevitably belongs to the same family.

FI may cover something other than living people, such as pet animals, aborted or miscarried fetuses, or dead people.

The case of Ms P., a company employee aged forty-five

Ms P. has long separated from her husband. She has an eighteen-year-old son and a seventeen-year-old daughter, who she thinks are independent from her. Ms P. is sure that her children will leave home soon. She feels lonely, but does not want to be comforted by someone. She has had enough of men – her husband was enough for her. Ms P.'s parents are dead. She has an older brother but has become estranged from him. These days Ms P. deeply misses her younger brother, who died at the age of twenty-seven. She thinks that her true family consists of her dead parents and younger brother only.

Figure 1.22: FI of Ms P.

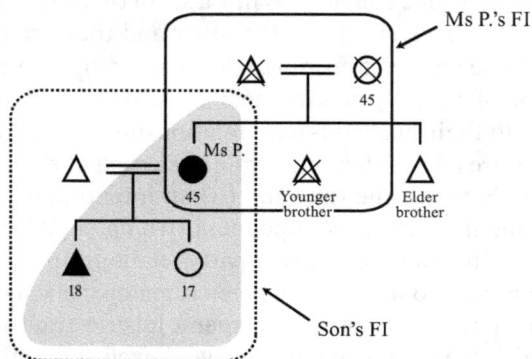

The gray area indicates the extent of co-residence.

The fact that Ms P.'s FI (Figure 1.22) covers her family of orientation (the family to which she was born) rather than her family of procreation (the family she created herself) may represent her psychological regression. However, it is true that one can romanticize dead siblings more than one's own children who grow up and go further and further out of one's way.

Next, a case of a gay man who stays ideologically single.

The case of Mr Q., a high school teacher aged thirty-five

Mr Q.'s only family member is a cat. After graduation from university, Mr Q. lived with another gay man but broke up the relationship after he was convinced that it is most natural for him to live alone. Mr Q. has lived alone since then. He does have a boyfriend now whom he is in love with, but he never wants to live with him. Mr Q.'s parents seem to assume that he will 'get straight' some day. Mr Q. is the eldest son, but does not want to attend his parents' funerals when they die and he did not attend his younger sister's wedding ceremony. Mr Q. has already asked his parents to dispose of the family's Buddhist altar. He does not count on his family's assets and is ready to die 'like a dog' when he becomes old. For the past several years, he has not returned to his parents' home, even for the New Year or the Bon Festival.

Even though Mr Q. is an ideological anti-family man, he lives with a cat and says that his pet is the only thing for which he feels responsible (Figure 1.23).

Figure 1.23: FI of Mr Q.

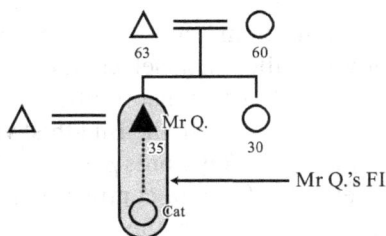

The gray area indicates the extent of co-residence.

New illusions of family

If you can expand your FI to include dead people, friends or non-human beings without actually living with them, you could, conversely, include imaginary family members in your FI while living with your blood relatives like a normal family in terms of appearance. If a family consists of more illusion than substance, you could even start with an illusory (imaginary) family. It is well known that religious communities attempt to rely on a fictitious family often by using kinship terminology.

In this section, let me foretell the outlook for families by studying the details of new illusions of family that have emerged in the Japanese pop culture scene.

Banana Yoshimoto's novels, which are influenced by girls' comics and whose style and sensitivity have brought her works a burst of popularity among female readers of her generation, frequently uses the term *minashigo* (orphan) (Yoshimoto, 1988). Although it is unnatural for the protagonist of a story to make his or her appearance as an orphan right from the beginning without much explanation, this setting has a long tradition in the history of stories for young girls. This is because by defining the protagonist as an orphan and identifying themselves with the protagonist, readers are able to deny their actual parent–child relationships and play in the world of make-believe just as they please. A twelve-year-old girl, whose parents are in the baby-boomer generation, imagines that she was actually adopted, and frequently writes letters addressed to her fictitious 'real father.' By creating an idealized, fictitious father, this girl denies her real parent–child relationship.

The media distributed in the world of these girls, such as girls' comic magazines and occult magazines, often contain works on the theme of family in a previous life, as seen in the *Genma taisen* (Great War with Imaginary Evils) boom that arose several years ago. In August 1989 a case occurred in Tokushima Prefecture where three junior high school girls killed themselves in order, supposedly, to see their previous lives, after they had written a scenario. Among these girls who are unfamiliar with the Buddhist view of the world, what is the role played by the keywords *previous life*?

First of all, a 'previous life' is in contrast with 'this life.' As is the case with the illusion of orphan, the idea of fate in our previous life helps us deny realities and escape to a fantasy by teaching us that our fate in this life is only temporary and that in our previous life it is absolute. Second, a previous life is always associated with specific relationships, or a fate. Again, this aspect is similar to the illusion of orphan, in which being an orphan does not mean isolation or severance but a starting point from which the person can start various relationships freely. Third, the fate in a previous life is often not retained in the person's memory but is told to him or her by someone else as his or her inescapable destiny. In this sense, the fate is absolute, something about which you have no choice. You must comply with something that (someone else tells you) lies in the subconscious. While the actual parent–child relationship should be experienced by children as something absolute and involuntary, why do children deny their actual relationship with their parents and look for a relationship that is even more absolute and involuntary?

One factor that I should point out as something that is probably behind this phenomenon is the difference between the prewar illusion of orphan and today's illusion of 'family in a previous life.' In former times, actual families had substantial power from which children might have had to escape by strongly denying their own families. In contrast, families experienced by contemporary teenagers have already become something unstable such that they might dissolve at the whim of the parents at any time. This instability of families is represented by a girl's words to her mother in the girl's comic, *Hotto rōdo* (Hot road) by Taku Tsumugi (1986–87); the girl, who lives with her single mother after her parents' divorce, asks her romantic mother, 'Why don't you behave a bit more like a mother?' Nevertheless, this is not attributable to any limitation of or any defect in the generational personality of the parents of today's *shin-shinjinrui* (new-new breed, which refers to those who were born in the 1960s) and baby-boomer juniors (which refers to those who were born around 1971–74). At this time, when, as discussed above, families have lost their substantial foundations (such as family property, family business and family name) and when their 'sharing of residence' and 'sharing of food' have been shaken, and, further, when even their 'sharing of sexual relationship' and 'sharing of blood relationship' are becoming shaky, people's FI is wandering about looking for its foundations. It is interesting that one such foundation happened to be previous life, a key word representing an absolute, subconscious and unselective relationship. It seems that, at a time when families have an increasing level of flexibility (thus instability), children are looking for a relationship more absolute than their real family.

This fact gives us a hint for the question of what a family is (thus what family illusion is). It is a paradox that after people's FI has shifted all the way from the conventional to unconventional models in both form and perception, there is a belief that there must be a relationship, although idealized, more absolute and fateful than one's actual family. This paradox reveals one of the essential characteristics of what people represent by the word *family*: if a relationship is voluntary and selective, and thus can be formed and dissolved, then people would not call it a family; therefore, when one selective relationship is described using the metaphor *family-like*, this represents the desire of the parties involved to change the foundations of the relationship from something selective to something absolute.

While people's FI has shifted from involuntary to selective relationships, the reaction to this shift has resulted in the fabrication of an even more involuntary relationship. This is a situation where religions and the occult prove themselves. The illusion of twins is one version of these ideologies. Members of a couple would be more stable if they perceive themselves and are perceived by others as '(fatefully) being two of a kind' than as 'loving each other.' If a couple's FI is based on the concept that 'we are two of a kind who happen to be a man and a woman,' even their gender difference and sexuality constitute nuisances. Similarly, what children are looking for, as expressed by the terribly retrospective phrase of 'fate in a previous life,' is a foundation for their existence that would assure them that they were born to this world according to the fate in their previous lives and not as a result of their parents' insecure love.

It has been demonstrated that the prewar concept of *ie* was a mere illusion once deprived of its physical foundations. In search of a new illusion of family that would replace the *ie* concept, people's FI has been wandering up and down and around such words as *previous life* and *twins*. While no strong candidate for replacing *ie* has emerged, there is no doubt that FI is associated with people's transpersonal illusion about the foundation for the necessity of their birth to this world. In this sense, a family is eternal, psychological 'security goods.'

Contrary to their unchangeable appearance, families actually dissolve when faced with a crisis and get rid of unfavorable members. On the other hand, contrary to the trend that seems to enhance the voluntary and selective nature of families, illusions that add an absolute nature to families are also enhanced. It seems that families are not necessarily making a one-way shift in the direction of dissolution.

2 Women's Transformation and the Family

Women's transformation during the shift of industrial structure

If changes for women during and after Japan's postwar rapid growth were to be summarized in a phrase, that phrase would be the 'women's participation in the workplace.' According to the 1982 Employment Status Survey (Shūgyō kōzō kihon chōsa) published in 1983, of all married women the proportion of working women was 50.8%, which comprised a majority at last. With more married women being working housewives than full-time housewives, 'becoming a housewife upon marriage' now represented the life course of a minority of all married women.

The true state of the 'emergence of women in the workplace'

How have Japanese women changed during the past two decades?

Emiko Shibayama, a researcher in economics of female labor, summarizes the changes in the Japanese female labor force after the 1973 oil crisis in the following eight points (Heiwa Keizai Keikaku Kaigi, 1987):

1. The labor force participation rate for middle- and older-aged women exceeded 50%.
2. The proportion of women in the labor force rose to 40%.
3. Of all working women, the ratio of employees rose to approxi-mately 70%.
4. Of all employees, the proportion of women rose to approximately 40%.
5. The average age of female employees rose to mid-thirties, and of all female employees, the percentage of married women (including married, widowed and divorced women) rose to 70%.
6. Approximately 70% of female employees were concentrated in the tertiary industry.

7. Of all female employees, the proportion of part-time workers rose to a little over 20%, showing the diversification and reduced stability of employment patterns for women, such as dispatch labor and employment on a temporary, casual or daily basis.
8. Women have been increasingly employed in high-technology areas.

These points indicate that the true state of 'women's participation in the workplace' was not an increase of 'super women' or 'career women' as once touted by the media, but an increase of middle- and older-aged female workers in unstable employment, a situation that can be termed the 'marginalization of the female labor force.'

In terms of life course pattern, these middle- and older- aged women who emerged in the workplace fall under the *suspension–re-employment* pattern, which includes women who temporarily left their jobs for marriage or childbirth. Women who fall under the *continuously employed* pattern have never left their jobs for childbirth or child-rearing, and, contrary to our expectations, their numbers have not increased remarkably.

Atarashii josei no ikikata wo motomete (In search of a new way of life for women) (Keizai Kikakuchō Kokumin Seikatsukyoku [ed.], 1987), published in 1987, reports on the results of a detailed survey – commissioned by the Social Policy Bureau of the Economic Planning Agency and undertaken by Kiyomi Morioka and his colleagues – on the relations between women's employment and family life by life courses. This survey classifies women's life course patterns into the following six patterns: Pattern I, unmarried, working; Pattern II, working, without children; Pattern III, continuously working before and after childbirth; Pattern IV, full-time housewife after marriage/childbirth; Pattern V, re-entering the workplace after childbirth; and Pattern VI, no work experience. Of these, Pattern III (continuously working before and after childbirth) represents only 21.7% of all samples. In terms of age groups, women who fall under Pattern III account for 27.8%, 25.2% and 27.9% of women in their thirties, forties and fifties, respectively. Employed (as opposed to self-employed) women who fall under the same pattern account for 14.3%, 14.4% and 12.1% of women in their thirties, forties and fifties, respectively, showing no significant differences between these age groups. Considering the reduction in the proportion of self-employed women, employed women who do not suspend work seem to progressively contribute to the total percentage of women in this pattern. However, this contribution has not brought such a major change to the majority that it can be termed an 'increase of career women who do not leave their jobs for marriage or childbirth.' Even in women in their thirties, the majority leave their jobs for marriage or childbirth at least for some time (i.e. women who fall under Pattern IV, full-time housewife after marriage/childbirth, and those who fall under Pattern V, re-entering the workplace after childbirth, which total 57.2%). The greatest change in the life course of women after the postwar rapid growth was that the suspension–re-entering the workplace pattern became the life course of choice of the majority of women in the past two decades or so, whereas there were practically no women of this type at the start of the rapid growth period,

As is generally known, however, the work conditions awaiting these middle- and older-aged women seeking re-employ-ment were extremely poor and included low wages in the unskilled sec-tor and little job security. While mentioning the diversification of employment patterns in the female labor force, Shibayama does not overlook the fact that this diversification included reduced stability. We must also pay attention to the data that says, 'Of all female employees, the proportion of part-time workers rose to a little over 20%.' If we look at the age group above thirty-five years, of all female employees the proportion of part-time workers jumps up to approximately one-in-three. In addition, still more women are actually likely to be in unstable employment if we assume that unstable employment includes women who are paid on a part-time basis (i.e. who work as many hours as full-time workers – and even extra hours – but are paid by the hour or day despite the govern-ment's definition of part-time work as being 'thirty-five hours or less of work per week'). We can therefore point out that 'women's participation in the workplace' was (1) brought about mainly by changes in middle- and older-aged women, and (2) was actually the 'marginalization of the female labor force.'

Transformation of the industrial structure

In order for 'women's participation in the workplace' as a social phenomenon to occur, the requirements of the demand side and those of the supply side needed to match each other in the labor market. On the supply side, factors pushing women out of home have consistently become stronger since around the 1950s due to a decrease in the number of children born and the electrification of households (Ueno, 1982a). However, it has been difficult to say that the demand side was ready to accept female workers. In this regard, it was, as Shibayama points out, the transformation of the industrial structure, or the so-called economic restructuring, after the 1973 oil crisis, that brought about the change (i.e. on the demand side, increased employment opportunities for middle- and older-aged women).

The transformation of the industrial structure resulted in a marked increase in the significance of the tertiary industry in the Japanese economy. This meant a shift of focus in the economy to software, or to information and services. Heavy industries such as steel and shipbuilding, which had supported economic growth during the 1960s, hit a ceiling and gave way to soft industries such as financial and distribution industries. The Japanese economy thus switched from the industrial age to a postindustrial age.

Veronika Beechy (1987) has demonstrated, using examples of countries in the Organization for Economic Cooperation and Development (OECD), that after the 1973 oil crisis a vast number of jobs for women were created in industrialized countries with few natural resources, such as Japan and European countries. Beechy points out that this is a paradox in that female employment increased during a structural recession, or when the unemployment rate was high. In this context, the 'high unemployment rate' means a high unemployment rate for adult male full-time workers, and 'female employment increased' means that unstable employment for middle- and older-aged women increased. This does not mean that, as people say, 'women deprived men of their jobs' because, first, jobs taken by women were of new types in the developing industry and had never existed before, and, second, jobs taken by women were of such poor conditions that no decent man would have taken them.

The transformation of the industrial structure caused direct damage to middle- and older-aged male workers in the skilled sector. While this appeared as high unemployment rates in OECD countries, Japan's unemployment rate did not increase. This was because in Japan the transformation of the industrial structure, or the replacement of the declining industry by the developing industry, occurred rapidly, with little time difference between the fall of the former and the rise of the latter, and because the reallocation of human resources occurred in a relatively smooth manner, although at some cost – as seen in the Jinzai Katsuyō Sentā (Human Resources Center) of the privatized Japan National Railways. Further, while victims of the transformation of the industrial structure were concentrated in middle- and older-aged male workers in Japan, the increased unemployment rates in OECD countries intensively affected young men who were about to enter the labor force, and middle- and older-aged male workers maintained their vested rights. This is associated with the strength of their labor unions.

Jobs for women increased during the transformation of the industrial structure for the following reasons: (1) the shift of focus in the economy to software made gender differences in labor less significant; (2) in the service sector, jobs with irregular shifts (i.e. jobs with wide seasonal/temporal variations) increased; and (3) such 'pink-collar jobs' were created as part-time jobs because they are jobs for women (Beechy, 1987: 163). Therefore, these new jobs that opened for women were 'jobs for pin money,' which were associated with low wages and unstable employment, and thus would never have been taken by adult men.

Let me mention here the special circumstance that existed in Japan but not in other OECD countries: the absence of immigrant workers. During its economic growth in and after the 1960s, the Japanese labor market consistently faced labor shortages because it was not given an option to introduce immigrant workers, who were available to markets in other industrialized countries. Under the strict provisions of the Japanese Immigration Control Law, foreign workers who are permitted to work in Japan are skilled workers who 'cannot be replaced by others.' However, it was unskilled labor that was in short supply during the economic growth. Companies managed to solve part of this labor shortage by factory automation and robotization, but had to rely on the latent unemployed population of married women to solve the rest of the labor shortage. Thus, middle- and older-aged married female workers were employed mainly as (1) unskilled labor, which could not be replaced by mechanization, and (2) in the types of jobs that were taken by immigrant workers in other industrialized countries. In conclusion, a trend in the introduction of immigrant workers and in the introduction of female employment are, therefore, closely connected with each other, because these two types of labor forces directly compete in the unskilled sector.

This 'marginalization of the female labor force' is paradoxically termed the '*housewifezation* of labor' by Claudia von Werlhof (Duden and Werlhof, 1986). Werlhof points out that not only women but men also are involved in this housewifezation process. Women's 'entry into the marginal labor market' refers to a situation where the barriers between paid labor in the formal sector and unpaid labor in the informal sector are lowered, allowing women to easily go back and forth between the two sectors. *Housewife* refers to a being who must always be ready to comply with a request from the informal sector (which is exactly why a housewife can only become a second-class worker). Likewise, a man can also become a 'housewife-like being' by being incorporated into the marginal labor market. Men and women together constitute marginal labor as the 'reserve army of labor' by, in the case of men, leaving the labor market (i.e. becoming unemployed), and by entering the labor market in the case of women.

The diversification of women's life course patterns

The above discussion reveals that the true state of 'women's participation in the workplace' was not necessarily a change to be welcomed by women. If we focus on married women with employed work experience and children, their life course alternatives in terms of work and home can be summarized into three patterns: (I) the continued employment pattern; (II) the suspension–re-employment pattern; and (III) the full-time housewife pattern.

Increase of women in the suspension–re-employment pattern

Of the three patterns, type I, the continued employment pattern, represents approximately 14% of the cohort of women in their thirties and has not substantially increased, as mentioned above. According to the survey results on the 'reasons for women leaving their jobs,' approximately 80% of female employees leave their jobs for marriage or childbirth, meaning that the remaining 20% of women fall under the continued employment pattern. This percentage agrees with the fact that the employment rate of women is 70% (20% of 70% is 14%).

In contrast, type III women, in the full-time housewife pattern, are on the decrease. By the middle of the 1980s, the proportion of double-income households in all worker households had risen above 60%. Of all women in their forties, considering that the proportion of working women had also risen above 60%, the proportion of women in life stage III who are over thirty-five years of age and are 'housewives without a job' must now be as low as some 30%.

It is women of type II, the suspension–re-employment pattern, who have leaped from a negligible minority position to the majority in the 1970s and the 1980s. Historically, these women, who are now in the early 1990s[1] in their forties or fifties, arrived at adulthood during Japan's rapid economic growth, and when they left their jobs for marriage or childbirth they did not expect to return to work. At that time, women were not fully aware of the suspension–re-employment life course pattern, nor were they prepared to return to work; they had no information about the labor market that was awaiting them in their middle- or older-age period of life. Only during the following two decades, namely the 1970s and the 1980s, did female employment increase dramatically as a result of the economic restructuring. We can say that the structural change in the Japanese economy during the past two decades gave these women an experience unprecedented in history.

Selection of life courses and economic factors

The options of women's life courses have thus diversified. Now, the sociological question arises as follows: What are the decision variables for women's selection of their life courses?

In selecting a work/home life course from pattern types I through III, a married woman must make two decisions. The first decision is whether she leaves or keeps her job, and this decision is made upon marriage or childbirth. The second decision is whether she returns to work or remains as a full-time housewife in the post-nurturing stage. A woman's decision-making is affected by various factors, including her education, awareness of self-reliance and family structure. However, the most determinant variable is likely to be an economic factor – her husband's income.

According to the 1982 Employment Status Survey, in the quintile household groups that were determined by ranking households according to the income of the head of the household, the proportion of working wives is about the same for each of the first four quintile groups, all around 50%. The corresponding proportion for the fifth quintile group is 38.1%, approximately 10% lower than the other groups. The cut-off point between the fourth and fifth quintile groups is an annual income of seven million yen. This means that one requirement for a woman to remain as a full-time housewife is to belong to an economically advantaged class whose member households have an annual income of at least seven million yen. This is also indicated by the fact that the most common reason for married women to start working part-time is an economic one – to help family finances.

Incidentally, the proportion of working women is not necessarily higher in women with higher levels of education. In Japan, where there is a strong tendency for female hypergamy, most college/ university-educated women marry college/university-educated men. Men with high levels of education are likely to belong to an economically advantaged class. As a result, there is a tendency for more 'wives without a job' in women with high levels of education.

Women in the continued employment pattern are more likely to have specialist jobs. It is not clear whether they have been able to continue to work because they have specialist jobs or whether they choose specialist jobs because they are highly motivated to continue to work. However, the three major specialist jobs of Japanese women are actually semi-specialist jobs, namely, childcare worker, school teacher and nurse. If we add public servant to these jobs, we have a list of 'jobs in which it is easy for women to continue to work.' While a requirement for women to get specialist jobs is to be well educated, these women tend to marry co-workers who have similar specialist jobs of the same type. On the other hand, a workplace where it is easy for women to continue to work – in other words, a type of job with 'equal work and equal pay between men and women' – is a workplace where, from the viewpoint of men, men's wages are as low as women's. Among public servants and teachers, compared with other jobs, the reasons that less women leave these jobs for marriage or childbirth is not only because public servants and teachers have access to maternity leave and other entitlements (which make it easier for them to continue to work), but also because they cannot reduce the size of the family budget, which is maintained by the double income of two full-time workers.

A survey conducted by Hakuhōdō Institute of Life Style, entitled '90 *nendai kazoku* (Families in the 1990s),' indicates that a woman's choice from the three life course patterns is affected not only by her husband's income (as *flow*) but also by the assets (as *stock*) of her and her husband's parents (Hakuhōdō Seikatsu Sōgō Kenkyūjo [ed.], 1989). The survey results mention 'husband's family's assets' as one requirement for a woman to choose type III, the full-time housewife pattern. Even if her husband's annual income is below seven million yen, if the household receives extra income from his parents' stock, then the household has increased disposable income. On the other hand, a woman's choice of type I, the continued employment pattern, is supported by her own parents' assets. First, in order for a woman to be educated well enough to get a specialist job, her own family must be either well educated already or economically affluent. Under the current circumstances, where more than 80% of Japanese parents wish to give their sons education up to four-year college/ university and their daughters education up to junior college courses, respectively, one requirement for a woman to finish a four-year college/university course is to be from a family where her parents naturally expect her to do so or are willing to help her do so. Second, a woman with affluent parents continues to receive support from them even after marriage, which enriches her own household either directly or indirectly. Assuming that this support from the wife's parents, either in service or in cash, constitutes another source of income for her household, some people have termed this kind of household a *triple-income* family (Ueno, 1989d).

According to the Hakuhōdō survey, households of type II women, the suspension–re-employment pattern, receive support from neither the parents of the husband nor wife, and both the husband and wife are at a disadvantage in both flow and stock terms. The reason behind most of these wives resuming work is to 'help family finances' by earning extra income in addition to the husband's income. On the other hand, income earned by these wives in order to 'help family finances' is less than 25% of the household income because of the 'wall of 900,000 yen' (which was raised to one million yen starting from 1989) – the upper limit of income of a working wife under which she is recognized as a dependent of her husband for social security purposes.

Thus, type III, the full-time housewife pattern, represents a class of women who are at an advantage in terms of both flow (a good income by the husband) and stock (being from an economically advantaged class); type I, the continued employment pattern, represents a class of women who are from an economically advantaged class and are thus at an advantage in terms of stock and whose households enjoy double income with both husband and wife working; and type II, the suspension–re-employment pattern, represents a class of women who are at a disadvantage in terms of both stock and flow. Analyzing women's employment based only on economic factors sheds light on the plain and simple fact that women who have no choice but to work have already been working, while those who have no need to work have not.

Gender norms and views of husband and wife among women in the suspension–re-employment pattern

A question is that these 'working women' include both type I, the continued employment pattern, and type II, the suspension–re-

employment pattern. Type I women and type II women are significantly different from each other in employment pattern, type
of job, position in employment, wage and other respects. It is not
actually useful to put types I and II together as 'working housewives' and to compare them with type III 'housewives without a
job.' Type II women include those who had no intention to resume
working but had to do so and those who were willing to continue
to work but had to discontinue for various reasons. In either case,
these women gave priority to child-rearing over their jobs in their
nurturing stage. Various data indicate that type II women are much
more similar to type III than to type I women in their awareness
of gender roles between husband and wife and in gender norms
(Toyonaka-shi Josei Mondai Suishin Honbu [ed.], 1989). The way
in which type II women work has not reached such a level that
would shake the gender role between them and their husbands and
change the latter's domestic behavior. Therefore, the power balance between these women and their husbands are conventional.
As a result, these type II women bear a so-called dual role, or dual
burden, in that they engage in wage labor while continuing to bear
all responsibility for housework (Ueno, 1985d). However, the conventional sociological hypothesis that this dual role as housewife
and wage laborer results in *role conflict* has been rejected for type
II women. This is because, first, these women generally return to
work only after the post-nurturing life stage; second, their income
is spent mainly on mortgage repayments for their own houses and
on (out-of-school) educational expenses for their children; and,
third, after specialists took charge of the secondary socialization
process (making it a service that money can buy), earning money
in order to give children a 'better education' became one requirement for being a 'good mother.' As pointed out by Natalie Sokoloff
(Sokoloff, 1980), women now work in order to play their role as
good mother; therefore, their employment does not necessarily
result in a conflict with their role as good mother.

The reference group for type II women in terms of gender norms
and views of husband and wife is type III, full-time housewives. In
this regard, type II women can be described as 'housewife-minded
women who unfortunately failed to become full-time housewives.'
If the determinant of whether a woman falls into type II or III is
her husband's economic class, the breakdown of Japanese social
classes was one background factor involved in the division of these
women into those who returned to work and those who remained
as full-time housewives during the past two decades.

Division of women into classes and trends in these classes

The diversification of women's life courses and the division of women into classes during the past two decades has been a historically unprecedented experience for Japanese women. At the same time, these changes brought women a historical experience valuable enough to learn from it. The changes under way today in the 1990s are, in a sense, a type of historical judgment made by these women based on their experiences. Let us explore the trends in these women separately for working and non-working women.

Increase of housewife-oriented women

According to the results of a survey conducted by Lady's Forum in 1989 with 2,990 women who worked for 114 private businesses, including Fujitsu and NTT, 25% of all women wished to continue to work.[2] However, the proportion of women wishing to continue to work is lower in lower-age groups, with 16% and 6% of women in their early twenties and those below twenty, respectively, wishing to do so. The survey showed: 'In all age groups, a majority of women wish to become a full-time housewife sooner or later.' In the age group below twenty, 55% wished to become full-time housewives.

The results of this survey are consistent with those of other surveys with female students. In a survey of female students in a women's junior college class conducted by this writer in 1988, a little over 60% of the students wished to become full-time housewives later in life. A comparison of this result with the situation in the early 1980s, where the intention of a majority of women was to suspend and then resume working, reveals that the suspension–re-employment pattern has lost its appeal for young women, who have come to wish to be full-time housewives instead. The students wishing to continue to work have represented between 20% and 30% of the sample, with gradual increases – still very far from reaching a majority.

In a situation where full-time housewives have actually become a minority, what does this increase of women wishing to become full-time housewives mean?

There are a couple of possible answers.

First, the realities of 'working housewives' in the suspension–re-employment pattern (whose numbers increased with the decrease of full-time housewives) became obvious to any eye, resulting in the loss of appeal of the model. During the 1970s women in the suspension–re-employment pattern increased rapidly. This model of life course, which attempts to achieve a good balance between work and home in each life stage, was even recommended by the Japanese government at the time. The term *sengyō shufu* (full-time housewife) appeared in the early 1970s. Some of the full-time housewives whose identities were threatened by the increase of working housewives started to call themselves 'just housewives.'

However, when women in the suspension–re-employment pattern reached a majority, the realities of their lives were revealed – no reduction in housework responsibilities, poor working conditions and increased burdens imposed by the dual role. Faced with the reality that all they could get at the cost of comfort was pin money, some of the women at the borderline level began to choose to actively refrain from working despite employment opportunities offered to them. This life course pattern, which had appeared to satisfy women's desire to balance both work and family, lost its luster in the face of reality.

Second, the accelerating division of women into classes revealed beyond question that it was actually a woman's economic class that determined whether she returned to work or remained a full-time housewife. Being a full-time housewife now became a 'proof of affluence.' This is confirmed by results of surveys of female students about what they associate with housewives. In the 1970s full-time housewives were associated with 'smells of the kitchen,' 'being worn out with domestic chores' and 'lack of individuality.' In contrast, ten years later, in the late 1980s, full-time housewives were described as 'stylish' and 'living in comfort.' In the decade from the 1970s to the 1980s, the image of the full-time housewife changed 180 degrees from negative to positive.

At the same time, full-time housewives did not actually stay home. They certainly did not go to work, but came to be often away from home for community activities and networking. Yoshiko Kanai named these housewives as *katsudō sengyō shufu* (full-time activist housewives), meaning that they were full-time housewives working full-time on activities instead of housework.

According to the results of a survey of grassroots networkers among housewives in the Kyoto–Osaka–Kobe region conducted by myself (Ueno and Dentsū Nettowāku Kenkyūkai, 1988), the requirements for housewives to be able to go out of the home are time and money resources. In fact, these women have higher levels of education and belong to higher economic classes than average women.

Full-time housewives are no longer the 'captive wife,' as described by Hannah Gavron (Gavron, 1970). They are beginning to form a privileged class of women who chose not to work in order to do what they want to do. The increase of housewife-oriented young women is, therefore, not unrelated to their wish to climb the social ladder by marriage (the Cinderella complex). The only problem is the gap between their wish and reality. While nearly 60% of women wish to choose the full-time housewife pattern, the reality is that men who belong to an economic class where these women can remain as full-time housewives represent less than 40% of all men who are now in their forties. This percentage is expected to decrease to around 30% or less in two decades, when men now in their twenties become forty-something-year-olds. This means that many women who wish to become full-time housewives and fail to do so in reality will inevitably fall into the suspension–re-employment pattern, in which they resume working to 'help family finances' after a period of full-time parenting. These women, who will be middle- or older-aged by then, and all unprepared, will be thrown into the marginal labor market with poor working conditions. Awaiting these women will be the same realities tormenting most of the women in the suspension–re-employment pattern today. This is the process of the reproduction of wives with much frustration because of their failure to become full-time housewives despite their reference group being the full-time housewife pattern.

Effects of the Equal Employment Opportunity Law

I would like to point out here the effects of the Equal Employment Opportunity Law (EEOL) enacted in 1985. According to Akiko Chimoto, a specialist in economics of female labor, housewife-orientation among young women paradoxically increased because of the EEOL rather than despite it. The EEOL is actually full of loopholes, guaranteeing equal employment opportunities without offering protection for women ('equality without protection'), and obligating employers simply to use efforts without subjecting them to penal provisions. Despite these realities of the EEOL, the impression the law gave to female students before its introduction to the labor market was that, even if it was only tokenism, the law would allow women to work equally with men – an image of fair competition. In response to the enactment of the EEOL, most corporations immediately introduced a double track system, which divided employees into career track and non-career track.

Using this system, employers replaced gender discrimination with 'individual choice.' However, women who are employed on a career track account for less than 1% of new graduates employed. Moreover, since 'equal opportunity' applies only to those with the same level of education, female junior college graduates are openly subject to discrimination based on education. Despite the sloppy realities of the EEOL, the law has spread the illusion of 'equal opportunity' that a woman can, if she will, keep up with a man on a career track. This illusion, however, is not very attractive to today's female students, because it means that women will be thrown into competition under equal opportunities, just like men are. This competition is welcomed only by a fraction of women who are high school achievers; namely, those who have accomplished achievements at school and have confidence in themselves after having ended up the winner in the competition. In addition, today's female students are aware that a woman can become successful in this game of competition only if she makes extraordinary efforts and bears extraordinary burdens. The background factors of the slow increase of women in the continued employment pattern during the past two decades are likely to include (1) the fact that the objective conditions surrounding working women who wish to successfully handle both parenting and a career have not improved in the least, and (2) the situation that a woman can handle both parenting and a career mainly by bearing personal burdens and making personal sacrifices, where this life course pattern has not been attractive to young women.

In the process of its formulation, the EEOL significantly declined from an *equal employment* act. It is not well known that Fujin Mondai Konwa Kai (the Japan Women's Forum), Watashitachi no Danjokoyōbyōdōhō wo Tsukuru On'natachi no Kai (the Women's Group for Making a Gender Equal Employment Law) and other feminist groups strongly opposed the contents of the bill. Their opposition was based on the anticipation that the EEOL's equality without protection – in exchange of the protection of women in the Labor Standards Law – would intensify competition among female workers and would result in the deterioration of the working conditions of women. It seems that these opponents' anticipation has proved to be generally correct, considering the subsequent developments of the Worker Dispatching Business Law, which was enacted at the same time as the EEOL, and the introduction of the irregular working-hour system under the Labor Standards Law.

The EEOL promoted the division of female workers into the elite and the non-elite. The fraction of elite female workers got opportunities to be employed on a career track and to receive the same treatment as men. On the other hand, awaiting the majority non-elite female workers was the marginal labor market, ready to accept those women who cannot work as hard as men. After the enactment of the EEOL, the employment pattern of women diversified. There are now not only part-time workers but also contract workers, dispatched workers, home-based workers and rehired retirees. Some companies, like Isetan, a major department store, introduced a 'some-timer' system to arrange shifts for employees' convenience. Jusco, a supermarket, has long had a re-entry system in which retired workers are registered and employed on a priority basis, although it is difficult for the system to ensure that retired workers return to their original positions as they have to go through many steps before regaining full-time positions. While the 'incorporation of women into the labor force' is loudly touted, this means a diversification intending only to incorporate women into the marginal sector of the labor force.

Under these circumstances, a quiet change is under way among female workers who joined the workforce before the enforcement of the EEOL. The Basic Survey on Wage Structure conducted by the Japanese Ministry of Labor revealed that the average length of continuous employment of female employees (except part-time workers) increased from 5.3 years in 1976 to 7.0 years in 1986, showing a 1.7-year increase in a single decade. The number of women who have worked continuously for ten years or longer also increased to one-in-four (25.4%). Women who had worked continuously for seven years in 1986 had certainly joined the workforce before the enforcement of the EEOL. These women were not given the choice of being employed on a career track. They were assigned 'jobs for women' in their companies and became experienced office workers without job transfer or promotion to higher positions. While one factor affecting the increase in the length of continuous employment of women is the growing tendency to marry later, another factor is their sense of self defence: after seeing the realities facing women in the suspension–re-employment pattern, these women who have worked continuously do not want to give up their stable employment for fear of not finding jobs again. These women have not necessarily been big assets to their companies, nor have their companies expected them to be. They have remained in their positions beyond their companies' expectations. This owes more to women wanting to secure stable employment despite boring tasks than to being highly motivated to work. One recent trend in employee training provided by companies is an increasing number of revitalization seminars for female employees working continuously for more than five years. This, too, must be because these companies, faced with female employees remaining in their positions longer, have started to think seriously about incorporating these female employees into the workforce, rather than because management has changed its attitudes towards female employees in response to the EEOL. For personnel managers in companies, differences in treatment and morals between female employees who joined the workforce before the enforcement of EEOL and those who joined later are emerging as a new problem.

Women's networking activities

A new movement is emerging among housewives without a job. Full-time housewives currently in their forties or older include the following two types of women: (1) those who intentionally chose not to resume working in the face of the increased employment opportunities for middle- and older-aged women; and (2) those who failed to catch up with the changes in the labor market and were too old to find a job when they wished to resume working. While gender discrimination in recruitment and employment has been prohibited by the EEOL, age discrimination is still quite common, making it difficult to provide employment opportunities for women over forty years of age.

Women who work at the core of women's networking activities belong to this age group (they are now in their late forties to fifties). The primary requirement for these women is that they have entered the empty nest life stage and have been completely released from parenting, education expenses and other child-related burdens. Even if a woman works part-time, her income is not 100% disposable unless her children have become independent. Women in this age group are in the best position in terms of both time and money resources (plus physical strength), after being freed from parenting burdens and before their husbands reach retirement age.

Concurrently with the emergence of other women in the workplace, these women have accumulated their experiences in community activities and networking. These activities have been developing into new independent businesses run by housewives. These are new, urban-style self-employment businesses whose members determine and manage the quality and nature of labor by themselves.[3] These businesses include former volunteer groups that decided to charge for their services; circles that began to gain income from their activities; and workers' collectives of consumer cooperatives. Unlike conventional family-owned independent businesses, most of the husbands of these women are employees.

These new self-employment businesses run by housewives are a result of the exclusion of women from the employed labor force and are also a product of their choice, in that they chose not to become employed workers. According to labor economics, self-employment businesses are found more often in social minorities that are systematically discriminated against in the labor market. In this sense, it seems that it is only because women are a social minority that they have been attempting to create work patterns other than employment. Amid the obvious trend for an increase in employed workers, work styles that question the quality of labor are paradoxically being explored among middle- and older-aged women who have dropped out of the labor market. Some of these businesses have been successful. However, an 'alternative work style,' which may produce smaller wages than those of part-time workers on an hourly basis, would seem to be another product of an affluent class.

Disintegration of family and diversification of lifestyles

I have discussed that the structural change of Japanese society during the past two decades has resulted in the division of women. This transformation of women will inevitably result in diversification of the family subculture. Now that 'becoming a housewife upon marriage' is no longer the only choice of life course for women, women's choices make a great difference in the realities of life.

While women's life courses have diversified, changes in their life courses will, for some time to come, remain within the scope of the three basic patterns (type I, the continued employment pattern; type II, the suspension–re-employment pattern; and type III, the full-time housewife pattern) and their variations. The major determinant variable of these patterns a woman chooses is, as described above, an economic factor, or which class she belongs to. However, factors determining which class a woman belongs to now include not only her husband's income as the conventional factor but also her own income and the assets of her parents or her husband's parents or both. Although this may be criticized as economic reductionism, it is unfortunately true that the economic strength of a husband and his wife most strongly affects the power structure and interdependence between them. If the wife's flow and stock increase, the Japanese family system, which originally was somewhat bilineal, may develop an even more matrilineal orientation. This trend is indicated in the increase of parents living with their daughters' families, as well as by the increase of urban-style matrilocal residence. In addition, the fact that a wife has an independent income does not necessarily weaken the interdependence between her and her husband. Such a family may even have stronger ties among members in order to maintain the size of family budget that has been determined based on the wife's income. Furthermore, with the increase of the value of assets of the husband's or wife's parents, the ties among members of a family as a community for the protection of assets are becoming stronger instead of weaker. Hakuhōdō Institute of Life Style has termed this kind of strongly united family *rikei kazoku* (literally, benefit-connected family), meaning a family whose members are connected based on benefits, unlike *chokkei kazoku* (stem family) whose members are connected by blood (Hakuhōdō Seikatsu Sōgō Kenkyūjo [ed.] , 1989).

Specifically, the lifestyle of a husband and wife or a family differs significantly depending on which life course type (I, II or III) the wife falls in. Today, working housewives and their non-working counterparts are totally different from each other in the structure of living and time budget, such that they could be described as living in different ecosystems from each other. They not only differ in the times of day and places they are seen outside their homes but may also have conflicting needs or interests regarding a parent–teacher association or garbage disposal. They also differ in consumption behavior, such as higher percentages of social expenses and communication/travel expenses in the expenditure of working women's households. Other differences between working and non-working housewives include awareness of housework rationalization and the priority order given to different types of housework.

Above all, working and non-working housewives are likely to differ greatly from each other in what they expect of their husbands and the requirements on which they base their choice of husband. While type III women expect economic power from their husbands, type I women expect their husbands' participation in housework instead. According to a survey of Japanese housewives conducted by Anne Imamura, a housewife feels happy when concordance is achieved between what is expected of her and what role she actually plays (Kokusai Josei Gakkai [ed.], 1978). In this sense, mismatches such as a strongly career-oriented woman married to a husband who expects her to be a full-time housewife, or, conversely, a strongly housewife-oriented woman married to an economically weak husband, would result in feelings of unhappiness in these women. The problem is whether or not a diversification will occur in men to a level that would correspond to the diversification that has taken place in women.

Thus, depending on whether the wife is type I, II or III, the family lifestyle will differ significantly, including hobbies, how to spend leisure time, whether or not the husband and wife act as a unit, whether or not the family life is centered on children, and consumption behavior. The gender-role-assigned lifestyle of the modern family that consists of a housewife who works full-time on housework and her husband who works full-time on his job will become a subtype of the diversified family sub-culture. We are about to reach a historical stage in which the generalization can no longer be made of what a *husband and wife* are or what a *family* is.

Part II
Modernity and Women

3 Formation of the Japanese Model of the Modern Family

Invention of *ie*

The former Japanese family system, the *ie* system, has long been regarded as a feudal relic. However, recent findings in family history research have revealed that *ie* was an invention by the Meiji government and was made as a result of the enactment of the Meiji Civil Code. Strictly exclusive patrilineal stem families were certainly seen in the samurai (warrior) class before the Meiji era, but were not known to the common people. It has been estimated that in the Edo era, samurai represented 3% of the population; together with their family members, they accounted for 10% of the population at most. The remaining 90% of the population had diverse family structures. As Hobsbaum says in *The invention of tradition* (Hobsbaum and Ranger, 1983), *ie* was an invention of the modern age.

Before the Meiji Civil Code adopted an exclusively patrilineal inheritance system, the so-called Civil Code Controversy had continued for almost two decades. This conversely provides evidence that other options for the inheritance rule were available to the Meiji Civil Code.

In 1870 the Meiji government first planned to enact a civil code. In 1871 the government started to formulate a bill, producing a provisional bill for a civil code in 1873. Meanwhile, the government conducted a survey of customary laws governing inheritance and families in different parts of the country. Based on the results of the survey, the first governmental bill was drafted in 1878.

Customary laws in different parts of Japan included matrilineal inheritance and ultimogeniture (inheritance by the last-born child). Matrilineal inheritance, called *ane-katoku* (literally, inheritance by a big sister), was practiced commonly among wealthy farmers and merchants. In a farming or merchant family as a management body, in terms of family strategy it was more reasonable to select (from a wide range of human resources) a decent groom for a daughter rather than to count on a son who may not necessarily turn out well but in whom the family had no choice. In contrast, exclusively patrilineal inheritance was a custom unique to samurai families (i.e. families who served their master's family by providing military power). In the samurai class, a family with daughters only had to arrange an adoption in order to obtain a male heir. Farming and merchant families did not necessarily need a male heir. In the process of the formulation of the civil code, however, this matrilineal inheritance was eventually rejected as a barbarous custom of the commonalty.

After the first draft of the civil code was completed, it took ten years before the civil code was enacted in 1890. Following the enactment, the civil code was due for enforcement in three years, during which time the well-known Civil Code Controversy erupted. The Civil Code Controversy developed into a major political issue, in which the jurist Yatsuka Hozumi bitterly criticized the civil code, saying, 'Up comes the civil code and down go loyalty and filial piety.' In the end, the government gave up the enforcement of the civil code and worked again on revision of the bill. It was as late as 1898 that the final version of the civil code was finally enforced. The very fact that it took so long for the civil code to come into existence demonstrates that the family system stipulated by the civil code was a political production produced by selecting from many options and after much meandering.

The *ie* system was a family model formulated to suit a modern nation-state. Conversely, the nation-state was also formulated to suit the family model. In *Kazoku kokka-kan no jinruigaku* (An anthropology of the pseudo-family state ideology) (Itō, K. 1982), Kanji Itō discusses in detail how the concept of *ie* was invented by Meiji government officials. In 1890, before the enactment of the Meiji Civil Code, the *Kyōiku Chokugo* (Imperial Rescript on Education) was promulgated. In the following year, Tetsujirō Inoue, the government's favorite scholar, discussed the relationship between the state and its people in *Chokugo engi* (The commentary on the Imperial Edict):

A people's position as subjects is just like children's position to their parents, which means that a nation is an extended family and that commands and orders given by the monarch of the nation to his subjects are no different from instructions given with mercy by the parents of a family to their children. Therefore, if His Imperial Majesty now addresses the whole nation as 'you, my subjects,' all who are His subjects must listen to Him with the same respectful attention and deep gratitude as children pay and feel while listening to their strict father and merciful mother (Inoue, Tetsujirō, 1891: 10–11).

Inoue repeats the same argument in *Rinri to kyōiku* (Ethics and education), published in 1908.

If the spirit of filial piety towards the head of a family is amplified to the whole nation, it will, not surprisingly, correspond to the loyalty to the Emperor. In this regard, loyalty can be equated with filial piety. This is because the Emperor is in the position of the head of the family of Japanese people, and this is why people should be loyal to the Emperor, just like family members should be filial to the head of their family. Thus, loyalty is the same thing as filial piety. And this is why 'loyalty and filial piety is one thing' is a teaching of the national morals that has been passed down since ancient times. A national moral code like 'loyalty and filial piety is one thing' would not have occurred unless the society is structured as described above. It is a principal moral code that would inevitably develop in this type of social organization, and without this principal moral code this type of social organization would not be able to continue (Inoue, Tetsujirō, 1908: 474–5).

Itō comments on Inoue's opinion as follows:

Here the relationship between the Emperor and the people in the national level is understood using an analogy with the relationship between the parents and their children in the family level, where the Emperor and the people are compared to the parents and their children, respectively. Further, as seen in the statement, 'a nation is an extended family,' Inoue constructs an image of the nation based on *ie* (Itō, M., 1982: 8–9).

Itō finds the secret of this 'pseudo-family state ideology' in the 'loyalty and filial piety is one thing' ideology. The Meiji government adopted Confucianism as the official ideology for the Imperial Rescript on Education. As seen in the words, *shūshin seika chikoku heitenka* (Behave yourself, only then you can manage a household; only then you can govern a nation; and only then you can bring peace to the world), Confucian virtues place the self at the center, with ethics extending in concentric circles from the center. In this philosophy, filial piety towards one's parents comes before loyalty to the monarch, and there was even a possibility that filial piety and loyalty might conflict with each other from time to time. One example of this conflict is the 'blood tax' riots, which occurred in many parts of the country in opposition to the promulgation of the Military Conscription Ordinance in 1872. Another example is seen in Akiko Yosano's words, 'Oh, my brother, how I cry for you, please do not throw away your life,' in her famous anti-war poem written when the Russo–Japanese War broke out in 1904. Service to the nation and filial devotion towards one's parents are not always compatible. Therefore, a logical leap was necessary in order to say (as Inoue said) that loyalty and filial piety are the same thing.

Indeed, in the process of the formulation of the Imperial Rescript on Education, a trick of reversing the natural order of the Confucian virtues from *kō–chū* (filial piety–loyalty) to *chū–kō* (loyalty–filial piety) was used. Nagazane Motoda, a Confucian scholar who served the Meiji government, published *Kyōgaku taikō* (General principles of education) in 1879. In this essay, Motoda emphasizes a Confucian teaching that people's loyalty to the Emperor corresponds to children's filial piety towards their parents. At that point in time, the virtues were still in the original order, with filial piety being given priority over loyalty. However, in *Yōgaku kōyō* (The elements of education for the young), published by the same author in 1882, the order of loyalty and filial piety has been reversed. The following year, Japan's first moral textbook was created based on Motoda's views. The textbook emphasized that people should 'serve the monarch just like they serve their parents.' Confucianism, as adopted by the Meiji government, contained a clearly different interpretation from that which had prevailed until the Edo era.

Tadao Satō, a self-taught film critic, made the same discovery as Itō on his own by observing domestic dramas on the silver screen. In *Katei no yomigaeri no tameni – Hōmu dorama ron* (For the re-birth of the home: Theorizing soap operas, 1978), Satō (1978) noticed that the patriarch of a family in European films and his counterpart in Japanese films behaved in contrasting ways. If a member of the family had committed a crime and sought shelter in the family, a French or Italian patriarch would refuse to hand the criminal over to the police and would, instead, attempt to privately punish the offender. In contrast, a Japanese patriarch would hand over his offending family member to the police authorities, instead of sheltering him/her, and would even disown or otherwise break off relations with the offender for fear of being involved in the trouble. From this observation, Satō noticed that while there is confrontation between family ethics and social ethics in Europe, a

Japanese patriarch behaves as though he is an agent for the external authority. The film critic attempted to solve this mystery by tracing the origin of the family system. In the end, he reached the Imperial Rescript on Education and its drafter, Nagazane Motoda. Satō then found that 'the ranks of loyalty and filial piety in the list of virtues was reversed between the publication of *Yōgaku kōyō* in 1882 and the promulgation of the Imperial Rescript on Education in 1890' (Satō, 1978: 50). He concluded that 'making the two virtues into the single word *chū-kō* (loyalty-filial piety) to create an impression as if filial piety is a concept inseparable from feudalistic loyalty is itself a creation of the Meiji government' (Satō, 1978: 262).

> Loyalty and filial piety, which are two totally different moral concepts in Confucianism, were forcibly put together and called *chū-kō* (loyalty-filial piety) to create an impression as if they are two inseparable concepts that are neither too close nor too far from each other. This made us believe that children serving their parents and people sacrificing themselves for the nation are doing the same thing…
>
> Thus, the two concepts, which are totally different or may even be opposite from each other, were connected, and *kuni* (nation) was called *kokka* (literally, nation-family), creating an impression that nationalism and familism work together to confront individualism. I do not know who did this, but I think this person is a genius (Satō, 1978: 176–8).

Satō thus demonstrates that the Meiji government artificially created the *ie* system so that family ethics would be subject to national ethics. He concludes that if familism refers to a view that gives priority to family ethics over any other ethics, Japanese family, or *ie*, does not represent familism in the European sense of the word.[1]

Yayoi Aoki confirms a similar process from the viewpoint of women. She demonstrates that Japanese 'femininity' is not a product of tradition but was formulated under the influence of Confucianism in the process of modernization (Aoki, 1983, 1986). Books of precepts for women, such as *On'na daigaku* (Code of conduct for women), were distributed only in literate classes. The concept of chastity or virginity was unknown to the common people. Until the middle of the Meiji era, high divorce rates and remarriage rates were recorded. Such a virtue as 'a good wife will remain faithful to the memory of her husband' was unrealistic to ordinary people.

Ie and patriarchy

As described above, there is a strong relationship of interdependence and interference between family and state or, in other words,
between the private and public spheres. This is because the
separation of the public and private spheres was brought about by
modernity, as revealed by findings in family history research. It
was modern society that divided the autonomous, communal living
sphere into the two interdependent spheres. In addition, the two
spheres were programmed to have an asymmetric relationship with
each other, resulting in the private sphere becoming invisible as a
'shadow' of the public sphere. Therefore, the *ie* system, which was
created in this process, was not in the least a traditional feudal relic.
Ie represented family reorganized in the process of modernization
or, in other words, the Japanese version of modern family.

However, the view that regards *ie* as a type of modern family and
emphasizes the continuity of prewar and postwar family has been
incompatible with the existing view on family. This existing view regards *ie* as feudal relic and understands that this vestige of feudalism
was swept away by the postwar new civil code, which put an end to
the history of patriarchy. The view holds that there is a discontinuity
between the former and current civil codes, and that the postwar
reforms achieved the democratization of family, making patriarchy a
relic of the past, together with the *ie* system.[2] When radical feminism
in the 1970s criticized modern family by raking up the concept of
patriarchy, most opponents would have expressed bewilderment, as
if they had been discussing a ghost from the past, and would have
responded that patriarchy no longer existed. However, patriarchy
had been redefined and used by feminists as a concept to explain
gender domination that was unique to modern family. According
to the *Encyclopedia of feminism* by Lisa Tuttle (1986), 'patriarchy'
means a social structure in which 'male shall dominate female;
elder male shall dominate younger.' Both the 'father's control' in an
extended family and the 'husband's control' in a conjugal family are
varieties of patriarchy. After the war, democratic 'companionship
family' seemed to have been established under the appearance of
the agreement of both sexes. Still, the 'husband's control' continued
in postwar families in the private sphere where gender roles result
in social or economic inequality behind legal equity.

Therefore, there are dual issues that I would like to point out
here: first, *ie* is another version of the modern family and, second,

patriarchal oppression has continued throughout the prewar and postwar periods.

'Descriptive model' and 'normative model' of family

The factors that have caused resistance to the view that *ie* is the Japanese version of modern family can be divided broadly into two categories. The first includes ideological factors, while the other includes theoretical ones.

With respect to the first, ideological factors, most historians have regarded *ie* as a feudal relic without questioning its historical origin. In this sense, these historians seem to have fallen into the trap of the *ie* ideology. This is because one function of an ideology is to conceal its origin and make people take it for granted. By regarding the ideology existing in their day as a tradition instead of deconstructing it, these historians lent a hand to strengthening the ideology. Actually, there is a grain of truth in regarding *ie* as a tradition; *ie* was certainly modeled after a tradition in samurai households. Positivist history, which relies on documentary materials, has limited its research to the history of literate classes. Until popular history and social history brought about the recognition of the diversity of the histories and cultures of illiterate people, historians had given priority to the history of the ruling class over that of the general public. However, we should understand that tradition varies from place to place and class to class, and that throughout the historical process one cultural item that fits with the times has continuously been chosen from the diverse cultural matrix and been redefined as a 'tradition' every time there is a change in the historical situation. Therefore, what has survived as a tradition has undergone changes over time. There is nothing like 'timeless' tradition. The truth is that the source of a tradition is concealed by the ideology that names something as a tradition.

Another factor in the ideological category is gender bias. When the private sphere was created as an indispensable but invisible twin of the public sphere, the private sphere was meant to be a shelter, or a sanctuary of love and comfort, from the public sphere, which was full of stress from competition and demands for efficiency. As this kind of shelter, the home was regarded as omnipresent beyond time and space, and people were not allowed even to question the reason for its existence. However, the meaning of the private sphere is totally different between men and women. Even though home may be a shelter for men, it is but one kind of workplace for women who are expected to supply love and comfort there. When feminists made an issue of women's 'shadow work' (Illich, 1981) in the private sphere and violated this 'sanctuary' by questioning the historical and ideological construction of family, historians and family sociologists – many of whom were men – were bewildered and showed their anger. This is because they, as men, had a shared interest in keeping this family system, which involved gender domination, the way it was then.

The second type of factors are theoretical. It was thought that one requirement for the modern family, which was modeled after those of Europe, was to be a nuclear family. Japanese *ie* was considered not to meet this requirement.

In *Kindai kazoku to feminizumu* (Modern family and feminism) (Ochiai, 1989), the characteristics of the modern family are summarized by Emiko Ochiai into the following eight points:

1. separation of the domestic sphere and the public sphere
2. strong emotional relationship among family members
3. child-centeredness
4. gender division of labor in which men and women are responsible for the public sphere and the domestic sphere, respectively
5. stronger collectivity of family
6. decline of sociality
7. exclusion of non-kin
8. nuclear family.

In 'Kindai kokka to kazoku moderu (The modern state and the family model)', Yūko Nishikawa (1991) points out Ochiai's inconsistency in her use of 'nuclear family.'

When the same eight points were listed as the 'characteristics of the modern family' in Table 1 of the article, 'Kindai kazoku to nihon bunka: Nihonteki boshi kankei no tokiguchini (The modern family and Japanese culture: In consideration of the Japanese-style mother-child relationship)' published in Number 10 of *Joseigaku Nenpō* (The annual report of the women's studies), item 8 was put in parentheses and described as 'Takes the form of a nuclear family.' This must be because in the case of Japan, in particular, the prewar family cannot be regarded as modern family without putting item 8 in parentheses.

Nishikawa says, 'When discussing the modern family, I would also like to put item 8 in parentheses' and adds the following two items:
9. the family is controlled by the husband
10. the family constitutes the basic unit of the modern state.
Nishikawa continues, 'This way, both the prewar and postwar families of Japan can be regarded as modern family. One characteristic of the Japanese version of the modern family might lie in the point that item 8 must be put in parentheses.'

Putting the 'nuclear family' item in parentheses has two theoretical implications. Specifically, putting this item in parentheses emphasizes the continuity of prewar and postwar families and this, as Nishikawa points out, makes it possible to discuss (1) the modern nature of the prewar family and (2) the patriarchal nature of the postwar family at the same time. Nishikawa points out the 'modern nature of the prewar family' and the 'patriarchal nature of the postwar family' in her items 9 and 10, respectively. This is because the shift to nuclear families involved only the shift to husband's control from father's control in the patriarchal system.

Ochiai's eight items represent a summary of modern family studies, but their source is not clearly specified. It is not clear, either, why there are eight items or whether the eight items are meant to be a complete list. Nor is it clear how many items we will end up with if new items are added to the list, as Nishikawa did. For example, item 1 (separation of the domestic sphere and the public sphere) and item 4 (gender division of labor in which men and women are responsible for the public sphere and the domestic sphere, respectively) nearly overlap each other. Item 2 (strong emotional relationship among family members), item 3 (child-centeredness), item 5 (stronger collectivity of family), item 6 (decline of sociality) and item 7 (exclusion of non-kin) can be summarized into a single item: autonomy and exclusivity of family.

Ochiai's list relies on findings of European family history studies. According to *The making of the modern family* by Edward Shorter (1975), a leading British family historian, the modern family has the following three requirements:
1. 'romantic love' revolution
2. emotional bonds between mother and child
3. autonomy of the household.
Shorter himself does not list 'nuclear family' among the requirements for the modern family. We can only infer that the husband–

wife relationship emphasized by the 'romantic love revolution' might result in a conjugal family system and thus in nuclear family households.

The view that the modernization of family is associated with the increase of the nuclear family has already been disproved by the finding of Laslett and his colleague that the nuclear family is universal (Laslett and Wall, 1972). According to this finding, the nuclear family is dominant in all societies, whether in modern or premodern times. It is easy to validate this finding for Japan. According to the data obtained in 1920 from Japan's first national census,[3] the nuclear family already accounted for 54.0% of all households at that time. The stem family represented only about 31%. According to a recent historical demography study, it is known from religious census registers that even in the Edo era the number of household members was as small as fewer than six people (Tsubouchi, 1992).

If we follow up the census data obtained once every five years from 1920, we find that during a little over half a century between 1920 and 1975 the proportion of nuclear families increased only by 10%, from 54.0% to 64.0%. It is doubtful whether this 10% increase of the nuclear family rate, which occurred during the discontinuity of the interruption of the war and the postwar rapid growth, can appropriately be called the 'increase of the nuclear family.'

The high nuclear family rate in prewar days can be explained by the prewar family cycle determined by Yasuhiko Yuzawa between 1935 and 1944 in the Suwa district, Nagano Prefecture (Yuzawa, 1987: 19). According to Yuzawa's findings, in stem family households joined by the wife of the eldest son, the average period before the deaths of the father and the mother was six years and ten years, respectively. Since the average family cycle was twenty-six years, if we assume that all married couples lived with the parents of either spouse, the probability of a given household being a nuclear family at a given time is sixteen years out of twenty-six years, or roughly two-thirds. This is in substantial concordance with statistical data (Seiyama, 1993). In addition, if we take the number of births into account, the average number of children per woman was five to six children during the Meiji era. Assuming that half of these children were boys (i.e. three boys per mother) and that the eldest son took a wife and ran a stem family household, the probability rate of occurrence of the stem family would be one-third. The high proportion of the nuclear family in prewar days can be explained by the shorter average life span and the larger number of children. In this regard, the 10% increase of the stem family in half a century may seem to be a relatively considerable change. On the other hand, in light of the fact that the average life span jumped from the fifty-year range to the eighty-year range and that the number of children per woman decreased to less than two, the fact that the proportion of the nuclear family is still increasing suggests that even the eldest son, who is naturally expected to live with his parents under the stem family ideology, may be increasingly choosing to live separately from his parents.

As far as statistics go, there is in fact no significant gap between prewar and postwar families. The 'universality of the nuclear family' that was found, and which was based on historical demography, applies to Japan as well, as far as the size and structure of households are concerned. However, social historians introduced the concept of 'change of mentality' to the theories of an historical change. They argue that even if Japanese nuclear family households look similar to their Western counterparts, they cannot be called the modern family unless the mentality of the members is that of members of a modern family.

Let us leave the matter of what the mentality of modern family members is for the time being and look at the behavior of the members of a Japanese nuclear family household. Their behavior indicates that they define their own family as a defective form of stem family in that the family wishes to be, but cannot be, a stem family, or, in other words, that it is a transitional form of stem family in the process of change from a stem family of orientation to a stem family of procreation. Their behavior of purchasing tombs and family Buddhist altars reveals that even the second and third sons, who are required to live separately from their parents upon marriage, behave as the 'founder of a branch family' established by them so that they will eventually be able to run a stem family household with their own sons when they grow up. Certainly, it was modernization itself that has allowed the households of these second and third sons to become independent from their parents' households without counting on inherited assets. However, these younger sons who live in nuclear family households behave more as patriarchs of the branch families they established than as members of the household of their elder brother. For these younger sons, being consigned to their elder brother's family tomb is a sign of their incompetence in that they have failed to establish a branch family. In this sense, if we focus on 'mentality,' we must say again that there is little gap between the prewar and postwar families.

This is because, at the common law level, the practice of demanding waiver of the second and younger children's right of inheritance is still very common, despite the new civil code, which secures equal inheritance among all children instead of primogeniture.[4] In some cases, the responsibility to support the parents is imposed solely on the eldest son, while the other siblings demand equal inheritance of family property among all children, resulting in the eldest son being put at a disadvantage under the transitional circumstances. Under the current circumstances, where more than 60% of parents in their forties who were born after the war say they wish to live with their sons in the future, we must say the change induced by the postwar civil code did not affect people's mentality. As a matter of fact, the explosive tomb boom occurred after the postwar rapid growth. After the large-scale separation of households caused by urbanization, what the heads of nuclear family households sought next were family tombs. These heads explained that they needed family tombs more for the convenience of their children than for themselves, and this provided them with a new, postwar discourse on the 'perpetuity of family.' This indicates the 'descendant worship' proposed by the folklorist Masao Takatori[5] (Takatori and Hashimoto, 1968; Mori, 1987) instead of 'ancestor worship'.

We do not have to trot out the novel term of 'mentality.' In sociology and anthropology, the *normative model* and the *descriptive model* have long been distinguished from each other.[6] Under the universal dominance of the nuclear family, where it is difficult to show a specific family model for the society, it is generally thought that if there is a family model normatively intended by people who live in the society, that model can be regarded as the normative model of family for that society even if statistics show that the proportion of families falling under the model is fewer than 30%. In this sense, we are faced with a situation where people who live in stem families in terms of their norms actually run nuclear family households. In this situation, the stem family is an idealized model and people evaluate their actual families based on the distance from the idealized model. This again indicates that family is a concept more normative than descriptive.

The myth of romantic love

The norms of the nuclear family include relative priority of sexual dyad over lineage. This is expressed as the rule of household separation, which prohibits a household from containing more than one couple. In other words, it is a conjugal family system where a family is established by marriage. Under today's unquestionable conjugal family system, it seems natural that a family is established by marriage and is dissolved by divorce. However, in the stem family or extended family, which emphasizes lineage, or in the polygamous family, one specific sexual dyad is no more than an element constituting the family. Even if the sexual dyad is dissolved, the family will continue and the vacancy will be filled by another sexual dyad based on the priority of lineage.

Let us now define the 'romantic love revolution' (which is supposed to constitute a turning point from the institutional family to the companionship family by emphasizing conjugal love) – proposed by Shorter technically as the 'priority of the conjugal relationship in a family' – by eliminating the emotional and normative burden. The 'conjugal family system' in this sense has existed in the Japanese *ie* system since its beginning in the sixteenth century. Haruko Wakita points out that the housewife's authority was established at the same time as the establishment of the patriarchal authority, and that the legal wife was always given priority, even in a polygamous situation. The housewife had a high position in the family and often represented the family on behalf of the patriarch. This is a phenomenon incomprehensible from the viewpoint of Chinese or Korean familism, which emphasizes lineage. In Chinese and Korean communities, which are governed by the principle prohibiting marriage between people with the same family name, a wife who joins the family from another family by marriage remains an outsider throughout her life by keeping her family name. In this context, the wife's family name is a sign of her remaining as an outsider and also indicates the notion that the family is simply borrowing her womb.

In contrast, the Japanese practice of regarding a woman who joins the family from another family as a formal member of the family indicates the Gesellschaft-like nature of the Japanese *ie*, which is not always governed by the principle of lineage, as seen in the frequent occurrence of adoption arrangements. This is also symbolized by the Japanese marriage protocol. In the performance of the ceremony of the three-times-three exchange of cups of sake at a wedding, the bride must first exchange cups with the parents of the groom. Only then, cups are exchanged between the groom and the bride, now in the capacity of a quasi-daughter who has joined the family. Another practice that is not uncommon in Japan, but is exceptional in the East Asian Confucian zone, is to allow a widowed woman to take over the family business. Even today, far more Japanese small and medium businesses are managed by female proprietors than are their foreign counterparts. This does not at all represent Japanese women's participation in the workplace, but is a mere consequence of the *ie* system in which a widowed wife commonly takes over the control of the family business (Komatsu, 1987). This is evidenced by the fact that female business owners are concentrated in small and medium-sized businesses and are virtually nonexistent in companies with more than 500 employees. However, the Japanese practice of allowing the patriarch's wife, who is an outsider in terms of lineage and who joined the family by marriage, to represent the family (as seen in the widow of a Diet member who runs for election to the office previously held by her husband) draws a line between the Japanese *ie* and Asian familism and suggests the priority of the conjugal relationship in Japan (if the East Asian principle of lineage, which gives priority to blood relationship, is what 'familism' is, then the Japanese *ie* system should not be regarded as based on familism).

However, would Shorter say that this conjugal relationship lacks romantic love? It is easy to assume that comradeship will occur between the patriarch and his wife in the *ie* as a management body. Can't we call them a *companionship family*? However, there is a historical requirement for this companionship; in studies of modern family, 'companionship' has referred only to emotion that has been reduced to sexual affection, and is felt when the family is viewed purely as a unit of reproduction instead of a unit of production.

By the way, what in the world is romantic love? Shorter defines romantic love as the non-utilitarian choice of spouse. If a daughter marries a poor young man against her parents' will, romantic love is deemed to exist. According to Shorter (1975: 80–83), the wave of extramarital births from the mid-eighteenth to the mid-nineteenth century in England indicates a surge of eroticism among young people. This means that young men and women began to act faithfully to their emotions and sexual instincts instead of for utilitarian motives. This change in the mentality of people is what Shorter calls the 'romantic love revolution.' However, isn't Shorter, a family historian, emphasizing mentality, romanticizing the romance?

A time of historical change is also a time of transition of power between classes. A daughter who rejects her fiancé, chosen by her parents from her own class, and marries a young man from a lower class may be buying futures in that she chooses a man from an emerging class over the other man from a declining class. In fact, young men who appear in romance novels (the word 'romance' itself is a synonym for a narrative) written at that time are from lower classes and are described as 'ambitious,' like Julian Sorel in *The Red and the Black* (Stendhal, 2002). Using their wisdom and wit, these men gain the love of women of high birth. The high extramarital birth rate was, as Shorter says, a consequence of marriages that failed to be achieved against expectations (i.e. out of negligence on the part of men). There has been controversy among family historians as to the interpretation of the surge of extramarital births in the late nineteenth century. There is a confrontation between two views: one is a victim-oriented historical view, which asserts that the increase of extramarital births was a result of the sexual exploitation of maids, who were fresh from the country, by their masters or the masters' sons; the other view argues that it resulted from contact between two different cultures in London, where these young women from rural communities, which originally had lenient sexual norms, met hypocritical Victorian morals associated with the sexual double standard. It may be true that urban upper-class men might have taken advantage of country girls, but these girls might have simply acted faithfully to their sexual codes. There must also have been maids, like the one in *Pamela* (Richardson, 1741), who attempted to climb to an urban upper class by making use of her sexual appeal. It seems that the surge of extramarital births was one social phenomenon representing two different realities, which were brought about by the two social groups who belonged to two different cultures and who acted in accordance with their respective codes.

In times of modernization and with great social mobility, men were able to climb the social ladder by making use of their education, but for women marriage was the only chance in a lifetime to transfer to another class. In taking a chance, isn't it a reasonably utilitarian choice for a woman to choose a poor but promising man?

In *The Rape of Clarissa*, Terry Eagleton (1982) applies feminist criticism to an eighteenth-century romantic novel and discusses how 'romantic love' contributed to the establishment of the modern patriarchy. In the eighteenth-century popular novel *Clarissa,* written by Samuel Richardson and published in 1748, the main character, Clarissa, is betrayed by a man whom she has chosen against her father's wishes, and she kills herself in disappointment and despair. To Clarissa, 'passionate love' meant escaping her 'father's control' and entrusting herself to her 'husband's control' with no protection.

In order for a daughter under patriarchy to escape her 'father's control,' she needs a huge centrifugal force. Romantic love can be a source of passion that gives her the destructive energy she needs to escape her father's control, but it also results in her losing her 'father's protection.' Paternal authority and husband's authority are in competition with each other, and no situation is more favorable for the exercise of the latter than a wife without a line of retreat in the absence of intervention by her father. Modern patriarchy is full of plots to cut women off from their parents in order to enable their husbands to control them in their nuclear families. In this sense, we might as well say that love represents the explosive energy for a woman to voluntarily transfer from her 'father's control' to her 'husband's control.' Women's internalization of the concept of love was one requirement for the establishment of modern patriarchy.

In France in the twentieth century, Pierre Bourdieu regarded marriage as a family strategy for the maximization of social resources and demonstrated, based on empirical research, that this applies also to times after the 'romantic love revolution' (Bourdieu, 1979). The same can be said for Japanese families after the postwar reforms. In the 1960s 'love marriage' gained an advantage over 'feudalistic' arranged marriage as spouse-selection behavior – although, in fact, 'arranged marriage' is nothing but an invention of modernity (Ueno, 1990b). However, an analysis of love marriages in terms of such variables as education, birthplace and parents' occupations reveals that the 'rule of homogamy' applies surprisingly well to love marriage.[7] In terms of the geographical range of marriage, the range of marriage may be smaller for love marriage than arranged marriage (Yuzawa, 1987). While arranged marriage allows interregional marriage through a matchmaker, feelings of love, which may lead to love marriage, often occur as a result of the proximity of residence or workplace. In addition, love between different classes, as typified by love between two people with different levels of education, is surprisingly rare. In fact, married couples whose wives have higher education or are older than their husbands are more often found in cases where the husband enters into an adoption arrangement with his wife's parents upon marriage. This indicates that even in modern times, love between different classes was exceptional and was often recognized as a serious incident only because it was exceptional.

The tendency for class endogamy is even stronger in love marriage than arranged marriage. It is as though feelings of similarity are the essential precondition for feelings of love. How should we interpret the fact that love marriage, which seems to assume a 'free market' system of marriage, results in even stronger class endogamy than an arranged marriage? This means that the criteria for a family strategy in marriage, which used to be judged by the parents on behalf of the bride and groom, have now been internalized and practiced by the bride and groom as individual free choice. While choice by the parents may seem to be compulsion, choice by the bride and groom themselves is regarded as made of their own free will. The result of the choice is substantially the same between arranged and love marriages. This means that love occurring in marriages between co-workers or in a 'feeling couple' game is nothing more than a game played by participants who have already been screened as belonging to the same class and who offer substantially the same choice. (A 'feeling couple' game is a game in which usually five men and five women sit at a table and ask questions to find out about each other; at the end of the session each person secretly and simultaneously pushes a button embedded in the table to indicate his/her favorite person of the opposite sex, upon which one or more bright lines of light appear on the table connecting one or more couples, if any, who liked each other). To become a free, independent actor in the laissez-faire, free market meant nothing but to internalize the rules of the game. This was exactly the formation of the modern 'subject,' or what Foucault describes as *subjectification* or *assujettissement*.

The autonomy of *ie*

Of the three requirements of the modern family listed by Shorter, the 'autonomy of the household' is a somewhat ambivalent concept. One can argue that *ie* has had autonomy as a management body from its beginning. To begin with, the emergence of *ie* from a community was intended to release households from the premodern control of the community. Conversely, however, this also seems to have resulted in *ie* being isolated from the community and being exposed defenselessly to control by national authorities. The 'pseudo-family state ideology' meant the breakdown of intermediate communities that posed obstacles to putting *ie* under direct control by the state.

As described above, Tadao Satō was the first to point out the vulnerability of the Japanese family system, which is not only defenseless against, but also acts as an agent for, public authority. *Ie* is thus without the autonomy of households as the jurisdiction of private law (as opposed to public law), which is another reason for not being able to regard *ie* as representing familism (as opposed to nationalism). *Ie* invented by the Meiji government as an agent of the imperial system was more an element of nationalism than of familism.

Yasumasa Kojita, having reviewed Volume 4, 'Kindai (Modern times)', of *Nihon josei seikatusu-shi* (A history of Japanese women's lives) (Joseishi Sōgō Kenkyūkai [ed.], 1990), which is a product of recent family history research, makes the following favorable comment in response to the issue posed by Yūko Nishikawa and her colleagues in the volume: '[The authors' view] put an end for the time being to the view that regards *ie*, as in the *ie* society in modern Japan, as a feudal relic and opened the way to the view that *ie* went hand-in-hand with increasing capitalism of Japanese society in all respects' (Kojita, 1993: 134). However, Kojita expresses a dissatisfaction that the 'autonomy of *ie*' is underestimated by the authors. Based on Junichi Murakami's *Doitsu shiminhō-shi* (A history of German civil law) (Murakami, J., 1985), Kojita sees a 'possibility that *ie* may function as a fort to maintain the ethical autonomy of citizens against the modern centralized government' (Kojita, 1993: 135). Kojita criticizes Nishikawa for overlooking the fact that if she and her colleagues assume that the autonomy of 'intermediate communities' (which existed in premodern times) against royal power was taken over by the autonomy of patriarchs in the modern nation-state, then in modern society *ie* and the state have an interdependent but tense relationship with each other (Kojita, 1993: 135). Nishikawa refutes this strongly, arguing that if she and her colleagues are to discuss the tense relationship between *ie* and the state, they need to focus on the modern family as the basic unit of the nation-state and to compare it between Germany and Japan, but that 'a nation state is actually established by depriving those intermediate communities of their autonomy' (Nishikawa, 1993: 27). Nishikawa further adds:

> When starting to suggest that we should not focus only on the negative aspects of *ie* and family, isn't Mr Kojita's tone suddenly changing from an excellent historian making an analysis to a member or defender of the domestic sphere? This makes me feel that I have renewed my awareness of the strength of the ideological nature of the word 'family' (Nishikawa, 1993: 27).

The autonomy of *ie* works in two directions: one towards the community and the other towards the state. Kojita seems to believe at face value in the ideological view that idealizes *ie* and advocates the absolute superiority of patriarchal authority. As pointed out sharply by Nishikawa, the interests and nostalgia of men who want to protect patriarchal authority seem to lie in Kojita's belief. Contrary to Kojita's belief, the modern family's high vulnerability to control by the national government, after obtaining autonomy from the community, has been demonstrated in Europe, as well, by such works as *La police des familles* by Donzelot (1991). As argued by Nishikawa, modern nation-states have a pseudo-family state-like nature to varying degrees. What Satō saw in European films were idealized patriarchs, or patriarchs belonging to nostalgy.[8]

Whether the household structure is of the nuclear family or the stem family, the autonomy (i.e. isolation and exclusivity) of family as asserted by Shorter was realized in prewar Japanese family. While Shorter, too, seems to idealize the autonomy of family, women's studies have demonstrated how arbitrarily paternal and husband's authority controlled the modern family in the absence of communal regulation (which would have acted as intervention by a third party).[9]

Ie as an ideology

As discussed thus far, Japanese *ie* meets all the requirements of the modern family proposed by Shorter. The fact that Japanese *ie* took the form of stem family instead of nuclear family is not unrelated to the fact that the proto-industrialization of Japan was supported mainly by household industry and, even after the first and second industrial revolutions, relied much on medium, small and tiny family businesses under the dual structure of Japanese industry. Japan's situation cannot be explained by a simple process in which the progress of industrialization resulted in the breakdown of the old middle classes (farmers and commodity producers) and an increase in the proportion of employees. Unlike a society such as America, where the proportion of employees has exceeded 90%, in Japan the corresponding proportion has remained between 80% and 90%, with a slight increase in the proportion of self-employed people each time a recession occurs. There have always been employees switching to self-employed status. This suggests that *ie* has been taken over by management bodies as their ideology.

In *Senzen 'ie' no shisō* (The prewar ideology of *ie*), Masanao Kano (1983) includes a chapter entitled 'Strengthened ideology and disintegrating realities.' The *ie* of the samurai class rapidly broke down exactly when the *ie* system, which was modeled after the family system of the samurai class, was being established by the national government. Further, under the influence of the harsh original accumulation of capital and the Matsukata deflation,[10] urban lower classes were also facing the breakdown of families. While the *ie* system was being established as an ideology, in reality it was rapidly disintegrating. However, this was exactly why the ideology had to be emphasized.

Bunmei to shite no ie shakai (The *ie* society as a civilization), co-authored by Kumon, Murakami and Satō (1979), has a totally different ideological background from Kano's work but shares the same observation as Kano's. In this work, the three co-authors positively evaluate *ie* as a medium of the promotion of modernization rather than as a feudalistic system for suppression, creating a new wave in the studies of Japanese culture. In the process of discussion, the co-authors understand *ie* as an organizational principle rather than as an entity.[11] They argue:

> In prewar days, *ie* had started to head for disintegration and demise. The development of industrialization promoted the breakdown of small businesses run by *ie*-like management and caused an increase of urban salaried workers. This resulted in reduction in family size and the more extensive generation of nuclear families, which are extremely weak as a family system and have lost the *ie* principles almost entirely. The provisions of the new Constitution and the new Civil Code represented institutional confirmation of these realities (Kumon, Murakami and Satō, 1979: 476).

They go on to discuss this as follows:

> after people were no longer able to feel belonging to or identify themselves with the state or *ie*, virtually the only satisfactory relationship that remained available for people to have was with workplaces such as companies. This resulted in the increasing social necessity for *ie*-like companies, with many people turning into enthusiastic workers or activists who devoted themselves single-mindedly to their company or union movements in their attempt to identify themselves with their company and/or in-house union (Kumon, Murakami and Satō, 1979: 477).

The authors argue that the principles of *ie* as a management body survived, against its intentions, in business entities rather than in the nation-state or families. This is because, first, *ie* was, from its beginning, a management body existing beyond the principle of lineage; and, second, both the nation-state and families lacked physical foundations for realizing the *ie* principles compared to business entities. The *ie* ideology survived modern times as managerial familism.

Conclusion

It can be demonstrated that *ie* was, in many ways, a historical, social construct in the formative period of modernity. In this sense, *ie* was nothing but the Japanese version of modern family and established the modern patriarchy in the form of conjugal family.

If *ie* is thus neither a tradition nor a feudal relic, it will be difficult to discuss Japanese identity in terms of the family system. Even if we assume that there was some prototype of *ie* in premodern times, it would have transformed in the course of history. The new *ie* adopted by the Meiji government was selected from the diverse cultural matrix as suitable for the time. Once this *ie* was selected, its origin was justified as a tradition and various alternatives that could have been selected were forgotten. If *ie* is the Japanese version of modern family, it is questionable to discuss it in the context of the cultural peculiarity of Japan. It is true that *ie* is unique to modern Japan in time and space, but it is neither particular nor a non-historical, timeless, cultural tradition.

What we need to make an issue of here is whether or not it is appropriate at all to discuss Japanese society using family models. In other words, we need to explore how the social theory surrounding the overvalued *ie* was formed, by tracing the process of model formation. In *Tate shakai no ningen kankei* (Personal relations in a vertical society), Chie Nakane (1967) regards family as the basic unit of society and explains the social structures at all other levels as extending in concentric circles from family as the basic structure.[12] However, isn't this kind of assumption possible only because family was cut off from all other social organizations and was constructed as an autonomous unit that provided a model in society? As discussed so far, this autonomy of family was, contrary to its appearance, established for the very purpose of allowing control by broader society. There is not only confusion between the cause and the effects. Nakane and other researchers who bring up a family model as a principle for explaining the social structure are simply tracing the structures constructed by modernity, and are forgetting to question how they were formed in the course of history.

These researchers do not just repeat the social construction of family in their own theoretical construction; by doing so, their theory itself contributes to the reinforcement of the family model.

It is simply a tautology to say that the society constructs a family model and then the family model explains the society and that this is what the pseudo-family state ideology is. We should question modernity itself as the 'age of family' in which the family model has gained such dominance. Social scientists are also slaves to the family ideology created by modernity. They serve as ideologues of family by treating family as an explanatory variable instead of an explained variable. It is conversely the history (i.e. social construction) of family that must actually be questioned.

Considered this way, we can solve the mystery of why Freud's theory was so rampant in the twentieth century. While Freud's theory was perfect as a theory for explaining the modern family, it was conversely a product of the modern family. The fact that a theory constructed by the modern family can explain the modern family well represents nothing but redundancy. Similarly, the fact that the family model explains the nation-state well represents redundancy because the nation-state was constructed based on the family model.

The family model as an ideology serves only one purpose – to prohibit questioning of the origin of family by regarding its naturalness as inviolable. There was a secret behind the formation of the modern family: the separation of the public and private spheres. The public sphere (i.e. the state) needed to conceal its dependence on the private sphere or, more frankly, its exploitation of families. Constructing family as a sacred, inviolable sanctuary was a plot of the modern patriarchy. In this sense, it is just that the Japanese *ie* was no exception. This myth of the modern family continued to survive until this sanctuary was later violated by women's studies.

Appendix: About the concept of patriarchy

In the tradition of Japanese social science, the concept of patriarchy has been understood in association with Max Weber. In *Shakaigaku jiten* (A dictionary of sociology) published by Yūhikaku in 1958 (Fukutake *et al.* [eds.], 1958), 'patriarchalism' is defined as 'a form of family in which the male head of the family governs and controls the family members using his patriarchal authority,' with 'families in ancient and medieval times' being mentioned as an example. The only reference mentioned is Weber's *Kasansei to hōkensei* (1921–22;

the Japanese title means 'Patrimonialism and feudalism' but there is no corresponding original collection of works). In the 1993 edition of *Shin shakaigaku jiten* (New dictionary of sociology), also published by Yūhikaku, the word 'patriarchalism' has been replaced by 'patriarchal family' (Morioka *et al.* [eds.], 1993). The definition, quoting Le Play (1855), is 'a form of family in which the authority over family members is centered on the father.' By mentioning examples ('seen among Oriental nomads, Russian farmers, and the Slavs in central Europe'), the definition intentionally contrasts the patriarchal family with the modern family. In the Kōbundō version of *Shakaigaku jiten* (The encyclopedia of sociology), which was edited in 1988 by Munesuke Mita and others, and is supposed to cover new trends in sociology, the word 'patriarchy' is defined as 'a form of family in which the male head with patriarchal authority governs and controls the family members,' which is no different from the definition in the Yūhikaku version published in 1958. Relying mainly on Weber, this definition states that patriarchy was 'seen in ancient and medieval Europe and Japan.' It also says that in Japan, 'the patriarchal system seen in the Meiji Civil Code provided for the family order in feudal society.' The definition adds the following understanding: 'However, patriarchy is disappearing with the development of the modern family and the breakdown of the *ie* system after World War Two.'

When we compare the descriptions of patriarchy in these Japanese mainstream and alternative dictionaries of sociology with the corresponding descriptions in the *Encyclopedia of feminism* edited by Lisa Tuttle (1986), we cannot help being stunned by the differences. The latter encyclopedia makes the following general remarks (p. 242): 'Literally, it means "rule of the father", and was originally used by anthropologists to describe the social structure in which one old man (the patriarch) has absolute power over other members of the family.' This is followed by the observation that this term has been variously redefined and used by feminists. 'The concept of patriarchy has been an important one,' says the encyclopedia, which then states (by quoting Kate Millett (1970) and Juliet Mitchell (1975)) that patriarchy is a social structure in which 'male shall dominate female; elder male shall dominate younger' and that 'all known societies' in history are patriarchal. Published in England in 1986 and translated into Japanese in 1991, the *Encyclopedia of feminism* demonstrates, by its existence itself, that the field of feminism has an accumulation of knowledge that is rich enough to be compiled into a full encyclopedia. Nevertheless, it is also clear that this knowledge has had no influence at all on the field of Japanese sociology. Even the 1988 Kōbundō version and the 1993 Yūhikaku version, which were published in the period of post-feminism, make no mention of feminism. It is as though the twenty years of the history of feminist studies after the 1970s did not exist.

Certainly, the ambiguity of the concept of patriarchy is acknowledged by the *Encyclopedia of feminism*: 'The term is frequently used by feminists, who are not always in agreement as to what they mean by it.' Kaku Sechiyama (1990) points out the confusion surrounding the concept of patriarchy and argues that different terms should have been used to avoid the confusion. *Jendā no shakaigaku* (A sociology of gender) includes an essay by Kōichi Hasegawa entitled 'Kafuchōsei towa nanika (What is patriarchy?)' in which Hasegawa proposes that patriarchalism and patriarchy should be distinguished from each other and that the former should be translated as *kafuchōsei* (the conventional Japanese word for patriarchy) and the latter as *fukensei* (system of father's dominance). Hasegawa states, 'The term *kafuchōsei* should be used to refer only to the form of male control typically found in ancient Rome, in which the oldest man has absolute and exclusive power and authority over all of the family members' (Hasegawa, K., 1989). At the same time, Hasegawa does not fail to point out that the concept of patriarchy has been 'rediscovered' and used by feminists.

However, it is not a matter of translation of the word as *kafuchōsei* or *fukensei*. Feminists in English-speaking countries have always used the historical term of patriarchy. The word was intentionally chosen from the conventional vocabulary in order to indicate the historical omnipresence of patriarchy. Feminists redefined the term 'patriarchy' in order to express the various phenomena that had been called 'male dominance' or 'sexism' as a comprehensive structure by tracing the origin of these phenomena. Although Hasegawa asserts that the 'difference between feminists' usage and the conventional usage of the word' has caused 'confusion and misunderstanding,' such 'confusion and misunderstanding' has actually occurred outside feminism. Since the word 'gender' has become commonly used, there is no longer anyone who uses this word in the limited sense of the 'grammatical classification of words into different sexes.' Similarly, there is no longer anyone who thinks that 'feminist' means a 'gentleman who respects women.' As seen in these examples, a concept is redefined during its use in the course of history. It is absolutely odd that, twenty years after feminists first redefined and used the term 'patriarchy,' absolutely no mention was made of this change in the dictionaries of sociology published in the 1990s, when young sociologists such as Sechiyama and Hasegawa wrote their papers on the concept of patriarchy.

A similar lack of understanding is seen in *Ie to kafuchōsei* (*Ie* and patriarchy), published by Hikaku Kazoku-shi Gakkai (The Society of Comparative Family History) in 1992 (Nagahara *et al.* [eds], 1992). All twelve authors of this work are men, none of whom refer to the achievements of women's historians, with the exception of Itsue Takamure. Further, no notice at all is paid to the achievements of women's studies after feminism. Keiji Nagahara, who was one of the editors and wrote the introduction to the work, still emphasizes the 'hidebound nature' of patriarchy, saying that patriarchy was a 'fatalistic inconsistency' to the capitalistic economic development (Nagahara *et al.* [eds], 1992: 9). Hiroshi Kamata, who asserts that patriarchy was a result of the Meiji government's policy to intentionally establish it, also adopts the conventional view that the patriarchy represented a 'structural peculiarity of the Japanese society' (Kamata, 1992: 27). However, Kazuhiko Sumiya points out, in his work '"Kafuchōsei" ron no tenbō (A review of the discourse on "patriarchy")', that the issue of patriarchy has shifted from the stage at which it was discussed as a feudal relic to a new stage at which the issue is 'patriarchy in the modern civil society,' and that the 'issue of patriarchy seems to have now entered a completely new stage' (Sumiya, 1992: 298). Nevertheless, as the reasons for his argument, Sumiya points out only that the 'view proposed by the development stage theory' (in which Japan and Western countries are contrasted as backward versus advanced) was made less convincing by Japan's postwar rapid economic growth, and that Western social history research has made it clear that European modernity cannot be discussed without patriarchy. Thus, Sumiya makes no mention of the fact that the history of modern family formation broke new ground as a result of the participation by researchers in women's history and feminism. On the contrary, Sumiya proposes to discuss patriarchy in a 'typological' framework throughout history instead of in stages, based on an understanding of the situation that the evaluation of the '"feudal relic" or the ancient regime was completely reversed from criticism to recognition as a valuable traditional legacy of Japanese culture and as a key prerequisite for the rapid progress of Japanese economy' (Sumiya, 1992: 297). This represents a retreat from feminists' historical awareness, which made an issue of the 'patriarchy unique to the modern family.' Based on an understanding that 'it was not individuals but nothing other than families that provided the foundation for the modern civil society that was actually established,' Itsuo Emori (1992: 280) proposes a concept of 'patriarchy in civil society' and identifies patriarchal authority in civil laws such as the Landrecht of Prussia and the Napoleonic Civil Code of France. However, in Emori's statement that the 'patriarchal structure of the modern civil family was shaken by wives' return to the labor market as a result of the machine-based, large-scale factory system,' we see an influence of the Engels-style socialist theory of emancipation of women that the complete return of women to the public labor force is a requirement for the emancipation of women. Emori's view reflects none of the findings of women's studies obtained by the 1980s; these findings include that, contrary to the myth that 'working class families were free from sexual discrimination' (Inoue, Kiyoshi, 1948), the modern patriarchy does exist in the working class; and that 'women's return to the public labor force' as a result of patriarchal capitalism did not shake patriarchy but resulted only in the suppression of women in both the private and public spheres, in association with gender segregation in the labor market. Their book, which should represent cutting-edge results of studies on *ie* and patriarchy in the 1990s, ignores the twenty years' achievement of women's studies as if no such thing existed.

4 Modernity for the Family

The happiness of the home

Even sexuality and family, which are frequently considered to be closest to nature and instinct, change across time and space. As Japan entered the Meiji era, there was a dramatic shift in the way people viewed spousal relations, marriage, the family, men and women, love, and their bodies. Studying the process through which these views were formed reveals very well that many of these views, which are firmly believed to be part of commonsense today, roughly a hundred years later, are actually a relatively new historical construct.

Modern European history has repeatedly shown, under the influence of social history and women's history, that the domestic sphere is reorganized with wider social change. In fact, the private domestic sphere is itself a product of the modernization process, through which it was formed at the same time that there was a construction of the public sphere. The universal belief that the family is a refuge from the outside world is, of itself, a product of modernity.[1]

We can also trace the establishment of the modern family in Japan. The mad rush to modernize that Japan entered after the Meiji Restoration involved conflict between newly imported ideas and those that were already in circulation, and between those pushing forward Westernization and those opposed to this.

When looking at modernity for the family, we need to first look at how the concept of the home was established. The magazine *Katei zasshi* (The home magazine) published in 1892, as its name implies, was concerned with the home and played an important role in strengthening an ideology that praised home life:

> The home is an enchanted land. Flowers blossom, birds sing, there are beautiful skies and long days. A wall makes the boundary between the inside and outside world. Inside, everything is far removed from the rest of the world, like peach flower petals being carried far away by the flowing water...Here is the home of each one of us. Peaceful

and beautiful, this home is for happy children. This home maintains harmony and enjoyment, cleanliness, health and the unique family tradition. This is made possible only when it creates a distinction between the inside and outside world and opens up a small and separate space for each of us (*Katei zasshi*, 'Katei to jiji (Current topics in the home),' no. 24).

Charitable father and mother, siblings who get along well, a husband and wife devoted to one another, making a good-natured, loyal, diligent, simple and modest family. Is it not the happiness of people in the world, heaven or the idealized home that poets have daydreamed about while sitting under the roof of a thatched house? (*Katei zasshi*, 'Katei no fukuin (The good news for the home),' no. 24).

The peaceful home is a happy home. The husband leaves the home, but does not forget his family, the wife prayers for her husband's safety and the children respect their parents. Through frequent get-togethers, the family joyfully laugh and enjoy talking together. There is nothing more joyfull in life than this (*Katei zasshi*, 'Tanoshiki katei (The enjoyable home),' no. 26).

In issue number 15 of *Katei zasshi* we find the word *katei* given as the Japanese equivalent of the word 'home.' In an article written under the pen name of Miss Shūkō, we are told that it is 'the place where we can receive genuinely pure pleasure, or *katei* (home)' ('Kekkongo no kōfuku (Happiness after marriage)'). The adjectives attached to the noun 'home' include 'happy,' 'pleasant' and 'healthy.' The symbol of this 'happiness of the home' is the happy family circle: 'What can be called heaven at home in the evening? One can only point to the time spent together in a happy family circle, which is good in all its pure innocence' (*Katei zasshi*, 'Yoru no katei (The home in the evening),' no. 1).

The conditions structuring this 'happiness of the home' are:
1. mutual love between husband and wife
2. monogamous relationship and
3. unmarried children (excluding non-kin), thus forming a nuclear family
4. the employed husband, and
5. a full-time housewife, thus based on an urban worker's household with a gender division of labor.

The concepts of 'happy family circle' and 'chatting over tea' were introduced here for the first time, and with it 'conversation' among family members was stressed (*Katei zasshi*, 'Katei no danwa (Conversation in the home),' editorial, no. 6). The inaugural edition of *Katei zasshi* mentions an article in the *Kokumin Shinbun* (The people's newspaper), number 790. Here we are told that 'there is nothing more joyful for a family than sitting in a happy circle, the old and the young together, to chat and eat,' and eating together as a family is emphasized. Traditionally, family members ate their meals at different times on the basis of gender and age divisions, and chatting while eating was considered a breach of etiquette: from this perspective, eating meals together so that family members could mix regardless of gender and generation could only have led to confusion of categories and a breaking down of family morals.[2] Yet this was extolled as the beginnings of a new moral code. However, if we consider this from a different perspective, the emphasis placed on communication within the family in the form of 'get-togethers' can be seen as a necessary step to bind together family members who, as a result of individualization and urbanization, no longer share family businesses or assets. The traditional family, where there was an organizational foundation in the family business, did not have to emphasize communication.

The primary precondition for establishing this 'happiness of the home' was the mutual love of husband and wife. Ryōzō Kōda (1887) argued in *Kishi myōko shikijō tetsugaku* (New ideas and good attitudes: A philosophy of love and sex) that the 'greatest pleasure in human life lies in the existence of monogamy between husband and wife:'

> What we call the greatest pleasure in life at all would be best represented by conversation between a man and a woman who have nothing to feel guilty about and who feel very relaxed about each other.
>
> Only if a man and a woman keep the moral code of monogamy and stay faithful to one another in sexual relations, they can enjoy the supreme pleasure with innocent heart and mind.

Shikijō tetsugaku (A philosophy of love and sex), as the title suggests, is concerned with the metaphysics of love and sex; however, the moral code of monogamy represents a 180 degree about-turn when compared to the metaphysics of love and sex of the Edo era (for example, Kizan Fujimoto in *Shikidō ōkagami*[3] (The encyclopedia of amours, 1678) makes a distinction between the *yūjo* (courtesan/prostitute) of the pleasure quarters and *jiwon'na* (local women),[4] then proceeds to eulogize the *yūjo-sama* (honourable courtesan)).

There is no question that the notion of monogamy was an imported idea of modernization. In 1885 Jirō Inoue introduced in *Jogaku shinshi* (A new magazine for women's studies) the ideas of 'American scholar Mr. Cook' to explain the idea of 'spousal love:'

1. Those who are about to become husband and wife must ardently love each other above all others.
2. The ardent love that husband and wife feel for each other must never be extended to any other person.
3. If a man and a woman who love each other above all others are to become husband and wife, then, because only two people can love each other above all others, a marriage must consist of only one man and one woman (i.e. a man should not take more than one wife nor take one wife and keep a mistress).
4. Those who do not ardently love each other above all others cannot become, or are not allowed to become, husband and wife.
5. Whether or not a man and a woman love each other above all others can be judged on the basis of the following conditions:
    i   whether or not they feel that should their marriage be in danger for any reason, they would want to make it up
    ii whether the engagement to get married is based on an agreement between both parties or only one party forces the other to give an agreement.
    iii whether the couple to be married has the resolve sufficient that they would die for the other.
6. If two people who ardently love each other above all others as described above become husband and wife, their life after marriage will never be an unhappy one.
7. A marriage that is not entered into in this way does not only stand in opposition to natural law, but also to the rules of society (compiled from *Jogaku shinshi*, nos. 20 and 21).

From what can only be described as a strict puritanical moral standard, item 5.iii would probably cause particular fear in most people.

From this puritan morality, based on an assumption that love and marriage went together, arose the demand for 'free marriage.' Tetsujirō Miyagawa in *Nihon no jogaku* (Women's studies in Japan), number 21, made an argument for just this under the title 'Free marriage and arranged marriage:'

Can there be anybody in the world who does not desire to enter into marriage freely? Can there be anybody who does not feel an aversion to his/her parents' intervention in his/her marriage? Can there be anybody who does not desire the happiness of peace and harmony between husband and wife? We earnestly desire free marriage as quickly as possible.[5]

At least four problems arise when we consider the matter based on this idealistic concept of 'happiness of the home.'

First of all, there is the reality of male dominance in the Japanese family, which is far from the idealized happy home. In an article titled 'Genkon no katei (The home today)' written under the pen name of Kyūmei and published in the editorial section of the inaugural edition of *Katei zasshi*, the writer lamented the relationship between husband and wife of that time as one between a 'lord and a servant,' where 'the small state of the family [was], as before, akin to that of a despotic state:'

Nothing is more unpleasant than a disorderly home...In short, this occurs because the household head shares only hardships and no pleasure with his family. Whether a head of household does share any of the pleasure is entirely up to him, and this determines whether that home becomes a happy or unhappy one...The wife and children simply and meekly obey any orders the household head may give, including somewhat unreasonable ones, saying, 'Whatever you say, sir.' So the household head...acts like a lord in his own home and spends most of what money the family has for entertainment just for his own pleasure. He regards his family members as his servants and thoughtlessly uses them to satisfy his own desire. If he is not pleased with what they do, he scolds them with his eyes dilated. Family members try not to incur the wrath of the master of the house and live from day-to-day nervously and cautiously. When the master of the house goes out, there are laughing voices throughout the home, just as if a pest had gone out. Given this state of affairs, however much we may hope for a happy home, it is just not possible (*Katei zasshi*, 'Tanoshiki katei (The happy home),' no. 26).

This lament for '*genkon no katei* (the home today)' was based on a comparison with Westerners. The following passage, written under the pen name of Totsutotsu Koji, appeared in *Nihon no jogaku*, number 12, under the title 'Kijo shokun ni tsugu (An announcement for you ladies):'

In the case of those Western men, a husband will hold his wife's hand at all times and offer her help. Whether going on a long trip or attending an evening party, the couple stay together side by side without leaving each other's side. In contrast, the Japanese man will scold his wife arrogantly. He will be cared for by her but will never offer to help her. It seems common that a Japanese husband will at times sleep with a courtesan or flirt with prostitutes and will take a *gonsai* (concubine) and/or keep a *gaishō* (mistress) outside. When it comes to kindness, it must be said that a Japanese husband is extremely coldhearted.

Even *Kijo no tomo* (The lady's friend), which advocated 'wifely morals,' published an article entitled 'Nihon no danshi wa joshi ni taishite shinsetsu nariya (Are Japanese men kind to women?).' We are told that:

> it is indeed a pity that even wives, themselves, are bewildered by the situation, saying, 'Nothing is more boring and miserable than being a woman.' Men work actively outside the home and have many interesting and enjoyable experiences, so when they return to the home they should politely offer comfort to their wives (*Kijo no tomo*, no. 41).

When this article also says, '*Japanese* men and women should show each other love on a basis of equity' (italicized by the author quoting), it is clear that the writer is conscious of 'Western men.'

In the popular instruction book *Irogoto no shikata* (The manner of making love) by Gika Jōshi (a.k.a. Yoshio Kamine, 1883) there is a chapter on 'Fūfu no majiwari (Coitus between husband and wife),' which had the following to say on the subject:

> Please just take a look at foreigners out enjoying themselves in Yokohama or Kobe. Most of them will be accompanied by their wives. A husband and wife going out together is nothing to be ashamed of in the least. We would urge you to be intimate and become more intimate with your partner.[6]

This overlaps absolutely with what renowned Meiji intellect and educator Yukichi Fukuzawa (1835–1901) had to say in *Danjo kōsairon* (An essay on companionship between men and women, 1886). He writes, 'A *senryū* [a short sarcastic poem] goes, "A husband and wife walk together only after they have walked a few blocks from home." Intrinsically, in the natural affection between men and women, their real intention must be to head out for a walk together leaving the house behind them...'

The idealization of both the culture of Western home and the 'Western man' eventually led to self-contempt that 'the Japanese man is an animal without any redeeming features,' which went as far as a recommendation of international marriage: one magazine article addressed to women said, 'Let me advise you ladies... you should marry Western men' ('Kijo shokun ni tusgu (An announcement for you ladies),' *Nihon no jogaku*, no. 12). This was rebutted by *Kijo no tomo*, a magazine that loathed Westernization, and this contributed to the development of the controversy to the level where an unexpected debate blew up over Westernization versus ultranationalism. New views on family life, to the extent that these represented imported ideas, did not escape from the imputation that they were 'worshiping the foreign culture.'

In the second place, practicing prostitution and keeping concubines, many Japanese men violated the moral code of monogamy.

> The relationship between men and women is extremely great and important, and when husband and wife make a promise to share the same bedroom (i.e. make marriage vows) it must be regarded as an important code of conduct for human beings. It is the foundation of all happiness in society, while also the cause of all unhappiness ... If asked which party, whether in the ancient or modern period, is more likely to have violated this code I would have to answer that it is always the man (based on Gentarō Tezuka and Yukichi Fukuzawa, *Nihon danshi ron* (An essay on Japanese men), 1888).

The sexual double standard that Fukuzawa points to was revealed in the Meiji Criminal Code in the asymmetric gender differentiated standard applied to adultery: a wife who committed adultery was punished but not a husband.

Another liberal intellect, Emori Ueki (1857–92) set forth his ideas for the abolition of prostitution, for monogamy, and concerning the home, first in the magazine *Kokumin no tomo* (The nation's friend), founded by journalist Sohō Tokutomi (1863–1957), and later in the local newspaper *Doyō Shimbun*, which Ueki himself edited. However, in *Ueki Emori nikki* (Dairies of Emori Ueki), published in 1955 by Kōchi Shimbunsha (Kōchi newspaper company), there is the following entry for September 7, 1880: 'In the evening, I spoke at a forum in Sen'nichimae. I argued for the equal rights of men

and women. I called for a geisha named Kikue.' The fact that Ueki
so mentions his own two-facedness – one face being of a gender
equality stalwart that he showed during the day and the other of a
brothel customer for night – as if he had done nothing wrong, shows
that he was living by a sexual double standard himself.[7]

The idea was also proposed that the immoral behavior of men was
due to the lack of a happy home. In *Irogoto no shikata* the secret of
harmony between a husband and wife is being together: 'If husband
and wife accompany each other at all times, the husband will not get
blind drunk outside of the home and flirt with another woman, nor
will the wife resort to illicit dreams in her husband's absence.' This
is no different from the view suggested by Yukichi Fukuzawa.

> Some of the wealthy and noble enjoy pleasure by keeping concubines
> in and outside his home or by inviting geisha girls to his home. If we
> look at lower social classes, some men go to brothels and get drunk with
> prostitutes, committing every imaginable misdeed to take his mind
> off his own troubles...In consideration of the circumstances, I cannot
> say that there is absolutely no excuse for such behavior. Specifically,
> in the life of people in general who do not have peerless mental and
> physical strength, how can they enjoy themselves when they behave
> graciously with mannered behavior in a hard-hearted society like
> Japan? Because they cannot enjoy themselves, they seek ways to do
> so and find the only way out in engaging in those misdeeds – keeping
> concubines and inviting geisha girls. Although these misdeeds are truly
> disgraceful, they are not intended just to appease men's lusts. In fact,
> whether a man might set up a mistress's room or house or go to the
> pleasure quarters, these places provide enjoyable shelters where sexual
> relationships are offered outside the boundaries of social manners and
> customs, making him feel as if he could be free from social restrictions.
> This is why he uses these places, nasty though they may be, in order
> to satisfy his desire for illicit intercourse. Therefore, these misdeeds
> are not necessarily to be criticized; rather, they should actually be
> pitied (drafted by Yukichi Fukuzawa and transcribed by Hikojirō
> Nakakamigawa, *Danjo kōsairon*, 1886).

What Fukuzawa refers to as 'social restrictions' is a 'major
misfortune of our country, Japan,' whose society allowed 'no
friendship between men and women,' thus making the 'relationship
between men and women...awkward.' Fukuzawa had a sense of
gender equality, which made him feel that 'what is unpleasant to
women should be unpleasant to men' as well. However, it did not

match the symmetrical notion of sexual equality in *Irogoto no shikata*, which, under the heavy influence of Edo sex culture, refers to the possibility of misconduct by wife as well as by husband.

Thirdly, it was pointed out that the lack of love between husband and wife arose from the way they married.

> What I hear about how arranged marriages take place according to our traditional custom is that if the potential husband is pleased with the potential wife, then the arrangement is deemed accepted despite the fact that seven or eight out of ten potential wives do raise a complaint or objection of some sort against the potential marriage. Thus, it is usually the case that a woman must marry a man once he is pleased with her and that she will be abandoned once he is no longer pleased with her. This is indeed extremely lamentable ('Fūfu no ai (Love between husband and wife),' *Jogaku shinshi*, no. 21).

This is because marriage served as an economic institution:

> It seems that in the marital relationship today, men take a wife for their own pleasure as soon as they can afford to do so. Women who have reached marriageable age marry in order to obtain means of livelihood. Therefore, men always ask whether or not their potential bride is a beauty and women always ask whether their potential husband receives a high or low salary before they decide to marry each other. There can thus be no true love between husband and wife. A husband often threatens his wife with divorce, while the wife always pays insincere compliments to her husband. If there were no economic or social problems, most of the couples currently married would divorce at once (*Heimin Shimbun* (Commoners' newspaper), February 21, 1904).

This is because 'women have no way to earn their own living' (*Sekai fujin* (World's women), no. 14, July 15, 1907). Such 'loveless marriage' is 'particularly seen most frequently in marriages among the noble and wealthy classes' (*Sekai fujin*, no. 5, March 1, 1907).[8]

In *Shikijō eisei tetsugaku* (A philosophy on sexual hygiene) (Shizuya Kuroki and Chisato Iida, 1906), the authors pose a question: 'Aren't most of the marriages today similar to prostitution?' They continue, 'Haven't most [of the married women] married their husband's title, or his social status, or his financial power?' The authors go so far as to say, 'they regard marriage as one form of business and are being engaged in human trafficking.'

According to Kunio Yanagita's *Meiji taishōshi: Sesō hen* (Social history of Meiji and Taishō),[9] this period (particularly around 1907–12) coincides with the process through which marriage changed from intra-village marriage based on mutual agreement by institutionalized promiscuity, which was under the control of each village's *wakashū yado* (young men's association) and *musume yado* (young women's association), to inter-village/arranged marriage, which used matchmakers. The topsy-turvy seen in the reference of 'arranged marriages' as Japan's 'traditional custom' and in the argument that 'you should not demand free marriage' is nothing but a paradox of the time. At the same time as 'love between husband and wife' and 'happiness of the home' were being advocated, the trend for marriage to be an economic deal proceeded.

In the fourth place, the nuclear family model was introduced to serve the ideal of 'happiness of the home.' Emori Ueki's argument that 'a son and his wife should live apart from their mothers- and fathers-in law' derives from this ideal:

> [In order to create a] pure family with no outsiders, a family which is consistently faithful to truth, a family whose members always discuss before taking any action...it is best not to have any outsiders from outside the family...Wherever possible, a family should live only with their proper family members, particularly pure family members ('Uruwashiki kafū (Elegant family tradition),' editorial, *Katei zasshi*, no. 3).

The word 'outsiders' refers to 'spongers,' non-family dependents, servants and so on. It was further recommended that if economic circumstances permitted, a married couple should live apart from their mothers- and fathers-in-law. In the traditional stem family system, a son's wife, or a daughter-in-law, was considered an outsider. However, in the search for the ideal of 'happiness of the home,' mothers- and fathers-in-law finally came to be regarded as 'outsiders' or 'non-family dependents.'

This separation of traditional family members was further justified for the following two reasons:

> If the parent couple, or mother- and father-in-law, live with the child couple, or son- or daughter-in-law:
>   First, because the parent couple controls the child couple in an old-fashioned manner, they might hinder the progress of the society.

Second, when the parent couple grows old, they tend to feel like relying on the younger child couple, while, when the child couple is young, they tend to feel like relying on the older parent couple ('Kanai no bekkyo (Separation of family members),' *Kijo no tomo*, no. 51).

In other words, separation of traditional family members was recommended for the reasons of 'time gap' and 'generation gap,' In a time of rapid social change, a generation gap becomes wider and becomes more likely to cause conflicts. Thinkers of the Meiji era supported the separation of traditional households in the name of 'improvement of the home.'

I need to make some comments on the oft-stated bullying of a bride by her mother-in-law and the bride's low position in the household into which she has married. In his speech at a girls' high school, Arinori Mori said, 'Eight or nine out of ten brides tend to live in the same house as her parents-in-law upon marriage. In addition, the family finances are controlled by her parents-in-law' (*Jogaku zasshi* (Women's studies magazine), no. 120), which suggests that brides had absolutely no authority as housewives. Yukichi Fukuzawa also points out the 'inhumanity of parents-in-law,' saying, 'even when they are happy about the harmony between their child and his/her spouse, deep down they are hoping that the child couple's relationship will grow cold...' (*Danjo kōsairon*).

On the other hand, however, Kunio Yanagita reported cases in rural villages up to the mid-Meiji era where the distinction was still maintained between a wedding ceremony and the bride's move into her husband's family, and where the transfer of the housewife's authority and the bride's move into her husband's family took place at the same time (i.e. the bride joined her husband's family as fully-authorized housewife). In light of this fact, the bride's low position in her husband's family, which consisted of stem family members including his parents, must have occurred due to, among others, the following conditions:

1. it became common that a wedding and the bride's move into her husband's family took place at the same time
2. marriage came to be considered irreversible and a wife was no longer allowed to return to her own parents' home
3. hypergamy, or women marrying up the social ladder, became common practice, resulting in the lower social status of brides' families than their husbands' families, and

4. a bride was no longer counted on as a source of labor on the
   farm, but joined the family of her husband, an urban employee,
   as a wife without a job.

If this is the case, then the discord between wife and mother-in-law
is nothing but another 'modern' phenomenon. It may be likely that
the separation of traditional family members was proposed as a
measure against the intensifying discord. At any rate, the average
family cycle during the Meiji era suggests that after a bride moved
into her husband's family, her father- and mother-in-law died in the
average periods of six years and ten years, respectively, and she
most likely achieved the status of housewife by the time she was
in her mid-thirties (Yuzawa, 1987).

Household head and housewife

A man and his wife thus married became *shujin* (household head)
and *shufu* (housewife) of the family. The words *shujin* and *shufu*
first appeared as a pair during the second decade of the Meiji era
(1887–96). The responsibility of a housewife who was supposed to
manage the household was considered particularly heavy. Women's
role as housewife of the household was another idea imported from
the West during the Meiji era. The idea was introduced directly as
a Western concept, using katakana.

The woman is the key of the home ('Nihon no fujin: Sono 3 (Japanese
women: Part 3),' *Nihon no jogaku*, no. 10).

A Western proverb says, 'The wise woman builds her house.' This is
indeed true. The most powerful person in a household is the housewife
('Shōgaku keizai kasei yōshi: Kōhen (A study on economics: A
summary of home economy, part 2),' *Kaseigaku bunken shūsei*
(Collection of literature on home economics), quoted in Chūbu Katei
Keieigaku Kenkyūkai (ed.), 1972: 416).

What makes a home a home is, first of all, that the housewife of the
home is the queen of the home (Kanzō Uchimura, 'Kurisuchan hōmu
(Christian home),' *Jogaku zasshi*, no. 125).

A home is like a sovereign nation. Isn't it the housewife's major responsibility to serve as queen of this nation and manage everything? ('Kasei
tenka (The world of home economics),' *Jogaku zasshi*, no. 229).

The husband, as opposed to the wife, was considered her partner in building their home, but was a pale presence in the home. The articles titled 'Tsuma taru mono no tsutome (Wife's duties)' and 'Otto taru mono no tsutome (Husband's duties),' published in succession in numbers 2 and 3 of *Nihon no jogaku*, describe a prototype of married couple with a gender division of labor: 'household affairs should be under the control of the wife' and the husband 'should avoid as much as possible intervening in homemaking for which his wife is responsible.' Although 'what a wife does should be limited to home management,' the above description suggests high autonomy granted to the wife within the boundaries of homemaking. 'In particular, seen from the viewpoint of home economy, the husband is like the public, while the wife is like the government' (Shōgaku keizai kasei yōshi: Kōhen (A study on economics: A summary of home economy, part 2), *Kaseigaku bunken shūsei*, quoted in Chūbu Katei Keieigaku Kenkyūkai (ed.), 1972: 416).

It is misleading to flatter wives this much, but Kanzō Uchimura is correct when he points out that 'although Japanese women have traditionally seemed powerless on the surface of society, we should note that they actually have strong latent power in their households' (*Jogaku zasshi*, no. 489). It is worthy of special mention that Japanese housewives enjoyed high autonomy in home management compared to Western countries in which modern gender role assignment existed.[10]

In 1878 Makoto Mochizuki won a reputation by publishing two popular manuals on household management titled *Nyōbō no kokoroe* (Wife's rules) and *Teishu no kokoroe* (Household head's rules). While the wife's rules consist of a total of thirty-three articles, those for the household head contain a total of nineteen articles only. The author specifically adds the following statement below the title of the latter rules: 'Note that the use of the word *teishu* (household head) instead of *otto* (husband) in opposition to *nyōbō* (wife) in *Nyōbō no kokoroe* is not intended to mean *aruji* (the master of the house).' This is interesting when taken together with the fact that the Japanese folkloric vocabulary referring to housewife includes the word *enushi* (also meaning the 'master of the house'). As the word literally suggests, housewife might be considered the 'master of the house,' while Mochizuki declared that the husband was not. While the wife's rules are full of practical know-how, those for the household head have the flavor of an Edo comic novel. While a housewife as the person responsible for household management is required to have diverse skills ranging from housekeeping and childrearing to administration of servants, the most important is knowledge in economy or, more specifically, mathematical skills. In this regard, the wife cannot do without knowledge and resourcefulness. In Japan economics derived from a concept of government rule known as *keikoku saimin* (managing the state, governing the people) and was introduced to households during the Meiji era. It is interesting to note that this is the opposite of what happened in Europe, where *oikonomia*, which was originally a discipline in domestic science, changed into 'economy' as economic principles governing the nation and markets.

Women's occupations

'A sound community is built by sound households and a sound household is built by a sound married couple' ('Shin fusai (New husband and wife),' *Katei zasshi*, no. 4). Even such a conservative magazine as *Kijo no tomo* (no. 2) argued that, to this end, women's independence was a pressing need: 'As long as a woman has not achieved independence, there is no stable foundation for her husband's independence.' It was argued that in order for an independent man and an independent woman to continue the 'best-matched relationship,' they 'must have a stable job for each of them to do every day' because 'human beings are meant to work' (*Katei zasshi*, no. 4). However, this kind of argument limited 'women's jobs' to household chores, saying, 'society is men's battlefield, home is women's contribution to the state.' Kumaji Kimura timidly supported this argument in an article titled 'Kanai keizai no taiyō (An outline of home economics),' stating:

> When we say both husband and wife should work, this does not mean that the wife should work away from home like her husband does. What we mean is that the wife should be responsible for household management and economics, should keep her family healthy, should engage in home training of her children, and should pay attention to the use of male and female servants, so that her husband is freed from all domestic cares (*Jogaku zasshi*, no. 131).

However, Tōru Hattori argues: 'If a woman has already married into her husband's family and manages the household, her daily jobs should not be limited only to housekeeping and training of children but must extend to another business of her own.' His criticism of 'ladies' is harsh:

> [Ladies do] nothing more than scolding their male and female servants day and night other than a little bit of knitting in their leisure hours. They look down upon skills like sewing or weaving and regard them as lowly businesses. Whatever they do they get someone else's help and do not work of their own accord. This is just like a geisha, whose lover has paid her way out of bondage, is kept by him in a house as his new mistress and indulges in pleasure. What difference do these ladies have from her? ('Joshi shakai no shokusan jigyō (Promotion of businesses in women's world),' *Nihon no jogaku*, no. 25).

From the stance that 'wives, too, are obligated to engage in an occupation,' it was inevitable that 'noblewomen' were compared to 'parasites:'

> Please forgive my comparing these so-called noblewomen to parasites ...These women live the rest of their life without worries under the protection of another person and remain unable to get their own social position. Can't we refer to them as parasitic wives? ('Fujin mo mata shokugyō ni jūji suruno gimu ari (Wives, too, are obligated to engage in an occupation),' *Kijo no tomo*, no. 23).

It was well recognized that the relationship between wives' occupation and their independence differed across social classes. Kakei Atomi, the founder of the girl's school Atomi Gakuen, writes as follows in her article titled 'Fujin shokugyō ron (An essay on wives' occupations),' *Kijo no tomo*, no. 38:

> Try taking a look at upper-class ladies. Although they have noble titles and are always moving around the streets in four-horse carriages, if you turn your attention to their private activities, you will find that they are no better than housesitters...Let us go down and take a look at middle-class women. While their husbands, fathers and brothers work diligently on their respective businesses from early morning till late at night, women idle their time away day and night. Many of them simply read books and learn calligraphy while indulging in *koto* [a Japanese harp] or singing or dancing...Let us go down further and take a look at lower-class women. I cannot help being surprised at the fact that they are more likely to have occupations...Many lower-class women have occupations, while middle- and upper-class women do

not...Some attempt to expand their arguments on upper-class women to middle and lower, but I intend to support lower-class women's attitude towards occupations and to expand their practice to middle- and upper-class women.

...If a woman has no job and idly receives care and support from her husband, she will inevitably place herself at a disadvantage...If we look at those lower-class women, we find that they bravely stay free from their husbands' restraint by working hard on their occupation, with some even restraining their own husbands, on the contrary. Even though we should of course not follow their example in being uneducated and ignorant and being apt to be hostile to and swear at each other, we should regard them as an illustration of the fact that those who produce results are rewarded.

In this sense, Meiji Japan was a clear class society.

However, it was difficult to say that there had emerged a sufficient variety of occupations appropriate for women.

In Japanese women, those in the middle and upper classes do not have occupations, while those in the lower class often do. In many cases, it is inappropriate for these women to have occupations. It confuses the distinction between men and women, spoils the dignity of our culture, and makes us very unpleasant (Ryūkō Takeda, 'Fujin no shokugyō (Women's occupations),' *Kijo no tomo*, no. 29).

In Takeda's opinion, 'occupations appropriate for women' include 'handicraftswoman,' as well as 'schoolmistress, nursery governess, nurse, midwife, accountant, secretary, etc.' Number 31 of *Katei zasshi* reported Japan's first 'female bank clerk' employed at 'Mitsui Bank Osaka Branch.' This was exactly when new, urban-type occupations for women emerged one after another.[11] However, most of these occupations were what we call pink-collar jobs, or 'female ghetto' occupations, which make use of 'feminine characteristics' such as dexterity of the hand, patience and child caring, and in which women are not likely to compete with men.

Types of occupations considered compatible with family life and 'suited for women' in the middle and upper classes can be inferred from a series of articles titled 'Fujo shokugyō an'nai (A guide for female occupations)' published in numbers 15 through 32 of *Katei zasshi*. What are referred to as 'occupations' are, after all, handicraft work at home, or domestic piecework. Another article of the same magazine preached: 'Even in wealthy families where the housewife has no need to do handicraft to earn a living for her family, handicraft should never be neglected' ('Katei ni okeru shukō (Handicraft at home),' *Katei zasshi*, no. 2). However, the reality suggested by the serial articles was that 'upper-class people tend to feel somewhat ashamed of practicing domestic piecework'[12] (*Katei zasshi*, no. 18) and, as a result, there was a large response to certain types of domestic piecework that were 'gracefull-looking,' 'well-paying' and 'sophisticated.' At the same time, there was no end to the number of fraud cases and deceptive advertisements surrounding domestic piecework.

On the other hand, lower-class women were facing extremely miserable labor conditions. Factory girls' issues, including long work hours, poor labor conditions, resulting pulmonary tuberculosis (which should be regarded as an occupational disease), and sexual abuse by male supervisors, are detailed in *Meiji joseishi* (Women's history in the Meiji era) by Nobuhiko Murakami.[13] In response to this situation, the Ten-Hour Law was finally enacted in an attempt to limit work hours (which had previously been as long as twelve to fourteen hours a day) to ten hours a day (Tetsujirō Itō, 'Kikonfu no jitsugyō ni jūji suru gaiaku wo ronzu (A discussion on evils of married women's engagement in business),' *Nihon no jogaku*, no. 14). On one hand, this law was welfare legislation, but, on the other, it resulted in exclusion of women from the labor market.[14] Contrary to Ms Atomi's intention to 'support lower-class women's attitude towards occupations and to expand their practice to middle- and upper-class women,' it was actually the middle- and upper-class family model that was to spread to working-class families both in Western countries and in Japan.

5 Women's History and Modernity[1]

The liberatory and oppressive historical perspectives

Evaluating modernity from the viewpoint of women's history is an extremely ambivalent task. There has been, on one hand, a view that regards modernity as liberatory to women. On the other hand, another view regards modernity as oppressive to women. Let us refer to the former view as the *liberatory historical* perspective and the latter as the *oppressive historical* perspective. Representative works indicating the former view include Kiyoshi Inoue's *Nihon josei-shi* (A history of Japanese women) (1948) and Itsue Takamure's *Josei no rekishi* (A history of women) (1954–58). The latter view emerged in and after the 1970s under the influence of women's liberation and women's studies.

At the beginning of the 1970s, a controversy about women's history broke out, which was initiated by Nobuhiko Murakami. Murakami, a researcher in women's history with no formal institutional affiliation and the author of all four volumes of *Meiji josei-shi* (A history of women in the Meiji era) (1969–72), criticized Inoue's version of women's history as a 'history of liberation movements,' and proposed a more positivistic 'social history' approach focusing on the lives of common people. In his work, Murakami mentioned miserable lives of women, such as those experienced by factory girls and by poor families' daughters who were sold into bondage under the licensed prostitution system. However, because Murakami's emphasis was on women's strength and bravery in dealing with their lives under such oppression, his view was ridiculed by some as a 'bravery' historical view. This confrontation between 'liberatory history' and 'life history' resulted in a controversy among researchers in women's history.

Murakami's proposal of social history coincided with a methodological turn in studies in women's history. First, Japanese historical studies as a whole had increasing interest in social history under the influence of the Annales School in France. Second, the field of historical studies and that of folklore studies increasingly overlapped with each other, resulting in an increase of an oral history approach. Third, the counter culture movement during the 1960s provided increased momentum for 'people's history,' which attempts to reconsider history from the viewpoint of social minorities or the oppressed. The last factor to be mentioned is women's liberation movement during the period from the late 1960s to the early 1970s. Although Murakami himself was an independent researcher who did not organize any school, his proposal of social history came at the right time to attract the attention of many women who were not satisfied with liberatory history.

Japan's first women's liberation meeting was held in 1970. Groups of female researchers worked on women's history in their attempt to find the root of the oppression of women. However, virtually the only literature available to these researchers was Inoue's and Takamure's versions of women's history. These versions of liberatory history, which argued that women had been oppressed by 'feudal relics' and were then liberated by modernity, were not enough to explain these female researchers' actual feelings about the situation in the 1970s, at which time they asked why the oppression of women still remained in light of equal legal rights.

It was then that, for the first time, women's history researchers turned their attention to the oppression of women by modernity. A view emerged that questioned modernity itself, which had long been inviolable due to its association with such concepts as liberation and progress. In this sense, this turnabout in women's history was affected in part by the counter culture movement in the 1960s, which proposed the reconsideration of the value of development and production brought about by modernity. In addition, under the influence of women's liberation and women's studies, women's history came to represent an attempt to drastically shift the paradigm from women's history as a complement of men's history (which had been official history) to a completely revised version of history created by reconsidering conventional history from the viewpoint of women. Defiant researchers in women's history jokingly called their task *hikkurikae-shi* or *dengurigae-shi* (both literally meaning 'overturned history' and including a pun).

With *Josei kaihō shisō no ayumi* (Tracing the philosophies of women's liberation), Tamae Mizuta (1973) was the first in the field of women's studies to challenge the taboo associated with modernity. A researcher in history of European social thought, Mizuta minutely analyzed the works of Jean-Jacques Rousseau, who created the idea of 'human rights,' or literally *le droit de l'homme et du citoyen*, and is regarded as the 'father of the French Revolution,' and revealed that human rights as referred to by Rousseau were nothing but 'men's rights,' behind which women were systematically deprived of 'women's rights.' In other words, Mizuta argues, modernity brought about both 'emancipation of men' and 'oppression of women' as a package, and the 'oppression of women' originated in the concept of modernity itself. This was a shocking point of view for people who had understood modernity as a history of the emancipation of women – a history based on a series of classical textbooks about the thought of the emancipation of women, starting with *Die Frau und der Sozialismus* (Woman and socialism) by August Bebel (1895) and *Der Ursprung der Familie, des Privateigenthums und des Staats* (The origin of the family, private property and the state) by Friedrich Engels (1884). However, Mizuta, herself, was consistently a modernist. To her eyes, the problem was incomplete permeation of modernity, in that the ideal of human rights failed to permeate women's realities. The irony of modernity was, however, that the invention of the concepts of human rights and equality, and the extension of the scope of application of these concepts, resulted in resentment and anger among people who are excluded. In this sense, the concept of 'discrimination' was a by-product of the demand for equality.

In *Gender* it was Ivan Illich (1982) who pointed this out and took advantage of a blind spot in the feminists' hypothesis that modernism lurks behind the oppression of women. According to Illich, discrimination against women is exactly a product of modernity. Therefore, Illich argued, feminists who denounced discrimination and demanded the achievement of equality would not only be caught in a dilemma but would also assist the oppression of women by modernity by lending a hand in completing the concept of modernity. Illich outraged American radical feminists by referring to feminists as 'fem-sexists.'

While his earlier works, such as *Deschooling society* (1971) and *Limits to medicine: Medical nemesis; The expropriation to health* (1976), won him broad support among activists in the counter culture movement during the 1970s, after *Gender* Illich started to discuss gender discrimination in the framework of criticism of modernity. Illich argues that the main cause of gender discrimination is industrialization. His view eventually gained some influence with Japanese ecologists and feminists.

It is no coincidence that the oppression hypothesis of modernity emerged from the field of social history. Illich professed himself a researcher of medieval history and, considering his lists of references, was under the strong influence of the Annales School. Social historians overturned the image of 'dark medieval times' and vividly depicted the autonomous microcosm of the medieval masses. Illich argues that this ecological microcosm was destroyed by industrial society.

Illich tends to idealize societies before 'industrial society' as worlds of harmony and order. This is common to some feminist anthropologists, including Eleanor Leacock (1981). Based on research on native North Americans living in the Labrador region, Leacock argues that it was modernity (i.e. colonization) that introduced gender discrimination into their autonomous microcosm. According to her, there was no 'oppression of women' among these native Americans before colonization and, although there was some gender division of labor, both men and women were equal and harmonious. Despite Illich's insistence, however, sexual discrimination can be traced back before industrialization. We should say that industrial society is characterized by its specific historical form of gender discrimination.

The discovery of *ie*

The attention of social history researchers turned to the period of the formation of modernity. Family history and women's history revealed, in succession, the historical relativity of various factors characterizing the 'modern family,' including the worship of domesticity; the exclusion of women from productive labor; the birth of childhood; and the formation of the concept of 'motherhood.' In Japan this trend brought about a review of the concept of *ie*. While the *ie* system had conventionally been understood as a feudal relic, the review revealed and gradually established that the *ie* system was an invention of the Meiji government and was the Japanese counterpart of the modern family. The self-taught film critic Tadao Satō independently elucidated, at an early stage, the historical process of formation of the *ie* system based on the Japanese modernity he found on the screen (*Katei no yomigaeri no tameni – Hōmu dorama ron* (For the re-birth of the home: Theorizing soap operas, 1978). As a result, Satō revealed the process through which the concept of 'ethics,' which demands 'filial piety towards parents and loyalty towards the monarch,' was switched around to 'loyalty towards the monarch and filial piety towards parents' during the formulation of the Imperial Rescript on Education in the early Meiji era, and demonstrated the circumstances under which Japanese-style familism was created as a miniature of nationalism. According to Satō, Japanese familism is unlike any other familism seen elsewhere in the world. If we assume that Italian or Chinese familism functions as a base for private matters as opposed to public matters, Japanese familism functions as a private sphere where public authority exercises its power through patriarchs. Satō argues that such familism was invented and named the *ie* system by the Meiji government. Satō made this cross-cultural finding simply by peeping into foreign cultures through the silver screen.

Later, the cultural anthropologist Kanji Itō (1982) confirmed Satō's view in *Kazoku kokka-kan no jinruigaku* (An anthropology of the pseudo-family state ideology). Itō takes up the so-called Civil Code Controversy that occurred before the enactment of the Meiji Civil Code, and explains how the matrilineal inheritance supporting *ane-katoku* (inheritance by the eldest daughter) was turned down as a 'barbarous custom' of the commonalty and was beaten by unilateral patrilineal inheritance. Itō argues that the *ie* system was created as a miniature of the state by modeling it after the family system of the samurai class. The *ie* under unilateral patrilineal inheritance was conceptualized as a counterpart to the emperor system that boasts an unbroken patrilineal line of imperial succession. Just as the Tennoism state ideology based on the unbroken line of imperial descent was an invention of the Meiji government, under the pseudo-family state ideology the state was explained using the metaphor of family, and family was explained using the metaphor of the state. Thus, family and the state came to permeate each other after the Meiji era.

Yayoi Aoki (1983) discusses the formation of the *ie* system from the viewpoint of women in 'Seisabetsu no konkyo wo saguru: Nihon ni okeru kindaika to jukyō ideorogī ni tsuite no oboegaki (Exploring the root of gender discrimination: A note on modernization and Confucian ideology in Japan).' Similarly to Itō, Aoki traces the formation of the *ie* system and points out that women were gradually alienated and oppressed in the process of modernization.

The view that the *ie* system was modeled after the family system of the samurai class and was originally unrelated to the common people was strongly supported by a discovery made in folklore and in the history of common people, with the latter being influenced by the former. When a social structure changes, the new system selects a suitable cultural item from among the existing cultural items, at which point in time, the existing item, so selected, is placed in a new context. This was how the *ie* system was selected from the conventional cultural matrix. To this extent, *ie* can be regarded as a 'cultural tradition' or feudal relic of Japan. However, it is actually a cultural tradition of the samurai class only. When a certain cultural item is employed, 'historical identity' is given to it in order to make it look as though it was an eternal tradition. The fact that there actually were other alternatives when the *ie* concept was established is known from the shaky process of its formation.

Ie was a cultural tradition of the samurai class and not of the common people. During the Edo era, people who belonged to the samurai class accounted for less than 10% of the total population. A class society is a type of multicultural society in which different lifestyles are segregated from each other. The common people, who represented a majority of the population, lived in autonomous communities indifferent to Confucian samurai culture. The history of common people has revealed in succession, among other things, that inside these communities, horizontal age group order was given priority over vertical *ie* order; that there was freedom of marriage, including premarital sex, and people lacked the concept of virginity; and that there were high rates of divorce and remarriage.

According to studies in social history and popular history, modernization is the root of the evil of the oppression of women. They argue that it was modernity that excluded women from productive labor, deprived them of sexual autonomy, and confined them in the *ie* system as wife and mother. Since it was demonstrated that the *ie* system was far from being a feudal relic, but was an invention of the 'modern' state of Japan, the enemy against which women should fight shifted from premodernity to modernity.

For instance, a feminist literature group has been working on the challenging task of reviewing the entire history of modern Japanese literature from the viewpoint of women (Kimi Komashaku, *Majoteki bungakuron* (A witch-like theory of literature), 1982). A common view in the history of Japanese modern literature understands a first-person novel as an expression of the conflict between *ie* and the self, which means the conflict between a feudal relic and a modern individual, or between premodernity and modernity. However, the new feminist history of literature reinterprets both *An'ya kōro* (A dark night's passing) by Naoya Shiga and *Yoake mae* (Before the dawn) by Tōson Shimazaki as depicting moans of the weak self that cannot bear the responsibility as patriarch under the *ie* system. In fact, pillars of the 'literature of the weak,' such as Takuboku Ishikawa and Osamu Dazai, were not in the position of women or children but were in the position of patriarch in their own families. These first-person novels were not the 'literature of children' but the 'literature of patriarch,' and appeared to be the 'literature of victims' but were actually the 'literature of perpetrators.' As a matter of fact, there were wives and children who were victimized by these irresponsible, weak patriarchs, such as Takuboku's wife Setsuko and Osamu Dazai's wife and children.

Completion of modernity

The aforementioned review of history made by understanding modernity as oppressive instead of liberatory is itself very stimulating and interesting. However, the problem with the oppressive perspective is its one-sided, single-track evolutionary theory that regards modernity as the root of all evils. In this regard, the oppressive perspective is similar to the liberatory perspective in that it also employs a single-track 'development stage theory,' which is the negative of the liberatory perspective's evolutionary theory and is a type of reverse evolutionary theory. While one perspective considers that the development of modernization results in improvement of women's status, the other considers that the development of modernization results in deterioration of women's status. This difference in view results in a confrontation over the interpretation of historical changes in women. For instance, women's participation in the workplace is regarded by Engels as a path to gender equality and the liberation of women. According to Illich, on the other hand, it is indeed the worst choice; it will result in women being absorbed by the industrial society and being turned into 'homo economics,' which will finalize the self-alienation and the oppression of femininity.

This conversion from the liberatory perspective to the oppressive perspective occurred under the significant influence of the social change brought by the rapid economic growth of the 1960s. It was in 1963 that Betty Friedan (who later became the first president of the National Organization for Women, the largest women's organization in America) wrote *The feminine mystique*, which depicts the anxiety and dissatisfaction of suburban middle-class wives. The oppression and alienation of women in the advanced industrial society experienced by Friedan finally also became a reality among Japanese women by the early 1970s, after the postwar rapid economic growth.

The period of rapid economic growth was associated with significant demographic changes. There was a rapid shift of population from villages to cities, with the population urbanization rate exceeding 30%. At around the same time, the proportion of employees exceeded that of self-employed people, making the 1960s the 'era of salary men.' The average number of members per household rapidly dropped from more than five people to little more than three people. Urban employees' nuclear families were formed, which were characterized by a salary-man husband, a full-time housewife doing housework and parenting only, and no more than two children. It was at this time that the substance of the 'modern family' was finally realized in the Japanese general public.

By the end of the postwar rapid economic growth, Japan came to have the characteristics common to advanced industrial societies. It was no coincidence that women's liberation movements occurred in many different parts of the world simultaneously at the end of the 1960s. The Japanese women's liberation movement was not simply a ripple effect or an introduction of the American counterpart. Behind the Japanese women's liberation movement was the maturity of industrial society, which was sufficient to generate the movement.

Mioko Fujieda divided the history of feminism into two parts, and named the first and second parts the *first-phase feminism* and the *second-phase feminism*, respectively. First-phase feminism comprises the women's rights movements that occurred concurrently all over the world from the late nineteenth century to the early twentieth century. Second-phase feminism comprises the women's liberation movement's burst a half-century later, during the 1960s and 1970s. In '"Kindai" to feminizumu: Rekishi shakaigaku-teki kōsatsu ('Modernity' and feminism: A consideration of history and sociology)', Emiko Ochiai (1987) characterizes the first and second phases as *modernism* and *anti-modernism*, respectively. The reason for this is that, in first-phase feminism, both bourgeois women's rights activists and socialist women's emancipation activists shared the liberatory perspective and embraced a development-stage theory that believed in progress and development; and that in second-phase feminism, both radical feminists and ecological feminists shared deep skepticism towards what modernity brought to women. To put it another way, however, this skepticism towards modernity emerged only after modernity appeared as a tangible reality. The emergence of the criticism of modernity by feminists had to wait for Japanese modernity to be completed, a process that progressed throughout the 1960s. In *Fujin/josei/onna* (Lady, female, woman), women's historian Masanao Kano (1989: 130) reinterprets the first- and second-phase feminisms as a shift from 'women's problems' to 'women's studies,' stating:

> It seems that the studies on and movements for 'women's problems' overcame difficulties one by one to win 'modernity' and that, based on these achievements, 'women's studies' has begun to fight against the oppressive nature of 'modernity,' which has been revealed exactly as a result of these achievements...To put it conversely, the birth of 'women's studies' itself indicates the advent of 'modernity' in Japanese society in the sense of the eradication of 'premodernity.'

Modernism versus anti-modernism

The year 1985 saw the outbreak of the 1980s' Feminism Controversy, also known as the Aoki versus Ueno Controversy. In opposition to Yayoi Aoki's proposal of ecological feminism, Chizuko Ueno (1985b) pointed out, in 'Onna wa sekai wo sukueru ka: – Iriichi "jendā" ron tettei hihan (Can women save the world?: A thorough criticism of Illich's theory on "gender"),' the political pitfall and the reactionary nature of the 'feminine principle.' While Illich's view that regards women as victims of modernity appealed to some Japanese feminists, his one-sided anti-modernism, which proposes the abandonment of industrial society as the only way to solve 'women's problems,' carried with it various problems. In Japan in the 1980s there was a loud chorus of criticism of industrial society, and the feminine principle, which had been criticized with contempt, was now praised as a savior of the deadlocked male-dominated society.

In 'Midareta furiko: Ribu undō no kiseki (The erratic pendulum: Trajectory of the women's liberation movement),' Yumiko Ehara (1983) traces the history of the Japanese women's liberation movement and points out that it has had, from its beginning, an 'anti-modernistic' orientation, such as a community orientation, adoration of motherhood, and a return to the physical body and nature. Illich's anti-modernism fitted well with Japanese feminism.

We must also remember that there were special circumstances under which Illich, who had been virtually neglected in America, was enthusiastically supported in Japan. First, Illich's critical theory

on industrial society served as an intellectual weapon that had long been used by anti-American 'progressive intellectuals' in Japan. In this regard, Illich's view appealed to the nationalism and anti-modernism of these male intellectuals. Second, Illich's idealization of premodernity taught a way to confirm the present situation and affirm tradition not only to these male intellectuals who were beginning to feel threatened by the changes in women but also to some women. Illich was supported not only by some feminists who emphasized gender differences but also by clearly rightist women. Michiko Hasegawa, the author of an essay on Norinaga Motoori entitled *Karagokoro – Nihon seishin no gyakusetsu* (Chinese mind – A paradox of the Japanese spirit, 1986), opposed the enactment of a gender equal employment law (which was later enacted as an equal employment opportunity law) in '"Danjo koyō byōdōhō" wa bunka no seitaikei wo hakai suru (A "gender equal employment law" will destroy our cultural ecosystem)' (1984). In this work, Hasegawa declares her affinity with ecology, followed by an expression of sympathy with Illich. Hasegawa, a conservative female intellectual who wishes for the continuance of the Japanese emperor system and supports gender role assignment, shared an 'understanding' with Illich, who was the main guest of a symposium to which Hasegawa was invited. While Yayoi Aoki criticized Illich more strongly than before from the viewpoint of feminists, rightist female intellectuals and leftist male intellectuals sat in company with each other, with Illich sitting between them. This peculiarly Japanese situation fully symbolizes the complicated context of Japanese women's issues.

In the Aoki versus Ueno Controversy, while the two opposing views shared a criticism of modernity, they confronted each other over the form of anti-modernist versus postmodernist. Yūko Nishikawa (1985) summarized the course of the controversy and compared it to the motherhood protection controversy waged in the Taishō era ('Hitotsu no keifu: Hiratsuka Raichō/Takamure Itsue/Ishimure Michiko (A genealogy of feminists – Raichō Hiratsuka, Itsue Takamure, Reiko Ishimuta')). Nishikawa defined Akiko Yosano (who argued for the rights and independence of women as modern individuals), Raichō Hiratsuka (who argued for motherhood protection) and Kikue Yamakawa (who mediated the conflict between the above two and pointed out limitations of both) as a 'women's rights defender,' a 'femininity defender' and a 'neo-women's rights defender,' respectively. Based on this, Nishikawa argues that the status of a women's rights defender corresponds to modernistic feminists including Tamae Mizuta; that the status of femininity defender corresponds to Yayoi Aoki, who advocated ecological feminism; and that Kikue Yamakawa's status of neo-women's rights defender corresponds to Chizuko Ueno. Yamakawa was followed by Itsue Takamure, a successor of Raichō Hiratsuka. The confrontation of women's rights defender versus femininity defender was schematized by Takamure. Takamure professes herself as a 'neo-femininity defender,' who emphasizes Japanese women's 'maternal self' existing beyond individualism. During the 1980s' Feminism Controversy, this fourth status of neo-femininity defender represented by Takamure remained vacant. This was later taken over by the controversy between Mikiyo Kanō and Yumiko Ehara over the view urging wholesale withdrawal from corporate society.

The women's historians during the 1980s thus wavered as to the evaluation of modernity. In *Josei kaihō toiu shisō* (The philosophy of women's liberation), Yumiko Ehara (1985: 57) argues that the confrontation between modernity and anti-modernity is a 'dummy problem' imposed on women: 'The true issue in current feminism is to thoroughly analyze the views of both modernism and anti-modernism from the viewpoint of women. This is because the confrontation itself is part of the modern social system.'

The history of women as perpetrators

The maturation of feminism and women's studies in the 1980s made it possible to interpret the meaning of modernity for women ambivalently so that it worked both in liberatory and oppressive manners, instead of taking either the liberatory perspective or the oppressive perspective in a one-sided manner. For instance, family formation history during the early days of modern times revealed that the separation of private and public spheres and the formation of 'domesticity,' each of which was brought about by industrialization, meant both the isolation and confinement of women to the private sphere and the liberation of women from labor as the hostess of the women's sphere. Domestic feminism was formed paradoxically under the influence of the Victorian ideology, which is now regarded as oppressive to women. At that time, for a woman, becoming the lady of the house meant a rise in her status. The vestiges of domestic feminism have affected the history of women in modern Japan. Since the Meiji era, there has consistently been a desire to become a full-time housewife among Japanese women. This is an indication of a hidden desire to climb the social ladder by getting married and becoming the 'wife of a salary man.'

Viewing modernity in an ambivalent manner leads to a perspective that views the history of women not only as the history of victims but also as that of perpetrators. Mikiyo Kanō's 1987 study on the 'history of the home front' (*Onnatachi no 'jūgo'* (Women's home front)') is a laborious work that pursues common women's responsibility for damage in the Fifteen Years War. These women, dressed in white smocks, *voluntarily* participated in the war by waving flags to soldiers leaving for the front. Nobuhiko Murakami (1980) pointed out at an early stage that war experience had a liberatory effect on women (*Kindai-shi no onna* (Women in modern history)). Under the pretext of activities for the Japanese Defense Association of Women, young wives in rural villages obtained freedom to openly go out without worrying about their mothers-in-law. Murakami demonstrates that the Japanese Defense Association of Women was a decent means for women to participate in society and that these women vividly worked on their activities 'in that framework.'

Yūko Suzuki's *Feminizumu to sensō* (Feminism and war, 1986) pursues feminists' responsibility for war by describing the process through which the leaders of the women's rights movement, including Fusae Ichikawa, again voluntarily participated in activities supporting the war. For Ichikawa, who remembers the year of the legislation of male universal suffrage as the 'year of deprivation of women of their suffrage rights,' the Imperial Rule Assistance Association was a means for women to participate in politics and was a path to achieving women's suffrage, which had been so longed for.

Some have also started a task of critically reviewing the history of Japanese feminist ideology from the viewpoint of women's responsibility as perpetrators. In *Takamure Itsue ron* (A study on Itsue Takamure), Etsuko Yamashita (1988a), a young researcher of women's history, broke the taboo of critically analyzing Itsue Takamure, who is an original feminist thinker of prewar Japan and an independent researcher in women's history. In her work, Yamashita points out that Takamure's anti-modernism denied individualism and created a trend towards maternal feminism and, inevitably, towards fascism and the glorification of war. The selfless maternal feminism that made Takamure say 'This war is a war for us women' appealed to common women. In her next work, *Nihon josei kaihō shisō no kigen* (The origin of Japanese women's liberation philosophy), Yamashita (1988b) points out that Japanese feminism has continuously carried on the tradition of this maternal feminism and argues that it has affinity with imperial fascism. Maternal feminism has had deep-rooted effects, as seen in the postwar peace movements, mothers' conferences, consumer cooperative movements and anti-nuclear power movements.

The paradox of culture

Since the 1980s the situation surrounding women has become even more ambivalent. During the fifteen years after the oil crisis, Japan achieved the transformation of its industrial structure. The resulting trend for an information- and service-oriented economy significantly increased employment opportunities for women. In 1983 labor force participation reached over 50%. 'The era of part-time housewives' has come.

Women's participation in the workplace brought about the marginalization of female labor (i.e. low wages and unstable employment of women). The conversion of women from full-time housewives to part-time housewives brought dual roles for women to play – both work and family roles, instead of one or the other. This dual labor, or double burden, is referred to by Keiko Higuchi as the 'new gender role assignment.' In place of tyrannical control by husbands, women are now placed under soft control by economic incentives, such as housing mortgages and education expenses for children.

The enactment of the Equal Employment Opportunity Law in 1985 prompted the emergence of women seeking treatment equal to men. These working women were 'late-comers to modernity' who enjoined men to believe in occupational ethics in the industrial society. Some of these women might pledge a greater allegiance to occupational ethics than men, who have been tired of working hard. In 1988 a 'great national controversy' broke out over child-rearing by Agnes Chan, a Hong Kong-born popular singer, who brought her own child to work. Most elite working women assumed a critical attitude toward Chan, proving, conversely, that the type of occupational ethics that attach greatest importance to patience and endurance remains in these women.

It is interesting that the *postmodern* situation in Japan during the 1980s made various *modern* values look anachronistic and caused the re-appreciation of the values of *premodern* cultural traditions.

For instance, Agnes Chan brought her children to television stations, the world of high-tech media. Many opinion leaders say she was able to do so only 'because she is Chinese.' It is an accepted custom for people from Hong Kong to bring children to work. Chan simply introduced this custom to Japanese television stations, her ultramodern workplace. This difference, in context, gave Japanese people a shock. While Chan brought her children to work only because she was a traditional 'Asian mother,' her act was in line with the postmodern orientation, which seeks shorter working hours and a more flexible workplace.

During the two decades that followed the period of Japan's postwar rapid growth, Japanese women have become increasingly diversified. The existence of different working styles, such as full-time housewife versus part-time housewife and full-time worker versus part-time worker, is making it difficult to see women as a monolithic class. In one and the same phenomenon, women are victims when viewed from one angle but are beneficiaries when viewed from another. For example, while those women who remained as full-time housewives can be regarded as 'left behind' in one aspect, they conversely are also the biggest beneficiaries of the economic prosperity of Japan, in that they have the most abundant time resources. In *Joen' ga Yononaka wo kaeru* (Women's networking will change the world, 1988), published by Ueno and based on a survey of grassroots networkers among housewives in the Kansai region, Ueno demonstrates that the energy of housewives, which has begun to overflow in massive amounts in the name of social participation, is a product of the extra time and money available to these housewives. Many of these women, who were brilliantly named *katsudō sengyō shufu* (full-time activist housewives) by Yoshiko Kanai, have high levels of education and belong to high economic classes. This networking of women, which was named *joen* (literally, women's bond) by Ueno, was paradoxically a by-product of the strong gender discrimination in Japanese society. This discrimination consists of (i) gender discrimination in the labor market, which excludes women from decent employment opportunities; (ii) long working hours of husbands and their absence from home based on the deep-rooted gender role assignment; (iii) mutual indifference and nonintervention between husband and wife, who do their own work based on traditional gender division of labor; and (iv) the segregation of women to the 'world of women' under the cultural tradition of gender segregation. While *joen* is a by-product of the gender discrimination in society, women who participate in it are also beneficiaries of the discrimination. As a matter of fact, data from a survey on reduction of working hours demonstrate that the reduction of husbands' working hours is least welcome by housewives without a job among various gender, age and occupational groups.

This also reflects the division of women into classes, which became evident in the 1980s. It became overtly evident that full-time housewives, who had been regarded as 'left behind,' actually belonged to high economic classes, while working housewives, who had been regarded as 'advanced,' actually belonged to low economic classes in which housewives had to work to help family finances. In this context, the new 'housewife-orientedness' among young women, which is said to represent a return to conservative values, again indicates their latent desire to climb the social ladder.

In addition, the aging society has promoted optional co-residence of extended households, including three-generation co-residence and matrilocal co-residence in urban areas. Women's continued employment is often supported by a high rate of three-generation co-residence. This is another paradoxical phenomenon in which career-oriented women are supported by a traditional family system.

It is becoming an increasingly complicated task to determine what is modern, anti-modern or postmodern. It is also becoming more difficult to determine definitively whether modernity or postmodernity is oppressive or liberatory to women. Traditional cultural items work in both positive and negative ways, depending on the context in which they are placed. We are at last at the beginning of a time of 'single issue' research in women's history, in which these traditional cultural items will be discussed meticulously in different historical contexts.

Postmodernists versus materialists

During and after the 1980s, global trends in feminism concentrated on the critique of cultural works, such as literary works or the media. In the background of these trends were postmodernistic views that questioned and deconstructed certain modern concepts, such as an 'individual' and 'independence.' These trends resulted in the appreciation of the values of femininity and maternity, as opposed to the genderless (but actually masculine) concept of an individual. The French postmodern feminist Irigaray proposed *écriture féminine*, which was designed to release people's thought from the spell of 'man-made language' (Irigaray, 1977).

The factors behind these trends include the following: (i) many pillars of 1970s feminism had to face their own maternity as their own biological clocks ticked away; (ii) the disappointment with male-dominated society resulted in the rise of separatists, including lesbians, who took leadership in the movement and theory aspects of feminism; (iii) the 'market' of women's studies was established within the academic world, in which a large number of papers came to be produced, mainly in such fields as literature and psychology; and (iv) throughout the economic recession and reorganization of the 1970s and 1980s, political backlash (e.g. 'Reaganomics' and the 'Thatcher Revolution') and the resulting retreat of feminism caused a loss of hope for an institutional reform of society. In America the Equal Rights Amendment movement was defeated in 1982. In Japan, too, the enactment of the Equal Employment Opportunity Law in 1985 resulted in a significant failure to meet the expectations of most women's organizations.

Materialistic feminists were openly irritated by postmodernistic views of culturists. Marxist feminists, including Lynne Segal and Christine Delphy, argue that the emancipation of women can be achieved only by institutional reform of infrastructures and not by a 'cultural revolution.' However, while classical socialist feminism equated the emancipation of the working class with that of women, Marxist feminism, after second-phase feminism, aims at abolition of the patriarchy, or husband's appropriation of domestic labor, which provides a material basis for the oppression of women. The discovery of domestic labor as non-capitalistic labor under the capitalist system was a major contribution by Marxist feminism (Ueno, 1990a). This discovery revealed that as long as unpaid domestic labor exists, so does patriarchy in socialist society.

For Marxist feminism, the goal for a feminist revolution is to reform the family and the relations in terms of gender and generation in the family. However, patriarchy under the capitalist system has changed with the changes in the capitalist system. First, domestic labor has increasingly been commercialized and is losing its substance. Second, women have already changed into part-producer and part-consumer. It has been pointed out that this outsourcing of housework is nothing but the market-scale gender division of labor, in which what has been done by women at home is now done by women outside the home; that global-scale 'housewifezation of labor' (Werlhof, 1983) is put in progress by reorganizing female labor in the marginal labor market; and that, to this extent, patriarchy will not be abolished but will be reorganized and remain the 'main enemy' (Delphy, 1984).

In the process of the development of a new history of globalization and postindustrialization after the 1980s, such factors as gender, age, class, race and nationality have been taking on new importance. These attributional values, which had been regarded as premodern and should have once been dissolved into an abstract 'individual' by modernity, have reappeared in the context of postmodernity. The meaning of modern 'gender difference' will no longer hold, as is the case with such other modern concepts as the state and an individual. These concepts will not disappear, however; they will be reorganized in the context of other variables.

Part III
The Development of Home Science

6 The Evolution of Umesao's Home Science

The origin of Umesao's home science

As the editor of Parts I and II of *Shufu ronsō wo yomu* (A review of the housewife debate), which included three essays by Tadao Umesao ('Onna to bunmei (Women and civilization),' 'Tsuma muyō-ron (Superfluous wife theory)' and 'Haha toiu na no kirifuda (Mother as All-Mighty)'), I had wondered for a long time why an up-and-coming cultural anthropologist in his mid-thirties at the time of the essays' publication should have been interested in such things as theories on the home and housewives. The three stages of the so-called *Shufu ronsō* (Housewife debate) (Ueno, 1982b) after the Second World War involved a 'debate about women by women for women,' which was mainly conducted by female commentators in a women's magazine for its female readers. The 'women's issues' did not step out of a ghetto for a long time. Except for a small number of economists who were challenged directly or indirectly, the only men who took part in the debate were regular 'women's department' commentators who liked to lecture women on every possible occasion. Umesao's discussion stood out prominently from all the others for its clarity.

This mystery was finally solved twenty-five years after the housewife debate when I read a newly written supplementary note to his essays in *Umesao Tadao chosakushū* (The collected works of Tadao Umesao) published in 1991. According to the circumstances surrounding his 'participation in the debate,' as explained in the note, he did not know the existence of such a debate itself, nor did he realize that he was creating a stir at the time.

> I was completely unaware that I was taking part in a debate at that time. I did not agree or disagree to someone else's argument; I just wrote down my thoughts. When I look at the course of this 'debate' as compiled by Ms Ueno, however, I realize many people have criticized

and talked about my discourse. I became embroiled in the debate without my knowledge (Umesao, 1991: 132–3).

According to Umesao, it was the 'brilliant duo of Chief Editor Saeko Saigusa and Deputy Chief Masamichi Takarada' (Umesao, 1991: 4) who got him to write in *Fujin kōron* (Women's review). It is very like him to write 'as I pleased,' 'as my interest dictated' and 'at someone's request,' and he was naturally controversial even though he did not intend to be controversial. His message emitted such a powerful noise that it disturbed 'social conventions' of the time.

Umesao's supplementary note clarified how he was 'embroiled' in the housewife debate but it made the question of why he dared to step into the realm of 'theory on the home' all the more mysterious. When Naomichi Ishige proposed 'anthropology of food culture,' he had to break down an unspoken taboo of stepping into the kitchen, which was considered 'unbecoming for a man.' The academic world is neither fair nor objective at all; it is full of taboos. In fact, when I partnered with a male co-researcher in a research project on food culture, I was annoyed by his repetitive preemptive apologies and excuses for stepping into the 'women's domain,' which he said was not a research field for a grown man like him.

According to Umesao's note, it was 1957 when he 'addressed women's issues from the angle of civilization theory for the first time' (Umesao, 1991: 8). Prior to that, he visited Afghanistan, Pakistan and India as a member of the Kyoto University Scientific Expedition to the Karakoram–Hindukush in 1955. Anthropologists take interest in minute details of the lifestyle and culture of their research subjects. And, being outsiders, anthropologists can easily break through gender barriers within cultures:[1]

> In my mind…there are many unforgettable images in relation to the kitchen. I am lacking in common knowledge since I cannot often get a chance to intrude into the kitchens of other people's homes in Japan but I have taken a good look at the kitchens of several different peoples abroad exercising the anthropologist's prerogative. They are such images (Umesao, 1991: 10).

Based on his observations, he wrote a series of theses on women and home through a comparative cultural approach: 'Afuganisutan no joseitachi (Women of Afghanistan)' (1956), 'Onna no chirigaku (Women's geography)' (1957) and 'Tai no joseitachi (Women of Thailand)' (1958). It is no wonder that he looked at Japanese homes from the same perspective. It was, from the start, a comparative civilization perspective on Japanese culture, which he rediscovered through his observations of foreign cultures. At around the same time, he was a practitioner of 'homemaking' in his personal life. In view of his outstanding practical ability with *chiteki seisan no gijutsu* (the technology of intellectual production) (1969) in his professional capacity, I do not think he would have been inept in life skills, either. Daily life provided good opportunities for fieldwork for Umesao, who was creating a family, raising children and leading a home life.

To add some social background information to his personal historical background, the late 1950s, when he published a series of theses in theories on the home, was the age of technological innovation during which the energy revolution in the kitchen and domestic electrification advanced rapidly. It provided not only a good test ground to put the lifestyle revolution into practice for Umesao as a household member, but, as a thinker, it also provided an ideal experimental field for his contemplation of the history of civilization. I am still amazed by the accuracy of many of his predictions when I re-read his old writings. For example, he made the following prediction in 'Atarashii katei zukuri (New homemaking),' serialized in the *Asahi Shimbun* newspaper in 1959:

> This seems like a wild dream in the light of the present situation but it will become an issue in several years' time. It will soon become normal to see middle class salaried workers commuting to work by car. We are already seeing symptoms everywhere. The production of people's cars will start soon and there will be a large market for cheap used cars. The car will become something that anyone can afford to buy (Umesao, 1991: 190–1).

He therefore recommended that 'anyone who is planning to have a new home should take a car garage into consideration.' This prediction, which Umesao made in the 1950s, was surprisingly accurate considering that motorization in Japan took place in the late 1960s, defying the country's poor road and housing conditions and contrary to the prediction of most experts.

Umesao also made the following prediction about commodific-ation of housework at the time:

> After all, it is such a primitive practice for the housewife to make clothes for her family at home. She should buy ready-made clothes

at a shop or have them made by professionals. The self-sufficiency system is absurd...the women of the future will not need dressmaking skills. All they will need is a good enough sense to choose suitable clothes from the rack (Umesao, 1991: 193).

The *An-an* magazine was launched in 1970, heralding the arrival of a ready-made clothes era. Its fashion pages were filled with pictures of ready-made clothes and product information (i.e. where to buy and the price). Considering that the fashion sections of women's magazines were carrying dressmaking samples and 'how to make' information up to the end of the 1960s, Umesao's prediction in 1959 seems to have been made very early. This prediction offended the feelings of those who believed dressmaking was an essential skill for a good wife in those days. This is another example of the characteristic of his thinking that was so ahead of the times that it unintentionally emitted provocative signals.

At the same time, I cannot help but sense the presence of the mastermind, the editors of the *Fujin kōron* magazine who instigated Umesao to write this unorthodox home theory – some arguments are so orthodox that they often appear unorthodox in the context of the times – and set the stage to 'embroil' him in the housewife debate. 'Umesao's home science' would not have been born without the help of these 'midwives' working behind the scenes.

Characteristics of Umesao's home science

Umesao's home science has the following four characteristics.

First, it has a civilization historian's perspective, which looks at the home as a system incorporating the infrastructure of (life) skills, technologies and hardware. This dry, materialistic perspective separates the home from a very emotion-laden concept of the family, which is contaminated by values and feelings. It is a materialistic view that regards the institution and relationship of family as the dependent variables influenced by changes in the infrastructure.

Second, it has a cultural relativist's perspective, which attempts to understand gender as a variable inherent to a particular historical and social system, in thoroughly relative terms. Nothing offends him more than 'human nature' and 'human instinct' theories. Some people may think that it is natural for an anthropologist in comparative cultural studies to adopt a cultural relativist view of gender, but it is unusual to find someone with a mind so free from 'truism' in a society that firmly takes gender differences for granted. His perspective is also free from modernist values such as human rights awareness and humanism. Such a dispassionate gaze that is so removed from a given cultural system is rare among his contemporary anthropologists.

Third, it adopts a civilization historian's long time span, which in turn generates an amazing predictive power. In comparison with sociologists who are especially sensitive to the 'latest trends' in social phenomena and whose time spans are ten years or ten to the power of two at most, it is admirable when anthropologists cover a time span as long as ten to the power of three or four. Even in Annales historians' concept of *longue durée* (long duration) in social history, the length of a cycle is only 300 to 400 years. A cycle 'lasting' for 300 years is almost an 'eternity' to those who actually live in it. Umesao looks beyond this horizon and the ups and downs in the history of civilization with his dispassionate eyes. His predictions for the future are certainty underpinned by long-term cycles of civilization history.

Lastly, I would like to point out a viewpoint of Umesao's that can almost be described as nihilism of the civilization historian. His absolute cultural relativism tends to be mistaken for rationalism. However, he does not subscribe to modernistic Enlightenment rationalism or historicism, such as the theory of development stages. He does not share the optimism of futurologists, either. His gaze is too dispassionate to be rationalist. He does not believe in progress and is well aware that humans are irrational beings. Human history is anything but a history of reason and harmony; it is filled with human folly and destruction. Is there a better word than nihilism to describe a gaze that studies history as it is, without falling into pessimism or prophet's romanticism? The vision he gained from the history of civilization is so broad that it is a view from a spaceship rather than a bird's eye view.

I would like to examine his thought based on these four points.

Home as a system

One characteristic of Umesao's theory on home is 'the view that treats the home as a system' (Umesao, 1991: 322). It has three aspects: material, energy and information. It also has two phases: stable and fluctuating.

Such a textbook description may make one think that it is merely an application of systems theory to the home, but it was not until feminism and the social history of family began to exert their influences in the 1970s that analytical eyes were turned to the 'home,' which had been sealed in the name of 'love.' In fact, considering the present situation in which domestic science, which is supposed to be the 'integrated science centering on domestic life,' is disintegrating into small fields within the existing individual sciences, the 'science of home' is yet to be established, even after Umesao's proposal.

Assuming that home is made of the *metabolic system* (flow) and the *attachment system* (stock), changes in the *hardware system* (technology, tools and machines), that is the infrastructure, will change human behavior and relationships. It is not the other way around. This lucid *literal* materialism smashes all kinds of cultural theory and consciousness revolution theory. For example, Umesao finds a basis for the status of housewife in the establishment of the housewife status that was brought on by domestic labor-saving technological innovation and the *pseudo labor* – domestic labor performed to a higher standard than is necessary – that guarantees it. Technological innovation first drove out domestic servants from homes. Then housewives used pseudo labor to prevent men from participating in domestic labor in order to establish their domestic sovereignty.[2]

The hypothesis that gender-based division of labor in the home is defined by technological innovation and the level of infrastructure is also supported by the following facts. In China there is a shortage of domestic servants and the hardware system for domestic labor saving has not come into wide use. A heavy burden of housework necessitates the participation of the husband in domestic labor. On the other hand, in America, where an extremely high level of domestic labor saving has been achieved, the technological standard of domestic labor declines to the 'men's level,' enabling the husband to participate in domestic labor. This leads to the conclusion that exclusive housewife labor – that is, 'labor performed by the housewife' instead of 'domestic labor' – is nothing but a product of the transition process of the domestic technological innovation from a low level (as in the case of China) to a high level (as in the case of the United Sates) in the history of civilization. This explains the historical reason why Japan's 'housewife debate' was a 'housewife's labor debate' and not a 'domestic labor debate.'

At the same time, Umesao prophesizes 'the less housework, the better' from a civilization history perspective, but he is not advocating for mere domestic labor saving or home rationalization.

He does not neglect to point out that the home has the aspect of an attachment system as a junkyard to store 'stuff that cannot be thrown away' and that it is really the housewives who are resisting domestic labor saving (the 'irrational factor'). He even predicts that housework will again become a 'hobby' to fill in time once the ultimate domestic labor saving is achieved. The accuracy rate of his forecast is very high and almost the only prediction that did not eventuate was his prediction that the dishwasher would be the next high-demand appliance for domestic labor saving. This is because Japanese housewives would not try to 'rationalize' their eating habits to suit the automatic dishwasher. Japanese housewives have, so far, not shown their support for the idea of replacing their existing ceramic ware, china ware, lacquer ware and other dishes of various materials and shapes (for a wide-ranging menu of Japanese, Western and Chinese food) with a set of standardized multipurpose dishes. Conversely, it can be said that the level of domestic technology is not advanced enough for the automatic dishwasher to cope with the diversity of their food culture. As Umesao states, 'cooking has nothing to do with rationalization of domestic life and it actually has been very much a hobby-like labor from the start' (Umesao, 1991: 177). And he does not necessarily support 'rationalization of domestic life,' as we can see from this statement.

Umesao's gender theory

Umesao wrote, 'What are women? As for the total quantity of energy, women have almost as much as men have. Or they have more energy than men have' (Umesao, 1991: 144). He also says, 'There is no difference between women and men in intellectual ability, as well as administrative ability and coordination ability' (Umesao, 1991: 139). This kind of view has gained currency following the enforcement of the equal employment opportunity law – some may be loathing it but they at least hesitate to say so openly – but it is unusual for a man who was born in 1920 to express such a view in 1963. How did Umesao form the 'assumption that men and women are completely equal human beings' (Umesao, 1991: 80)?

After pointing out that 'the powerlessness of the wives of salaried workers' stems from 'the powerlessness of the wives of feudal warriors' and 'vertical division of labor rather than horizontal,' he laments 'the wife turning into a prostitute' and 'the wife turning into a pet.' He sees 'terrible inhumanity' in a wife's existence as a 'provider of comfort entailing a sex life' (Umesao, 1991: 67), and watches 'with sadness their situation in which they have to bury themselves in the role of mother' and 'forfeit their own lives' (Umesao, 1991: 80).

Is Umesao a feminist and a humanist? Considering that 'fundamental differences between men and women are often emphasized in the views of the conservative circle of society' (Umesao, 1991: 154), as he acknowledges, his view of gender was exceptionally egalitarian in his generation and days. However, it was the perspective of an unequivocal civilization historian and cultural relativist that fostered such a view in him: 'I am not discussing fundamental differences between men and women. I am discussing the roles of men and women in the history' (Umesao, 1991: 155).

From this perspective, Umesao brushes aside biological gender difference theory ('Pregnancy and childbirth are the only prerogatives of women and the rest are not women-only tasks' (Umesao, 1991: 74)) and rejects maternal instinct theory ('Some may say that maternal love is instinctive and not something that is developed but such a view is actually the product of the new times' (Umesao, 1991: 77)).

This view of gender became an accepted argument in feminism after the experiences of radical feminism in the 1960s and social-historical studies of maternal love such as *Purasu rabu* (Plus love) by Elisabeth Badinter (1981), although it has not gained consensus outside the feminist circle, and it is surprising that it was uttered by a man in 1959. At the same time, it is not hard to imagine that this kind of statement would not have attracted support and understanding of the readers in those days. These arguments were extraordinary in the 1950s. Provocative essay titles such as 'Tsuma muyō-ron (Superfluous wife theory)' and 'Haha toiu na no kirifuda (Mother as All-Mighty)' suggest the author's awareness and pride that he was rubbing the nerves of commonsense the wrong way.

While prescribing that women should 'quit as a wife' and 'quit as a housewife,' Umesao made the following prediction about the future of gender relations as early as 1959: 'Masculinization of women would be an exaggeration but I believe that the social homogenization of men and women is inevitable. Marital life will gradually shift towards co-habitation of socially homogenized men and women in the future' (Umesao, 1991: 68). Quoting this in 1989, he declared with pride that 'my prediction has come true.' However, it was not due to the advancement of feminism or 'woman power,' which are merely the effect and not the cause. It is post-industrialization that has minimized gender differences. He firmly maintains his civilization history approach: 'The ground swell of woman power should be understood in this broad framework of the human, hardware and institutional systems and should not simply be interpreted in terms of relations and contrasts between men and women' (Umesao, 1991: 138).

In 1957 Umesao had already proposed the following 'hypothesis' in his account of a journey to Thailand: 'Our culture has evolved with an exaggerated sense of gender differences. Women's liberation in modern times may be just a process of overcoming such sentiments of sexist culture' (Umesao, 1991: 40). As a feminist who has worked within this process, I feel speechless and wonder if I have merely been a pawn used by history when the origins of feminism as a modern thought is exposed by Umesao's hand.

Transitions in the history of civilization

Umesao is a remarkable trend watcher, and a major difference between him and other forecasters of the 1980s trend boom is that instead of making short-term predictions from the wave crests of trivial phenomena, he accurately predicted changes that are logically deductible from much longer cycles of civilization history. Backed by the 'inevitability' of these changes, his predictions are highly probable and do not fail.

The biggest such change is post-industrialization, a historical transition from the industrial age to the information age. The first consequence of post-industrialization involves a shift from physical power to intellectual power. The second consequence is the resultant 'minimization of gender difference:'[3] 'The industrial age had a tendency to increase gender difference. However, the gender difference is likely to be minimized in the age of information industry' (Umesao, 1991: 157). Umesao is not discussing the nature of gender difference or whether he believes in it or not. He states that the 'minimization of gender difference' is the 'trend in civilization history' and no one can contradict this 'historical inevitability.' And his prediction proved to be true in its broad outlook.

The third consequence of post-industrialization is a value shift from production to consumption:

> Men should be consumers more. To put it in extreme terms, a very small proportion of the population will be producers and a large majority will be consumers. Or looking from a different angle, people can spend a very short period of their lives as producers and live the rest of their lives as consumers. In that case, the significance of women

as consumers should be reassessed. Since a majority of women who account for one half of the population are non-producers, perhaps we have already made considerable progress toward the shared human goal. The modern era has created a belief that production is good and consumption is bad but it is a groundless assertion when we think about it. Production has been given value unconditionally with no basis at all (Umesao, 1991: 148).

Here, the gender division of labor between 'men-producers' and 'women-consumers' in the industrial age, the paradox of 'ascendancy of women' by post-industrialization during the transitional period, and the feminization and consumption-orientation of men are amazingly foretold and explained.

The fourth consequence of post-industrialization is the limitations of rationalism: 'To begin with, rationalism was a very effective and efficient way of thinking in the early industrial era. However, we are discovering many problems with it these days...the principle of rationalistic thinking itself is inherently defective' (Umesao, 1991: 108).

According to Umesao, 'the family is the least rationalistic of all human groups...Rather, it is its irrational aspect that we should value...[alienation of human by rationality] should not be brought into the home' (Umesao, 1991: 100).

Umesao is neither a simple rationalist nor a futurologist who believes in progress. His cynical view towards this modern 'belief' called 'rationality' enables his theory on the home to reach the profundity of human history.

The nihilism of civilization history

My esteemed friend, T., names *Fūryū Mutan* (The tale of a strange dream) by Shichirō Fukazawa and *Watashi no ikigai-ron* (My view on the meaning of life) by Tadao Umesao (1981) as two of the best works of postwar nihilism. Umesao explains the future direction of civilization history as follows in the transcript of his 1970 lecture, 'Mirai shakai to ikigai (Future society and the meaning of life),' which is contained in the book:

After all, I think this is the direction in which we are heading. We will strive to find a way to waste our lives. We will live as idly as possible. Let's not try to do anything useful.

> Let's not do anything. If we are to make things, we make useless
> things. I think we are moving in that direction inch by inch. I may
> be a little too optimistic but I think it is a better direction...as we
> make more things, more useful things, we push ourselves into a
> difficult position in a broad sense – that's how it works (Umesao,
> 1981: 140–1).

Behind the self-described 'optimistic' outlook of civilization is
his pessimistic view that 'it may be possible to save ourselves if
we can stop making progress...civilization is a troublesome thing'
(Umesao, 1981: 121). In this case, the challenge for individuals is
to think about 'how to while away the time until the end of one's
life' (Umesao, 1981: 141).

Many people are probably puzzled why the man who developed
the anthropology of postwar Japan into a fully fledged academic
discipline and who created a giant 'toy box' called the National
Museum of Ethnology, and published a fifteen-volume collection
of writings, would make such a statement. His 'pastime' seems
too grand to be called a pastime. Yet, I cannot find any word other
than an intellectual 'monster' to describe the man who already
had such a penetrating insight into the future of humans and
civilization in 1970 when Japan was still basking in the afterglow
of high economic growth. As he predicted, the subsequent Japanese
economy produced 'useless things' such as Walkman products and
computer games and created the 'consumer class' called *Heisei-
kizoku* (aristocrats of the Heisei-era) amid the prosperity brought
on by the bubble economy. On the other hand, developed countries
have been developing 'useful things' and are now plunging the earth
into crisis with their efficient weapons and mechanisms.

Umesao discusses women and the home in the same tone of
argument. He raises the following question after pointing out
that 'women have free energy:' 'Women's energy is not used
productively...almost one half of humankind's energy is currently
wasted or not bearing much fruit. What should we do about it?'
(Umesao, 1991: 146).

This 'free energy' is directed at 'meddling with children (more
than is necessary)' or 'consumption of information:'

> As the result of enthusiastic consumption of information, women
> tend to have more knowledge in the average household. However,
> this is consumption of information in the true sense, a time-filler,
> a pastime. It can hardly be called productive. What will transform

it into something productive? This is the very question we need to consider. Before that, however, we must ask ourselves whether it is really better to turn women's energy into something productive (Umesao, 1991: 147–8).

His answer to the last question is 'No.' Umesao proposes that women should use their energy on *hanami-zake* (drinking rice wine while admiring cherry blossoms) – spending energy on useless consumptive activities among women. This is similar to my description of various women's grassroots networks as 'terminal care' – various activities they cheerfully pursue without annoying anyone in order to fill their time until they die.[4] Umesao says that 'this is the ideal life' and 'women have realized a life's dream ahead of everyone else.' And he encourages women to 'be proud and become exploiters,' just like aristocrats, specializing in information consumption activity (Umesao, 1991: 131).

Is it really so? Aristocrats exploited serfs; who are housewives supposed to exploit? Isn't it deceitful for him to encourage women to 'be proud' when he is well aware that housewives' rights are a 'limited sovereignty' subordinate to husbands' rights? Is he an enemy or an ally of women?

Umesao is neither. He is just an extraordinary observer of civilization history. However, I do have some reservations about his observations. For example, the infrastructure for consumption activity is, in the end, provided by husbands to wives and by the third world to Japan. Production activity is not going to be performed by 'a small minority of people' but it will be performed solely by many people under poor working conditions in the third world. It is possible to criticize Umesao's vision for missing the issue of disparities between the North and the South, gaps between advanced and developing countries.

Also, there is evidence that women have already made a transition from 'full-time consumers' to 'producers.' A large majority of women have at least become part-producer and part-consumer.

His argument on childcare, which made him the greatest 'enemy of women,' offers the discovery that modernization has reduced the total quantity of 'childcare labor' but the isolation of the nuclear family and the demise of communal childcare have placed the burden of parenting on the mother alone more than ever. His observation that 'at the moment, the cost of living alone for a man is a little higher than when he is living with a wife' can be explained by the finding in women's studies that wives' 'unpaid labor' is, in fact, underpinning the reproduction cost of men's productive labor.[5] After the women's liberation movement in the 1970s and the accumulation of knowledge in women's studies, his analyses and predictions are found to contain both valid ones and those hinting at his 'historical limitations.' Still, the incredibly long range of his prescience is truly amazing.

I shall no longer speak of the urbane coyness to recast his own respect for women as historical inevitability or the reversed shyness to deliberately disguise the gloomy outlook of civilization history as the 'optimism' that permeates his predictions. We are witnessing an extraordinary 'seer' of civilization history peering into the not-so-bright future of our civilization. And I shall welcome the contributions this intellectual monster makes when he looks toward the home, a 'domain of women and children,' with the same far-reaching and penetrating gaze as when he looks at other domains of civilization.

7 Technological Innovation and Domestic Labor

History of domestic labor

The history of domestic labor in the form of 'unpaid labor performed at home' as it is known today is not so long. It is difficult to distinguish domestic labor from a series of productive labors in pre-industrialized society, and part of domestic labor became outsourced services quite early. The first domestic service product in history is said to be pre-cooked food sold at markets. If domestic labor is literally defined as labor performed inside *domus* (household), the history of confinement of this type of labor to the household is very short. Domestic labor has existed both inside and outside the household.

Early domestic service workers included laundrywomen, nursemaids and bakers. The job of a laundrywoman was the first option for poor widows without capital to earn cash. It is said that about 20% of children were put out to nurse in eighteenth century Paris. To bakery proprietresses who were part of important productive labor, childcare was a low priority that could be delegated to others. And few households needed full-time domestic workers because a majority of household chores were simple in those days.

Aristocrats and wealthy households employed domestic servants. The number of these domestic servants multiplied as the urban middle class developed in the early part of modernization. Domestic servants did not form a clear labor market because they often worked without contracts and found employment by word of mouth or through territorial or blood relations, hence they did not show up on statistical data as clearly as factory workers did. Based on what is happening in Asia and Africa, which are undergoing rapid urbanization today, however, it is estimated that these domestic servants accounted for a substantial part of the population that drifted from rural villages to cities in the modernization process.

This is also applicable to prewar Japan. For girls from poor farming families who were put out to work, there were three available jobs according to their class and economic circumstances: factory worker, maid/nursemaid and prostitute. As the wage level for factory workers rose, a shortage of maids occurred.

It is known that prewar urban middle-class households – even the household of someone like Sōseki Natsume, who always complained of lack of money – generally had one or two maidservants. In the Taishō era, a typical salaried worker's house – a single-storied building with a middle corridor and a floor space of about 60 square meters (approximately 650 square feet) – used a room of 'three *tatami* mats beside the front entrance' as the maidservant's room. House size was not directly relevant to the employment of domestic servants. It was rather a matter of the difference between the wage level of a domestic servant and the income of the employer.

The term *shufu* (housewife) originally meant 'the mistress of a house' in both the European and Japanese languages.[1] To be a housewife, one had to hold the right to command and control the household by managing underlings such as *onagoshi* (housemaids) and female relatives, as well as being the wife of the head of a family. However, 'housewife' became popularized (and its status declined) in the process of urbanization and nuclearization of the family. The housewife in the nuclear family lost not only her housemaids but also other adult female members of her extended family. The whole burden of domestic labor was shifted onto the shoulders of the housewife, who was now the sole adult female member of the family. This is how the housewife became the full-time domestic laborer in a household. To borrow Anne Oakley's words, the housewife is 'the wife of the head of a household who has lost her domestic servants' (Oakley [1974] 1986).

Accordingly, domestic labor and housewife's labor are different. Housewife's labor is labor performed by a housewife but domestic labor is not always performed by a housewife. Housewife's labor came into existence when the housewife (i.e. the wife in a urban worker's nuclear family who engages in full-time domestic labor) came into existence. While it is difficult to distinguish domestic labor (or labor for direct consumption) from other productive labor, what is at work here is the 'urban criteria for domestic labor' as described by Christine Delphy (1984). That is, the housewife came into existence in the urban area first and the range of labor performed by the housewife came to be called 'domestic labor' later.

Technological innovation and the energy revolution in the kitchen

If the definition of domestic labor is historical and its scope is variable, its content must change considerably in response to changes in the household structure and technological standard. When a household is considered to be a type of system acting as an interface between humans and technology, technological innovations that have been taking place outside of it have inevitably had impacts inside it.

Domestic labor remained at the ancient technological level of the kitchen hearth, firewood and charcoal long after technological innovation in production machinery brought about the industrial revolution. Major changes in domestic labor only occurred because of the following factors: the spread of waterworks, the energy revolution created by the introduction of clean energy (gas and electricity) into the kitchen, and, as technological innovation reached consumer goods, the availability of affordable consumer durables such as electrical appliances. These changes transformed the structure of housing and even influenced the status of members and role relationships within the family.

In the United States domestic electrification was already taking place in the 1930s after the First World War. According to Susan Strasser's history of domestic labor in the United States entitled *Never done: A history of American housework*, '95 percent of Cleveland homes cooked with gas or electricity' as early as 1935 (Strasser, 1982: 264). In Japan the timber-floored kitchen with a gas range and a sink was proposed for new urban housing as early as the Taishō era, but it did not come into wide use. Many an urban house kept its earthen-floored kitchen with a connecting corridor and simply replaced the wood-fired oven with a new gas range. Rural households, which accounted for a large proportion of the population, continued to use firewood and charcoal.

The kitchen energy revolution finally spread nationally during the 1950s upon completion of Japan's postwar reconstruction. The transition from dangerous, inconvenient and soot-generating energy sources such as firewood and charcoal to clean and convenient gas and electricity made it possible to shift the kitchen from an unsealed floor space to a floored space in a house and to build one house on top of another in multiple dwelling complexes. The kitchen hearth had been the center of the household since ancient times and the housewife had a duty to protect a fire. A fire is difficult to make and maintain with firewood and charcoal and requires much care once it is lit. The 'god of fire' was the god of the house, as well as the kitchen, and had to be served carefully in order to prevent a disaster. But then fire became easily controllable by a flick of a switch.

The housewife's sacred duty to manage a fire, which required skill and responsibility, was simply abolished by the kitchen energy revolution. It had to have an impact on the power structure within a household.

one elderly California woman, remembering the day her parents bought a gas stove and relegated "that old wood-burning thing" to the barn, recounted her grandmother's distress. She "just felt terrible. She knew just how to put a piece of wood to make it that much hotter. Or not to put in the piece of wood if she had an angelfood cake in the oven" (Strasser, 1982: 264).

A similar change took place in Japan during the 1950s. The first household appliance that came into popular use was the electric (or gas) rice cooker. It had already reached market saturation during the 1950s before the 'three sacred treasures' (refrigerator, washing machine and vacuum cleaner) found their way into every home in the 1960s. The practice of cooking rice on the hearth was the first practice to be abandoned as a result of technological innovation in the kitchen. Rural families, who were fussy about the taste of their cooked rice, preferred gas cookers, which had greater thermal power, to electric cookers, and this released older women who were not familiar with the handling of gas from rice-cooking labor (Figure 7.1). They were highly skilled fire controllers as far as rice cooking on the kitchen hearth was concerned (a well-known technique required 'low flame at first, high flame in the middle') but technical innovation rendered their role, together with their skill, obsolete. While management and distribution of the rice as the staple food was a major element of the housewife's rights, older women had to relinquish it because of their inability to adapt to a new technology. In light of the lessons learned from defeat in war, people in the rural area were encouraged to increase their fat intake as part of the country's campaign to improve the physical and nutritional standards of the nation and they incorporated fried food in their menu under the slogan of 'one pan-fried dish a day.' These changes in cooking know-how and technology hastened a reversal of status between the wife and the mother-in-law.

Figure 7.1: The annual output of electric rice cookers

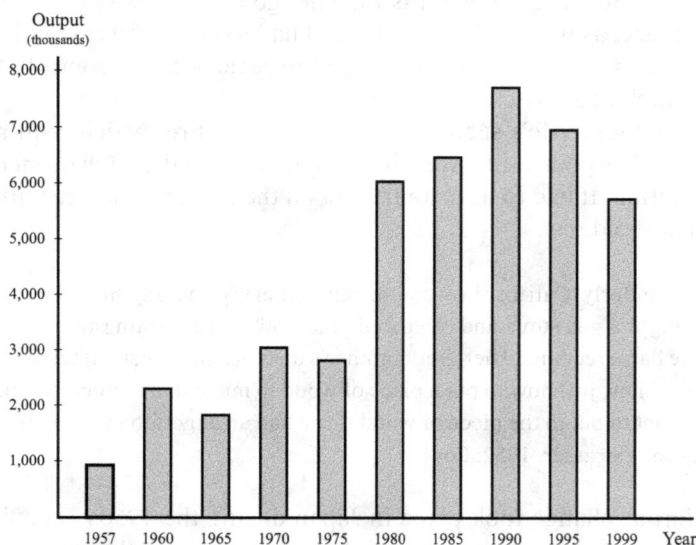

Output
(thousands)

Source: Tsushō Sangyō Shō, (Ministry of International Trade and Industry), *Kikai tōkei nenpō* (The annual statistical reports of machine production).

A paradox of domestic labor saving

The market penetration rate of all major household electrical goods rapidly reached saturation point in the space of a decade or so during the 1960s (Figure 7.2). Although household appliances are often called domestic labor-saving equipment, we must examine whether technological innovation in domestic labor has really reduced the burden of domestic labor.[2]

Let us take laundry, which was the hardest of all domestic labor tasks, as an example. Figure 7.3 is from an advertising pamphlet published in 1944 by Westinghouse, an American washing machine manufacturer. Its catchphrase – declaring 'an entire new day has been added to your week' – clearly points to labor saving and time saving. Conversely, it meant that housewives had endured a day of heavy labor called the 'washday' every week prior to that. However, they did not do all the laundry at home:

> Among a group of semiskilled workers' families in the East Bay area, about 60 percent sent some laundry out, but the small size of their

laundry bills made it "evident that even in these families the wife did the bulk of the washing" (Strasser, 1982: 268).

They used outside services mainly for 'flatwork (sheets, tablecloths and other linens) and men's shirts' (Strasser, 1982: 270). Such services were used because the former are large and difficult to

Figure 7.2: The diffusion rates of major household electrical appliances

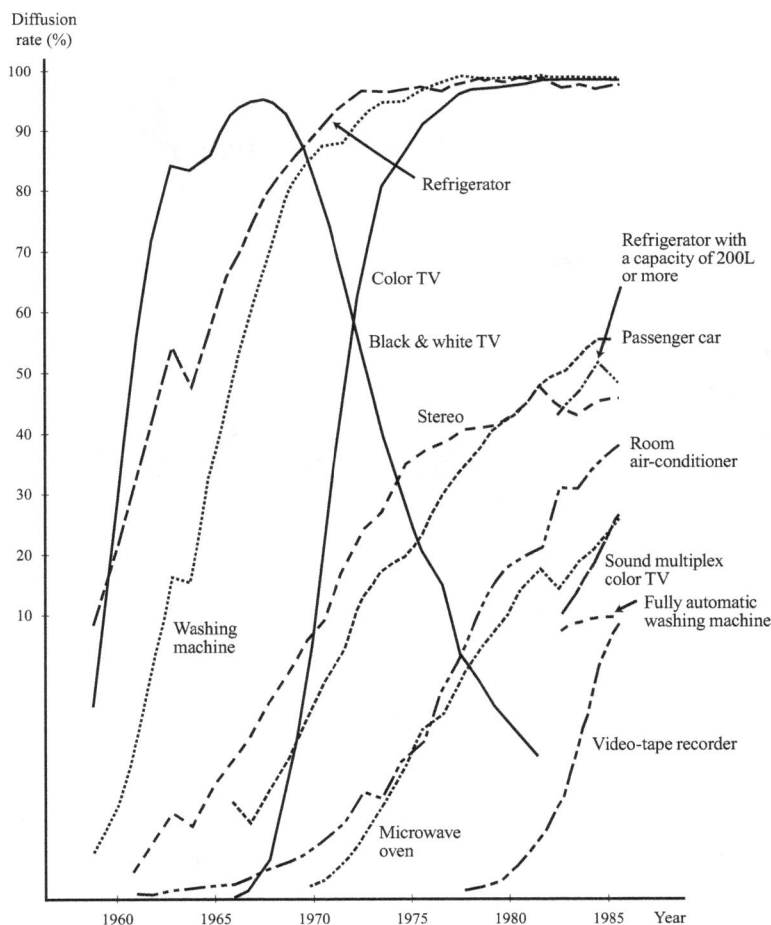

Diffusion rate (%)

Refrigerator

Refrigerator with a capacity of 200L or more

Color TV

Black & white TV

Passenger car

Stereo

Room air-conditioner

Sound multiplex color TV

Fully automatic washing machine

Washing machine

Video-tape recorder

Microwave oven

1960   1965   1970   1975   1980   1985   Year

Source: Keizai Kikaku Chō, 'Kakei chōsa no dōkō (shōhi dōkō chōsa) (Trends in household expenditure and income survey (consumption trend survey))' and 'Shōhi to chochiku no dōkō (Consumption and savings trends)'

Figure 7.3: Westinghouse advertisement in 1944

Source: Strasser (1992: 269).

squeeze dry and the latter required careful ironing. Laundry bills 'peaked in 1929' (Strasser, 1982: 270). The purchase of a washing machine therefore also meant laundry cost savings.

However, the washing machine, which was supposed to save labor, had some ironic consequences.

First, the introduction of a washing machine into the home meant that the housewife had to do laundry that she had previously sent out. Household appliances brought some of the domestic services that had previously been outsourced back into homes.

Second, the catchphrase, 'Wash any time, whenever you get a load' (from Westinghouse's pamphlet) dismissed one washday each week but turned everyday into a washday instead. Regardless of time or place, the housewife had to wash whenever she got the laundry.

Third, each load of washing was easier but the frequency of the washing increased. Early washing machines were mechanically simple and often caused wear and tear on garments. Housewives contributed to an improvement in hygiene standards instead of labor saving, even at the expense of the life of the laundry.[3]

Strasser points out that the electric washing machine has turned washing from a 'once-a-week nightmare' into 'a never ending job:' 'Over the long run, the automatic washer probably restructured rather than reduced laundry time' (Strasser, 1982: 268).

Cowan also points out some paradoxical consequences of technical innovation in domestic labor: 'Labor-saving devices were invented and diffused throughout the country during those hundred years that witnessed the first stages of industrialization, but they reorganized the work processes of housework in ways that did not save the labor of the average housewife' (Cowan, 1983: 45). She concludes, 'What a strange paradox that in the face of so many labor-saving devices, little labor appears to have been saved!' (Cowan, 1983: 44).

Cowan speculates several reasons for this. First, the wife in America's middle class is the 'housewife' in name only and she is merely a full-time domestic laborer without domestic servants. Cowan quotes the testimony of the daughter of a Norwegian who migrated to the United States in 1852:

We are told that the women of America have much leisure time but I haven't yet met any woman who thought so! Here the mistress of the house must do all the work that the cook, the maid and the housekeeper would do in an upper class family at home. Moreover she must do her work as well as these three together do it in Norway (Cowan, 1983: 43-4).

The 'mistress' referred to by this Norwegian woman is simply a mistress who has already lost her domestic servants.

Second, domestic labor-saving devices had the objective of saving on expenses for domestic service products. As Strasser's study found, 'sending out' the laundry was considered to be a usual practice prior to the advent of the washing machine. Not all domestic labor was procured within a household. Bread making became an established profession in very early times in Europe and the brewing of rice wine and soy sauce has been done outside of homes for many centuries in Japan. The introduction of domestic labor-saving devices facilitated the internalization of domestic labor; one reason for this was the rising value of domestic service products in response to an increase in other employment opportunities.

When we look at societies with wide wage differentials, such as India, it becomes clear that the level of investment in domestic labor-saving devices is closely related to the level of wages for domestic service laborers. The rate of washing machine ownership is not so high in India, even among households with an economic capacity to purchase one, because investment in expensive household appliances is not cost-effective in a place where the labor supply of housemaids and laundrymen is cheap and abundant. The diffusion of household appliances in Japan during the 1960s also coincided with a rapid decline in the number of domestic workers who moved from villages to cities.

Third, Cowan refers to the fact that domestic labor, which used to be hard but was shared by family members, has become the sole responsibility of the housewife. The husband used to chop wood, children used to fetch water, and the wife used to cook meals. Thanks to labor-saving devices, the housewife no longer has the help of her husband or children. The separation of work and home as a result of industrialization and the modern school education system is, of course, the background factor that took the husband and children away from the home.

The fourth reason is an increase in the quality and standard of domestic labor. The introduction of the washing machine changed 'once a week washday' into something that can be done 'any time and any number of times.' While it saved on labor for each load of washing, it increased the frequency of washing. People became more conscious of cleanliness and hygiene and began to replace sheets weekly rather than monthly and to change underwear more frequently. However, it is easy to guess (based on the frequency of underwear change among the Japanese) that people's sense of cleanliness does not change naturally if it is without any change in technological means. The Japanese customarily changed their underwear when they took a bath but they did not bathe daily, except for busy seasons on the farms. They developed the habit of changing underwear daily, regardless of the frequency of bathing, only when the electric washing machine came into wide use during the 1960s. Housewives did not make a proposition to their families that would increase their own domestic labor burdens until the washing machine came into their homes.[4]

Tadao Umesao used the term *pseudo labor* to describe the housewife's labor that was being done to an increasingly higher standard, instead of being reduced by labor-saving devices.[5] According to Umesao, clean and well-starched sheets, perfectly polished floors, elaborate dishes, homemade snacks, handmade clothes for children and so on are the types of skilled labor that have been created by the housewife for the purpose of protecting her status and this has made it more difficult for the husband and children to take over such labor. Umesao incurred the wrath of housewives when he argued in the 1950s that the housewife did not become a full-time performer of domestic labor because of these tasks (which were already in existence) but that, *after* the status of housewife was established, tasks of domestic labor suitable to them were invented.

A time-use survey by NHK (a Japanese national broadcasting company) shows that full-time housewives spend seven hours a day doing the same housework that is performed by part-time housewives in three-and-a-half hours. If they spend two of the seven hours doing knitting, it is difficult to say if knitting should be classified as 'housework' or a 'hobby.' It means that full-time housewives either fill up the seven hours by performing superfluous labor, as Umesao argues, or they are very slow and unskilled workers compared with part-time housewives. On the other hand, full-time housewives pride themselves on not contracting out domestic labor and on performing it to a much higher standard than part-time housewives (i.e. not cutting corners). However, the common perception that part-time housewives 'buy pre-cooked meals' or 'cut corners in housework' is not necessarily true. In view of data showing that full-time housewives are less reluctant to procure domestic service products externally than part-time housewives, it is difficult to judge the domestic labor standards of full-time and part-time housewives solely on the basis of the time spent.[6]

Looking from a different angle, it can be said that the standard of our subsistence has risen in all areas, including housing, food and clothing. Despite the technological advancements, housewife's labor has become the labor that requires more skills in order to serve hot meals and increase the number and variety of 'extra' dishes on the table. Consequently, it has become more difficult to delegate household chores to other family members. We cannot easily affirm that it stems from the housewife's desire to protect her status, as Umesao suggests, but it is true that some housewives show resistance to delegating their role to others. As Caroline Davidson points out, domestic labor follows Parkinson's Law: that is, 'work expands so as to fill the time available for its completion' (Davidson, 1982: 192).

If domestic labor-saving devices are *actually reducing the time required for domestic labor*, how do housewives use their spare time? Umesao says that they are using the time to perform domestic labor to a more sophisticated level beyond the required standard. It may be true in some cases. However, let us look at Davidson's data from her empirical study of the history of domestic labor at working-class homes in England.

In 1934 the average time spent on domestic labor by housewives at 1,250 urban workers' households was 12 to 14 hours, from 6:30 in the morning to 10:00 or 11:00 at night. In 1935, in the same social class, the average domestic labor time decreased to about 49 hours per week or about 7 hours per day in the households that had completed electrification: 15.5 hours were spent on cleaning, 14.2 hours on cooking, 7.5 hours on dish washing, 6.4 hours on mending and sewing, and 5.5 hours on washing. The average housewife's labor in 76 workers' households in 1948 was 12 hours a day, which was unchanged from 1934. However, a breakdown shows that 9.3 hours were spent on domestic labor and 2.2 hours were spent working outside for wages (Davidson, [1982] 1986: 191–2).

Davidson concluded that women's domestic labor time had been reduced but the total labor time had not changed. Women were spending the freed up time on labor other than domestic labor.

The same is suggested by the correlation between the diffusion of household electrical goods and married women's entry into the workplace during the period of Japan's rapid economic growth (Figure 7.4). Household electrification became a push factor that increased housewives' spare time and pushed them out of their homes. In turn, it gave housewives a greater motivation to earn wages in order to purchase more electrical appliances and accelerated their entry into the workplace further. In other words, women helped expand domestic demand by driving the cycle of going out to paid labor by 'investing in plant and equipment' within the household and purchasing more durable consumer goods with earned wages.

Figure 7.4: Pull and push factors of female labor in household and market sectors

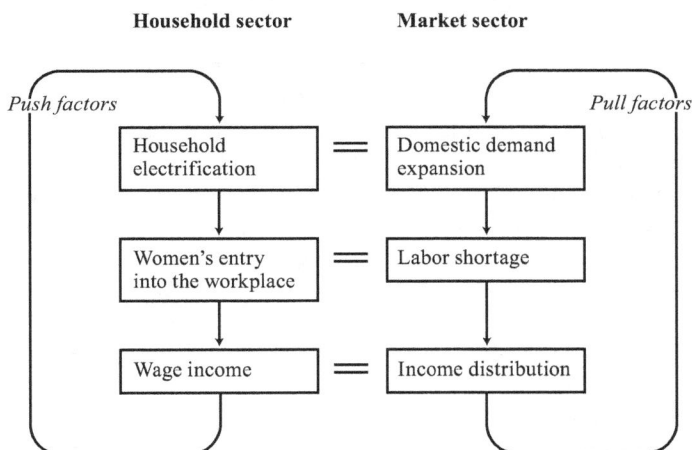

This cycle is also consistent with the correlation between an increase in the ratio of part-time farming households and the diffusion of farming machinery. Labor saving in agricultural work prompted more farming households to carry on part-time farming and, in turn, farmers made 'capital investment' in labor-saving machinery so that they could have a side job. It compelled them to go out to work for cash income.

It was no coincidence that Japan's rapid economic growth during the 1960s was driven by the expansion of the workforce to include part-time farmers and part-time housewives; this boosted domestic demand through the distribution of manufactured goods to workers while cultivating the last 'frontiers' of capitalism – the rural area and the home – and turning farmers and housewives into a workforce. It was ironic that both the part-time farmers and housewives tended to find jobs in inland manufacturing companies producing farming equipment and durable consumer goods.

Electronic revolution and de-skilling of domestic labor

Technological innovation in domestic labor progressed from the application of electrics to microelectronics from the 1970s onwards. Further, the restructuring of the economy into a more information- and service-based economy and innovations in the distribution system had to have impacts on the hardware system of the household.

The impacts of the electronic revolution can be found in every household appliance. Almost all household electrical appliances are controlled by integrated circuits (ICs). The application of microwave technology to new heating devices has especially contributed to the de-skilling of the once-skilled domestic labor and the resultant individuation. The de-skilling and individuation process was foreshadowed by the emergence of the electric rice cooker with a keep-warm function (now the IC-controlled electronic rice cooker and warmer). With the electric rice cooker, anyone can cook rice consistently and, as it automatically keeps the rice warm, does not need to keep an eye on a fire. The emergence of the microwave oven has enabled people to heat and serve pre-cooked or pre-purchased foods at any time. The practice of eating meals together as a family, and the housewife's right and obligation to distribute food at the table, has been rendered meaningless by the three-piece set of freezer/refrigerator, microwave oven and electronic rice cooker. The trend of *konabedate* (food cooked and served in a small pot individually), mentioned by Kunio Yanagida in *Meiji taishō-shi sesō-hen* (A social history of the Meiji–Taishō era: Social conditions) (1931, 1976), has finally developed into the phenomenon of *koshokuka* (eating individually). Now all family members can eat meals separately, thanks to these changes in the hardware system of the home. According to a survey of working households in the Tokyo Metropolitan Region, family members gather to have dinner together only twice a week on average. It has been reported that all four members of a family eat their dinners separately in some cases. With the introduction of the microwave oven, the individualization of family meals does not necessarily mean a longer standby period in the kitchen for the housewife (Ueno and Dentsu Nettowāku Kenkyūkai, 1988). The electronic rice cooker and the microwave oven have usurped the housewife's monopoly on the rice scoop and turned domestic labor into something that men and children can do.

When we consider the levels of domestic labor skill and the extent of participation in domestic labor by men and children in relation to the stages of technological innovation, we find something interesting. China and the United States are two societies with a much greater level of participation in domestic labor by men than Japan, but their men's stronger sense of gender equality and women's greater contributions to household finances are not the only reasons for this. It is difficult to imagine that societies with extremely different cultural backgrounds such as China and the United States would share the same ideas about the home or women. In China, men participate in domestic labor because they are compelled to help for the following reasons: first, they have the custom of serving their meals hot; second, this custom means that domestic labor is complicated and needs many helping hands; and, third, the low level of household electrification means that domestic labor is hard work. On the other hand, many husbands say that 'clearing up after meals is my job' in the United States, but it often means simply carrying dirty dishes to a dishwashing machine. In addition, a low level of sophistication in their food culture and the popularity of processed foods have turned their concept of 'cooking' into markedly low-skilled labor.

It is possible to explain the emergence of the full-time domestic laborer based on the technological level of the hardware system of the home by comparing Japan with China and the United States. It may be reasonable to say that the full-time domestic laborer called 'housewife' is a transitional existence that appears in the intermediate stage of household technology development between a low-tech stage, as in China, and a high-tech stage, as in the United States, or in the intermediate stage in the process of change of domestic labor from skilled labor to non-skilled labor.

Another consequence of the housework revolution is the further externalization of the once-internalized domestic labor. It involves, first, the commodification and socialization of domestic labor in all areas (including housing, food, clothing, childcare, education and nursing care) and, second, dramatic changes in the distribution system (home delivery, convenience stores, 24-hour shops etc.) brought on by the distribution revolution (Table 7.1). Inside the household, electrical appliances have become individualized, and having two or more televisions or refrigerators for personal use has become common (Table 7.2). Some electric rice cookers even have the ability to cook rice to different softness or flavors with a differential cooking time function: they mark the appearance of cooking devices designed on the presumption that a family does not 'eat the rice from the same pot' any more. Once a room is equipped with a standard package of individualized appliances, it becomes easier to separate it from the existing household to create a one-person household. This change was foretold by Tadao Umesao in 'Tsuma muyō-ron (Superfluous wife theory)' in 1959. While Jirō Kamishima, in his *tanshinsha toshika-ron* (singles-led urbanization

Table 7.1: Convenience store growth

	Sales growth over the previous year (%)		
	1984	1985	1986
Non-store retailing	5.6	6.2	8.2
Convenience stores	22.3	21.2	17.5
Service industry	8.6	9.5	-

Source: Leading corporations in each industry, *Nikkei ryūtsū shimbun* (Nikkei marketing journal)

Table 7.2: The number of units of major durable consumer goods per home

	Diffusion rate (%)	Units (per 100 households)
Washing machine	99.2	106.3
Color TV	98.7	180.2
Refrigerator	97.8	115.2
Vacuum cleaner	98.1	124.7
Electric *kotatsu* (a table with an infra-red heater underneath)	91.0	147.4
Kerosene heater	82.8	157.8
Camera	83.8	129.4
Automobile	81.7	145.7
Radio/cassette player	74.9	106.5
Carpet	67.4	144.4

Source: Keizai Kikaku Chō

theory), argued that Japan's urbanization had been supported mainly by single people, the traditional image of urban singles was rather miserable. In particular, male singles lacking necessary domestic skills were dogged so much by a forlorn image that some of them even decided to get married to escape the 'inconveniences of life.' However, advancements in technological innovation in the hardware system of the home and commodification of domestic labor have enabled singles without domestic skills to survive more easily. In other words, the domestic technology required in a one-person household has been markedly de-skilled. Single households, which account for 30% of total households in the Tokyo Metropolitan Region, contain many single male households. They also include many middle-aged and older 'business bachelors,' or the new modern-day *dekasegi* (coming to cities for work) workers;

away from home, their single life has been made possible by these changes to the material infrastructure of domestic labor.

The progression of family individuation

The process of *kozokuka* (individuation of family members) – *individuation* is a more appropriate term here than *individualization*[7] – was completed by the introduction of interactive communication devices, specifically the cordless telephone, into individual rooms. Most households had only one telephone line until now and communication with outside parties could be monitored by family members because the telephone was usually located in the living room or the corridor. Then, the spread of cordless telephones rapidly accelerated the individuation of communication. Sending children to their own rooms no longer means isolation from the outside world. On the contrary, they are not only directly exposed to information from the outside world through their personal audiovisual equipment but are also able to interact with the outside world using interactive communication devices without any family supervision. Children who are older than the upper elementary ages tend to spend more time in their individual rooms than in family living or dining rooms – and they are in contact with the outside world during that time and for a much longer time than they are in contact with their own families. In terms of residential building structure, the living room is becoming a place for occasions where all family members gather once in a while.

With family individuation, the communality of a household symbolized by communal eating based on 'communal use of a fire' takes on new meaning. Where husband and wife are both working, dining out has become a routine practice to save time on busy weeknights, and homemade food, which is eaten by the whole family together on weekends, is becoming an occasional meal instead. The 'gathering of the whole family' is taking on special meaning. Another thing that adds meaning to it is commensality with the parents' household, which is the closest kinship family. Although the nuclearization of the family has promoted the separation of households to a considerable extent, the parents' household is compelled to keep a sufficiently large space and enough crockery in the home for when they are joined by their children's households. Getting together of parents–children kinship households is becoming a new family occasion.[8]

Technical innovation in the household as a hardware system has been promoting individuation. The family has been freed from the constraint of 'eating the rice from the same pot' and individual tastes can co-exist on the same dining table because a single 'family taste' does not have to be shared or imposed any more. This can be interpreted as a sign of declining family culture and diminishing parental authority or as greater respect for the individuality of family members, but it happened because the hardware aspect of home life made it possible. Housewives would have resisted it if individuation made their work more complicated. The segregation of sub-households within a household has advanced considerably in the areas of housing, food and clothing. It is only one step away from a total separation of satellite households, equipped with their standard package of personal household appliances, in the form of studio apartments. Along the same line of thinking, some people have begun to rent satellite study rooms for children in their school or university exam years or satellite offices for husband or wife near their homes. Architect Takashi Kurosawa (1987) proposes 'individual living unit cluster housing,' which consists of individual rooms for all family members plus a common living space. Reality may go even further and a household may look like a multiple single-occupancy unit complex. And it can be made possible not only by changes in people's attitudes but also by changes in the hardware system of the home.

Family individuation is progressing, but the cohesive power of the family is not necessarily diminishing. It has often been pointed out that intergenerational cohesion based on landownership has strengthened due to abnormally high levels of 'land-sharking activity'[9] in the Tokyo Metropolitan area in the 1980s. One can also cite the following two factors in terms of domestic labor. First, the rising employment rate among women at the child-rearing age means that children's (especially daughters') households expect support for childcare labor from their parents. Second, parents' concerns about their old age means they expect nursing care labor to be provided by their children. There are certain commonalities between childcare labor and nursing care labor. First, they are interpersonal domestic labor that is least suitable for automation. Second, wage levels for such labor, and hence price levels for outside services, are too high for middle-class people to use. Third, the standards of publicly provided services are too low and unreliable. Lastly, there are moral sanctions against procuring such labor outside the household. It is difficult to say which of these reasons is the strongest determinant. It has often been said that moral considerations have been hampering the outsourcing of childcare and aged care. However, people delegate childcare to strangers without hesitation in countries where babysitting services are very cheap and easily accessible (having a nursemaid is even a status symbol for upper-class families), and the experience of European countries with advanced welfare systems has shown that aged care promotes the separation of households. Moral reasons are frequently used to justify the status quo. The prime example is the 'motherhood' debate over the use of disposable paper diapers. American conservation groups and European environmental groups that advocate conservation, which criticize the use of disposable wooden chopsticks by the Japanese, do not criticize the use of disposable diapers in their own countries in the name of 'motherhood' on moral grounds. Only in Japan, where relatively high prices of disposable diapers have limited their popularity, do we see some people argue that 'disposable diapers are bad for babies' in order to justify the present situation. Yet, such moralistic accusations have not been directed at the use of paper diapers for elderly people. It demonstrates how inconsistent and expedient these social sanctions are.

Domestic labor in the near future

As we have seen above, domestic labor is greatly affected by technological innovations and changes in the industrial structure. So, what are the factors that are likely to trigger changes in domestic labor in the near future?

First, further advancements in technological innovation are likely to promote de-skilling of many domestic skills. It has already happened in cleaning and washing. Cooking is becoming a programmable task using ICs. It depends on people's choice as to the level of food culture they wish to maintain, but it may take a form of programmed reheating of professionally cooked gourmet food in a microwave oven. Since some housewives who are critical of pre-packed food products are quite receptive to gourmet dishes being sold at department stores, home cooking may become an amateur's hobby to those who have developed discriminating taste by eating out regularly. The automatic dishwashing machine is one of the larger household appliances that has been slow to enter Japanese homes. Japan's complex and diverse food culture, and so much time available to women, are the reasons for its low diffusion rate. For the dishwasher to gain wide acceptance, either people have to give up the use of lacquered wooden bowls and collector's ceramic pieces and simplify their crockery to suit the available technology or the dishwasher has to make a technological leap (just as the Japanese language word-processor did) to cater for Japanese eating habits. In either case, pressure towards technological innovation will come from the scarcity of women's time resource. And exquisite tableware and home cooking will be saved for special occasions such as family gatherings on weekends.

Participation by men and children in domestic labor is likely to be promoted by the de-skilling of domestic labor by technical innovation more than by changes in their attitudes. In other words, it will be difficult to force men and children to upgrade their domestic labor skills while the current high standard of required skills is maintained, but technological innovation will make it possible for them to share domestic labor without changing their current domestic skill levels.

Second, there is the issue of increasing commodification of domestic labor and its pricing. More and more domestic labor will be offered in the form of commodified services but high price levels will limit their accessibility. The accessibility to domestic labor products is determined by the opportunity cost of women's labor.[10] If a woman's wage is higher than the prices of domestic labor products that she can purchase from outside service providers, she will become a purchaser of such products. Since the unit price of her labor is determined by her education, qualification, occupation type and ability, this will create the division between women who can afford to purchase domestic labor services and those who cannot.

Third, there is the issue of foreign workers. European and American examples show that foreign countries can become sources of domestic labor supply when a country opens up its labor market substantially, just as the rural area became the source of domestic labor supply in the Meiji and Taishō eras. Foreign workers who have low education, or whose qualifications from the home countries are useless due to the language barrier, often engage in service labor at the bottom of the heap. In the United States, babysitting is the first opportunity for paid work for female refugees because it does not require qualifications or language proficiency. However, some mothers avoid using them for older infants as they do not want their children to pick up their babysitters' foreign accents. Foreign workers are most welcome in the nursing care industry for the sick and the aged. Sweden's welfare labor shortage is made up for by these foreign workers. In a society such as Japan, where people are reluctant to place elderly people in nursing homes and prefer to care for them in their own homes, it is easy to imagine that there will be a very strong demand for home care service workers – provided that there is sufficient supply. The aforementioned example of the urban dwelling with a maid's room during the Taishō era has demonstrated that the small size of Japanese houses is not an impediment to the popularity of live-in workers. The dwelling space per person has actually increased since the Taishō era. Each individual may require more physical and psychological space now due to a stronger sense of privacy but there is still demand for live-out nurses, carers and housemaids. What we find here are disparities between the Japanese and foreigners and between domestic labor and other types of labor. Discrimination still remains here: foreigners engage in low-wage labor and domestic service labor, with the lowest wage level, is at the bottom of the labor hierarchy.

The fourth factor is the option of the socialization of domestic labor. This is a welfare socialization option to provide, as a public service, labor (especially childcare and nursing care) that cannot be automated. Even if we manage to put a good institutional infrastructure in place, it will immediately encounter the problem of labor shortage in its operation. In order to solve this problem, the program must rely on foreign workers who are willing to work for low wages, or the unit price for labor must be raised. In the latter case, the increased financial burden will, of course, put the brakes on the expansion of welfare provision. The choice between this option and having a full-time domestic laborer at home will be made on the basis of the household balance sheet.

In any case, it is certain that housewife's labor is a temporary, transitional product in the long history of domestic labor. The questions of the quality and quantity of domestic labor, its scope and who is going to perform it in the future will be determined historically by interactions between the aforementioned factors. Prior to that, however, there is a need to de-mythologize the 'naturalness' of domestic labor based on the false assumptions that 'anyone can do it' and that 'it should essentially be performed for free' – which ranks domestic labor as the least valuable of all types of human labor.

Part IV

Postwar Economic Growth and the Family

8 A Postwar History of the Mother

The Japanese and ethics

Since Ruth Fulton Benedict made a distinction between *guilty culture* and *shame culture* in her classic work on Japanese culture, *The chrysanthemum and the sword: Patterns of Japanese culture* (Benedict, 1946), Japanese people have been regarded as lacking transcendental internal norms. Originally, Benedict belonged to the 'culture and personality' school led by Franz Boas, among others, who had been under the influence of Sigmund Freud. With the introduction of the psychoanalytical methods of Freud's and Jung's schools to Japanese culture studies, Japan as a maternal society was increasingly regarded as a society lacking paternity that was able to intervene in the close mother–child relationship and, as a result of this, was regarded as an immature society that failed to internalize transcendental ethics (known as *superego*). The influence of this kind of argument still remains influential even today, as seen in the postmodern school's view on Japan, Kōjin Karatani's argument on the 'bilateral system,' and Akira Asada's view on the soft suppression in the 'mother-complexed or computerized society.' The arguments of these researchers ultimately have only one point in common: the ethics of Japanese society is formed differently from that of Western societies and cannot be understood by theories of Western origin.

Not surprisingly, the kind of argument as represented by Benedict soon met with counterarguments. With regard to Benedict's view, the sociologist Keiichi Sakuta argued in 1967, in his book *Haji no bunka saikō* (Reconsidering shame culture) (Sakuta, [1967] 1981), that shame culture is a type of internalized norm, as is the case with guilty culture. As a matter of fact, the significance of *shame* and *dignity* is familiar to the Mediterranean culture area in terms of folkloric categorization. Sakuta demonstrated that the argument that shame is a type of contextual ethics that makes people worry about what others think and cannot be regarded as internalized transcendental ethics is merely a product of Western ethnocentrism and of some Japanese researchers who fell into line with it.

Doubts about the application of the Oedipus complex to Japanese people were shared by some psychologists from the early stages of Freud's school because it was self-evident that the mechanical application of Freud's development theory would lead to the view that Japanese people lack superego. As early as before the Second World War, Heisaku Furusawa, a Japanese who studied under Freud in the 1930s, invented the concept of the *Ajase complex* to replace the Oedipus complex. Ajase is a main character in a Buddhist tale – he imprisons and torments his own mother, who remonstrates with him not to kill his father. Furusawa thought Ajase was a better model to explain the Japanese mentality than Oedipus, the protagonist of a Greek tragedy who killed his own father and married his own mother. In Furusawa's model, the source for the formation of a Japanese person's superego is his 'suffering mother' instead of his 'punishing father.' In the case of a Japanese person, the internalized 'little God' or 'voice of conscience' (in Japanese, *ryōshin no koe*, which is a homophone for the Japanese words meaning the 'voice of parents'), which supervises a person's behavior, is formed through the mother who blames herself rather than punishing her child for his or her misdeed. In Japanese patriarchal families, this internal norm is nurtured in children who routinely witness their mothers being battered by their husbands, a torment that intends mothers to bear the blame for their children's misconduct or failure.

After Freud's theory was deconstructed and understood as a 'story of a son becoming a father,' which is neither universal nor historically consistent but is unique to modern Western families, the universality of the Oedipus complex was also denied. Furusawa's view was rediscovered and re-evaluated by Keigo Okonogi and his colleagues after the war (Okonogi, 1978). These researchers argued that Japanese people form their superegos through their own mechanism, which is different from that of Western people. They maintained that neither mechanism is better than the other because their difference is based on different states of families.

These arguments direct our attention to what family is to Japanese people, particularly the position of the mother within it. If family is not an eternal cultural tradition but an entity changeable with the times, it would be necessary to discuss family in different phases of such change. In the following, I attempt to discuss the Japanese and ethics by using as a clue the representations of *mother* in postwar Japanese literature.

'Dominant mother' and 'shameful father'

Nothing gives better clues than Jun Etō's *Seijuku to sōshitsu*
(Maturity and loss) (Etō, [1967] 1988 [1993]) when discussing the
representations of mother in postwar Japanese literature.

Seijuku to sōshitsu is subtitled 'The disintegration of motherhood.'
The author chose the word 'disintegration,' not 'loss.' This alone is
enough to indicate that this book is not about independence from
mother, as was the case with Freud's Oedipus complex theory, or
about matricide as asserted by Shūji Terayama (an avant-garde poet
and theatre director). It is all too common a view that a person's
maturation is achieved in exchange for a 'loss' of the utopia in
which he or she has lived with his or her mother. Instead of lyrically
describing a person's maturation as a story of the 'loss of mother,'
Etō described the required maturation as a story of the irreversible
process of 'disintegration of motherhood.' By this attempt, this
work of Etō, which discusses postwar literary texts, successfully
becomes a critique of civilization beyond the level of a mere study
of literary works.

It is often said that, compared to Christian civilization where
the father has his own place, Japanese culture is associated with
a society based on the maternal principle, or a mother-dominated
society in which children are not allowed to become independent
or mature. However, is culture or civilization unchangeable with
time, or independent of history, like Jung's archetype? As the author
of *Natsume Sōseki* (Sōseki Natsume) (Etō, 1956), Etō knew very
well that Japan had been, at least up until the Meiji era, a society
based on the Confucian paternal principle, or Tao of Heaven. For
Etō the issue of maturation was a historical task facing Japanese
intellectuals, who encountered the West for the first time since the
'shock of the black ships.' Etō's generation, which experienced the
'American shock' as a result of Japan's defeat in the Second World
War, took over this task from Sōseki Natsume.

Etō repeatedly describes the maternal principle as 'associated with
agrarian society.' Comparing the maternal principle and the paternal
principle by associating them with pastoral culture and agricultural
culture respectively is an almost outdated cliché. However, Etō
did not forget that the Japanese agrarian society had inevitably
undergone a baptism of modernity. Behind 'dominant mother' is
'shameful father.' Only because of this, a tacit understanding is
formed between the mother, who had no choice but to marry the
'shameful father,' and her son.

Referring to the mother–child relationship described in *Umibe no kōkei* (A view by the sea) by Shōtarō Yasuoka (Yasuoka, 1959), Etō comments as follows:

> If they lived peacefully with the traditional feelings of farmers/settlers, the mother and her son would not be able to share such an extreme feeling of shame about the father. This is because in that sort of static culture, a mother is required to bring up her children so that they will be exactly like their father and this, in turn, gives rise to the close mother–child relationship (Etō, 1993: 13).

However, these shared feelings do not guarantee that a son can maintain a peaceful alliance with his mother. To him, his father begins to look like a 'miserable father' who is a cause of shame to his wife, while she begins to behave like a 'frustrated mother' because she has no other way to live than serving her miserable husband. Still, the son cannot entirely dislike his father, as he knows that he is destined to become a father himself in the future. This makes him identify himself with his 'miserable father,' which, in turn, makes him an 'incompetent son.' His inability to meet his frustrated mother's expectation of saving her from her distressful situation makes him internalize a deep guilt consciousness. At the same time, the son is secretly aware of the fact that by remaining an 'incompetent son' he can meet, in a collusive manner, his mother's latent expectation that he will not become independent from her control. This is a distorted version of the Oedipus story that is unique to modern Japan. Etō says that the 'sensuousness and flexibility' of Yasuoka's literary style 'derives from his experience of enjoying the "freedom" of this childish world to his heart's content' (Etō, 1993: 17). This comment may betray the potential envy of Etō, who lost his mother early in life.

As was the case with Freud, Etō was interested only in the 'son's story' and did not mention the 'daughter's story.' In his place, let me discuss the 'daughter's story.' A daughter has no need to identify herself with her 'miserable father.' However, unlike a son, she is given no power or opportunity to escape from the misery by herself. She accepts that her life ahead is destined to become like that of her 'frustrated mother,' in which she will have to let a man, whom she will be unable to control, steer her life according to his own will. This makes her an 'irritating daughter.' Unlike a son, a daughter has no responsibility or sympathy for her 'frustrated mother,' which makes her irritation all the more unforgiving.

The mother's…feeling of shame about her own husband is, when viewed from the other side, directly connected with a feeling of shame about herself, who was unable to marry anyone but the shameful man…In addition, she cannot entirely trust her own son because of the fact that, despite her wish for him to become a different man from her husband, he is an offspring of that very husband of hers. Moreover, should her son turn out to be better than her husband, he would have to climb the social ladder, away from the culture to which his mother belongs. The mother would surely be left behind (Etō, 1993: 14).

Etō adds, 'this kind of psychological disturbance of a mother never occurs in a society with fixed hierarchical order' (Etō, 1993: 14). As is dimly sensed by Etō, the close mother–child relationship cannot occur in an agrarian society. Mothers are busy working and are simply unmindful of their children. In any case, children in a traditional society grow up without bothering their parents very much. At the age of seven or so, children leave their parents' world when they are sent out to live-in service or to join children's age groups. They have no freedom to move up the social ladder, nor do they need extraordinary resourcefulness to live like their parents.

The close mother–child relationship occurred only after modern times and only in the middle class. In other words, it occurred only after and only where mothers were expelled from production and became 'full-time mothers' whose identities relied solely on being mothers. In addition, from the moment they came into existence, these mothers were 'child-rearing mothers,' or 'educating mothers,' who were evaluated based on the performance of their 'products,' or their children (Koyama, 1991). From the beginning of the formation of the middle class, the close mother–child cooperation to achieve the same aims through education was programmed to occur. After it did occur, this close mother–child cooperation was nurtured in the isolated environment of the prewar uptown middle class where, as recalled by Etō himself in *Ōrudo fasshon* (Old-fashion) (Etō and Hasumi, [1985] 1988), which contains a conversation between Etō and Shigehiko Hasumi, a child would 'visit a friend after calling him on the phone [to make an appointment].' From its beginning, this close mother–child relationship has structurally been associated with the lack of stability of the basis of motherhood, with the isolation of nuclear families, and with the alienation of fathers in these circumstances.

It is amazing how strongly 'mother' lingers in the heart of general Japanese men. This pattern has remained even after a school education

system was introduced to the agrarian society, which has resulted
in the mother–child relationship being threatened by the effect of
'modernity.' Rather, the influence of mothers may even seem to be
becoming stronger. This increase of the influence of 'mother' in
modern Japan is probably in inverse proportion to the weakening
of the image of 'father.' With the establishment of school education,
'father' became...something 'shameful' for most mothers and
children (Etō, 1993: 37).

The close mother–child relationship is not a remnant of traditional
society. Motherhood worship of similar degrees can be found
in Mediterranean men and in Hinduism. What I discuss here is
a mother–child relationship that is unique to 'modern families'
and which is a phenomenon in a society that was forced to accept
an unhappy modernization. This unhappiness resulted from the
extraordinary rapidity of the modernization, which created a
situation where 'success' of children always meant to 'avoid being
like their parents.'

In this modernity, motherhood inevitably becomes ambivalent:
a 'merciful, tolerant mother' and a 'scolding, refusing mother.' In
Seijuku to sōshitsu, the 'mother' described by Shōtarō Yasuoka
and the 'wife' described by Nobuo Kojima are meticulously
contrasted. The mother and the wife represent 'merciful, tolerant
mother' and 'scolding, refusing mother' respectively. Yasuoka's
'mother' has no choice but to be a mother, and establishes an
absolute relationship with her child. In contrast, Kojima's 'wife'
has already established a relative relationship with her husband in
that she chose him by 'love marriage,' even though she is forced
by her husband to take on the role of mother. It is very significant
that Etō's work begins with a quotation from Yasuoka's *Umibe
no kōkei*, which portrays the almost obtrusive love of a mother
who might tolerate her own son even if he has committed murder.
However, Etō quotes this work simply to demonstrate the loss of
such unconditional maternity or, more precisely, the loss of the
unconditional trust in such maternity. Between Yasuoka's 'mother'
and Kojima's 'wife' lies a discontinuity known as the postwar
modernization.

'Incompetent son' and 'irritating daughter'

If we look around us with the above-described view in mind, the
world is full of 'shameful fathers' and 'frustrated mothers.' Their

'incompetent sons' marrying their 'irritating daughters' would be represented by Shunsuke and Tokiko respectively, who are characters in *Hōyō kazoku* (Embracing family) by Nobuo Kojima (Kojima, 1965). Etō explains the process described in this work as a 'psychological mechanism by which the son shares with his own mother a feeling of shame about his own father but grows up to become a "father" himself, who is regarded as "shameful" by his own wife and son' (Etō, 1993: 71). Even after becoming a wife, Tokiko remains an 'irritating daughter' and remains under the illusion that she could choose to live otherwise, despite her continuous reliance on her husband for her wellbeing.

In fact, very few patriarchs would be as unattractive as Shunsuke Miwa in *Hōyō kazoku*. The impact of the creation of this main character was such that most professional literary critics erred in their evaluation of the work after its first publication. The critics (most of whom were men) identified with the male protagonist and ended up simply 'hating' (instead of 'criticizing') him as an excessively stark portrait of themselves. For instance, Tetsutarō Kawakami wrote in his review in the *Shinchō* magazine issued immediately after the publication of *Hōyō kazoku*, 'The unattractiveness of this man discourages me from actively supporting this work' (Kawakami, 1966). Similar comments were made by Shūgo Honda in his review published in the *Tokyo Shimbun*: 'Wherever this protagonist goes, everybody breaks up, falls apart, and can no longer take care of oneself, and all this falls upon the protagonist. He is the cause of all the trouble' (Honda, 1965).

In his joint review with Kenkichi Yamamoto and Takehiko Fukunaga published in the August 1965 issue of the *Gunzō* magazine, Honda says:

If Mr Shōno's patriarch is the proper type of patriarch, this one seems to be representing the most improper type of patriarch... It seems that the protagonist is the one who caused his wife and children to go beyond control...It's no surprise that his family went out of control (Honda, Yamamoto and Fukunaga, 1965).

Through Honda's comments we can almost see his face as he thinks that he would not make things that bad and as he clucks to the 'incompetent husband' who cannot set a good example to his family members.

In the same joint review, Yamamoto and Fukunaga agree with Honda.

Yamamoto: ...this wife is not at all attractive to me...

Fukunaga: By tumbling for such an unattractive woman, at least he succeeded in giving us an impression that it is hard after all to stay married [laughs] (Honda, Yamamoto and Fukunaga, 1965).

These 'literary critics' equate the combination of an 'unattractive husband' and an 'unattractive wife' with the alleged unattractiveness of the work. They do not even imagine that the combination might be a product of the author's conscious criticism. However, even the seemingly most masochistic of first-person novelists secretly slip self-justification and narcissism into their works through 'self-exposure' (Hijiya-Kirschnereit, 1992), a paradoxically heroic act. In contrast, Kojima portrayed the protagonist, who seems to represent the author himself, in a caricature-like manner. If the critics are 'critics' at all, they should have noticed that this fact represents the author's clear, conscious criticism. Their failure to do so reveals the magnitude of their dismay at the realities of the couple described in the work. These are realities that they hate to see or hear. It is not that the work is 'turbid;' it accurately reflects the 'turbid realities' (Etō, 1993: 90). As Etō says, the author 'clearly understands the realities of [this] turbid world' (Etō, 1993: 93). This must be the strength of this work.

For his *Hōyō kazoku*, Kojima became the first winner of the Jun'ichirō Tanizaki award in 1965. In his post-selection comments, Sei Itō appreciated Kojima's work as follows:

Frankly speaking, male authors have never given any serious thought to their wives or, alternatively, have been afraid of doing so...It is fair to say that this work established what a wife is – in the sense that she takes hold of her household as her own nest and that she still is a women – for the first time in the heart of Japanese people (Itō, 1965).

As was the case with Ken Hirano, some critics showed their confusion honestly by first assessing the work as low and later withdrawing the assessment.

Later, on second thought, it occurred to me that I had probably made mistakes in criticizing this excellent work. Briefly, I had understood this work as depicting the essential differences between men and women and had focused on the comical ways the characters, mainly male ones, are portrayed. However, I should not have understood this work in that sort of abstract manner; instead, I should have reviewed it more concretely by understanding it as a work depicting the realities of men and women in their contemporary family life (Hirano, 1971).

Hirano made similar remarks in an article titled '1965-nen bundan sōkessan (Overall literary review for 1965)' and published in the December 1965 issue of the *Bungakukai* magazine.

Sei Itō's insight is outstanding compared to that of most other male critics, who, rather than assessing the work, showed dismay that might have been associated with their self-hatred, simply because they were so clearly faced with a 'shameful' self-portrait. The competence of a critic becomes clear when comments are reviewed after a time. Itō even commented, 'The creation of this work will change the image of Japanese women.' Itō was able to say this only because he, as a modernist, had clearly sensed the postwar changes in Japanese women.

It was Etō's comments that prompted me to read Kojima's *Hōyō kazoku*. Some literary productions become monumental works of their time owing only to the ways they are read by brilliant critics. Kojima's good luck of having Etō as a reader made the author unforgettable as one of the best writers in the 1960s.

Deletion of 'others'

In a tripartite discussion between Sei Itō, Shōtarō Yasuoka and Jun Etō, titled 'Bungaku no katei to genjitsu no katei (Family in literary works and family in real life)' and published in the October 1965 issue of *Gunzō*, Itō describes his 'family in real life' as follows:

> Most writers seem to sort of internalize their wife and write as a single representative of their family...Don't we describe our wife's sorrow as our own pain instead of another person's? So our wife is never another person to us but someone who exists in us at the same time...To us, a wife is not like what they say she is in the West (Itō, Yasuoka and Etō, 1965).

Etō, the youngest of the three, immediately ripostes:

> Etō: What you have just said, Mr Itō – that you internalize your wife and cherish her there – conversely means that you cherish yourself only, doesn't it?
> Itō: 'Exactly. I really don't know what that really is, and I can't explain it very well either (Itō, Yasuoka and Etō, 1965).

We know 'what that really is.' It is that they do not have a wife as the other. This indicates what is pointed out by Etō repeatedly: the childishness or, if it is rude to use this word, egoism, of Japanese men who attempt to identify their wives with their mothers. In their attempt to do so, their wives are forced forever to take on the role of 'merciful, tolerant mother.' In order to test her 'mercy,' a man even torments his wife by running the whole gamut of dissipation. Because a wife is not the other but a part of the husband, a man's acts of torture towards his wife become very much like self-injury. For men like Sei Itō, who says, 'Once married, all her failures become my wounds,' tormenting a wife would be self-punishment, or a type of self-torture. This has given a look of suffering to men's egoism and this look has caused this egoism to be ethically tolerated – at least in the existing first-person novels. Etō identifies this point precisely.

> ...after all, the relationship between Shunsuke and Tokiko has been maintained out of an impulse to restore a natural relationship between 'mother and child' rather than an ethical relationship between 'husband and wife,' and there is no standard of value in their relationship other than whether or not there is strong affection like the one between 'mother and child.' Needless to say, the attempt to find a sensuous relationship between 'mother and child' in the relationship between 'husband and wife' comes from an incestuous desire. This is an attempt to find 'mother' in sex and to see an illusion of repose at 'mother's' breast in the pleasure of sex. This might be understood as an impulse to identify non-blood related persons with blood-related ones. In other words, there is no 'other person' here (Etō, 1993: 86–7).

Etō is able to identify this point because he is aware of the trap in the 'natural' relationship between Japanese husband and wife. In this natural relationship, neither husband nor wife can be another person to the other: 'This is only because they are united out of a desire to restore the natural relationship between "mother and child" rather than an ethical relationship between "husband and wife"' (Etō, 1993: 47–8). Etō perfectly knows the 'present situation of Japanese husband and wife, both of who have accumulated irreversible "loneliness" but can never be "isolated"' (Etō, 1993: 48).

In *Seijuku to sōshitsu*, Etō refers to *Hoshi to tsuki wa ten no ana* (Stars and the moon are holes in the heaven) by Jun'nosuke Yoshiyuki (Yoshiyuki, 1966). He does so in order to demonstrate that even in a non-'natural' male–female relationship, the man eliminates the 'other person.' Etō is harsh on Yoshiyuki. This is because 'to regard women as mere "tools" [of sex] is to deny the "nature" or motherhood in women,' and because Yoshiyuki's 'artificial world' created by so denying motherhood represents a 'lack of critical consciousness of the author,' who is not even aware of the 'loss.' The protagonist of Yoshiyuki's work can have a relationship with a woman only if she is a 'women lacking motherhood' (that is, a prostitute) or by treating her as though she was a prostitute. This is nothing more than a commonplace story of a woman-hater who has encountered 'refusal by mother' or 'betrayal by woman.' Later, Eiji Sekine, who was born after the war, titled his book on Yoshiyuki *'Tasha' no shōkyo* (Elimination of 'others') (Sekine, 1993). This, indeed, is an excellent expression. It is suggestive that the author is a young Japanese man who married an American.

Industrialization and women's self-hatred

From the viewpoint of a wife, the torment imposed by her husband is, after all, pain inflicted by another person – it is not her husband but herself who suffers. Even if her husband never regards her as another person, she soon regards him as another person. Unlike her husband who refuses to recognize the existence of another person, she is long aware of the fact that, in the mother–child relationship in which no other person exists, she would be placed on the exploited side. Unlike Shōtarō Yasuoka's 'mother,' Tokiko is no longer a women who has no choice but to accept being a mother. Similarly, even though Yoshiyuki's 'prostitute' is depicted as a woman who feels sexual pleasure in self-torture, she represents the man's expedient fantasy. When woman ceases to act as a collaborator with man according to his scenario, she changes into an eerie, other person. The man's bewilderment and surprise at his wife becoming the other is described straightforwardly by Kojima (1995): 'he was overwhelmed by the fact that there was a woman there.'

More precisely, Tokiko is neither ready for, nor capable of, assuming the role of mother because her maternity was killed by modernity. Needless to say, it is Tokiko herself who gladly helped strangle her maternity. Etō points out that the 'self-destruction of maternity' is an 'essential subject inseparable' from the process of so-called 'modernization' (Etō, 1993: 108).

> Hidden in the innermost depths of Tokiko's sense of rivalry (against her husband) is her desire to become a man. She wants to leave 'home'

and make her own 'start' like a man would do. This represents nothing but her self-hatred for being a woman...In other words, she finds it detestable to be a 'mother' and a 'woman.'

I might be generalizing the issue too much if I say this is the innermost feeling planted in Japanese women by 'modernity.' In a sense, hatred toward being a woman might be common in women living in all modern industrialized societies (Etō, 1993: 64).

It is no surprise that this 'start,' which involved the entire feminine agrarian society, exerted the greatest influence on real women. If woman is destined to be 'left behind' because of being woman and 'mother,' she must destroy 'nature', i.e. 'maternity,' in herself with her own hand. In addition, the more rapid the industrialization is, the more thoroughly her self-destruction must be (Etō, 1993:113).

When people were reciting, 'Nature still remains even after the defeat of the state,' they were still able to believe in the existence of *nature*. Then, in the process of industrialization, Japanese people destroyed nature with their hand. The nature in women was no exception.

The fact that industrialization is a process of civilization that eventually leads to destruction of the female principle is so obvious that I should not need to mention *Gender* by Ivan Illich (Illich, 1982). Industrial society has created an image of human beings that is allegedly modeled after an abstract *individual* but is actually modeled after adult males. Each member of the society had either to follow the model or be ashamed of himself/herself for not being able to do so. This is where Freud's nonsensical concept of *penis envy* came from. The impudent 'masculine mythology' of modernity claims that because women are born emasculated they are imperfect beings compared to men and are destined to envy men. Freud's theory is not universal at all; it is only able to explain women's self-hatred so well because it focuses on 'modern family.' Erik Erikson, on whom Etō relies, is no exception to this criticism in that he, too, belongs to Freud's school.

In modern industrialized society, woman is assigned *nature* as opposed to *culture*. In this situation, she has no choice but to either accept her alleged inferiority or hate her own femininity. If she chooses the latter option, she would be declared 'neurotic' by Freud for allegedly 'wanting to become a man' and for having penis envy. For psychoanalysts, 'treatment' for such neurosis requires nothing more than to make her feel inferior in order to put her back where she belongs or, in other words, to make her accept her destiny as a 'second-class citizen.' For a women, this 'adaptation' means the 'slave's happiness;' that is, she who has already been emasculated by culture must re-emasculate herself. Women like Simone de Beauvoir, who deeply internalized modernism, regarded pregnancy and childbirth as something that brings humiliation to females (Beauvoir, 1953) in that these activities bind women to motherhood. The single-minded efforts by 1960s feminists, including Shulamith Firestone, to physically neutralize women are associated with this female self-hatred planted by industrialization. However, women's liberation would result in a paradox if the establishment of self-identity requires structural self-destruction. Women's liberation thought had to wait for the advent of the women's liberation movement in the 1970s to be released from the spell of modernism.[1]

Etō's insight is surprising in that, as early as the mid-1960s, when both men and women had no doubt at all about the value of modernization and industrialization, he pointed out the structural paradox imposed on women facing industrialization. Etō had correctly sensed early signs of what later led to the changes and feminism in Japanese women and became obvious only after the 1970s.

At this point, another factor, which was unique to Japan, emerged.

the idea that 'modernity' simply represents something sparkling, or happiness that should be sought, is probably unique to Japanese women, including Tokiko Miwa. And the fact that this women's yearning for 'modernity' represents their self-hatred turned inside out must also be a peculiarly Japanese phenomenon (Etō, 1993: 64).

In addition, this modernity takes on the face of America.

if Tokiko were not so obsessed with 'modernity,' she would not actively try to introduce 'modernity' represented by George [an American G.I.] into her 'home' and even to 'pull' it into her own womb. On one side, her act represents her desire to possess 'modernity' in herself. On the other side, it might be regarded as a ceremony to punish herself for never being able to reach 'modernity' (Etō, 1993: 66).

The 'shadow of America'

Does modernity inevitably have to take on the face of America? There must be a shadow cast over this obsession with America by the fact that Kojima experienced Japan's defeat in the war and that Etō, who tenaciously reproduces Kojima's obsession, also had hands-on experience in North America. Their experience might be common to the generation of 'men who were defeated' in the war. However, by forcing their common generational experience on women, both Etō and Kojima overlook another aspect: women could have chosen to be with victors to make their own 'start,' mercilessly leaving 'their defeated men.' In the war-devastated land, neither Japanese women who became 'war brides' nor Japanese prostitutes who supported their families by relying on American soldiers chose double suicide with Japanese men when faced with Japan's defeat. Most Japanese men must have a bitter feeling about this situation. For Tokiko, her adultery with George is, in a sense, her revenge on her husband, who would not let her make her own start. In fact, the author makes Tokiko say, 'If I were younger, I would leave my stupid home with George.' In these words, we can see her 'immaturity.' However, the way Etō identifies Tokiko's 'punishment' of her 'incompetent husband' (who cannot help her reach 'modernity') with 'punishment of herself' betrays his view of husband and wife as similar to that of Sei Itō, who identifies the wife with her husband. Alternatively, did Etō inadvertently let out his personal feeling as a man – an ordinary man whose disgust with the betrayal by a woman, who chose to yield to a 'victor,' is such that he turns a blind eye to her act?

Did George, whose name sounds similar to the Japanese word *jōji*, meaning 'love affair,' really have to be American? At some 'houses with a central heating system' in Japan in the 1980s, 'wives on Friday' were indulging in extramarital affairs, as the term replaced the word 'adultery' to refer to the same act. There, Tokiko's desire is no longer associated with self-punishment but is easily achieved. 'Love affairs' are a type of recreation for wives to relieve stress from their everyday lives as housewives and do not constitute a reason to break up the marriage. Tokiko remarks upon her husband's discovery of her affair: 'You must stand this kind of minor event...You'd even have to think it's a comedy, knowing so much about foreign literature.' The European-style decadence seen in these remarks has, after being changed into a caricatured form, completely taken root in Japanese family life. Wives know very well that nothing really changes in their everyday lives, even if they make their own start. Considered this way, 'wives on Friday' seem to represent the way Tokiko might be after two decades, and this kind of affair seems universal in a sense, despite the difference in nationality between the affair partners.

However, there is another difference between Tokiko, a housewife in the 1960s, and 'wives on Friday,' in the 1980s a difference that was brought about by Japan's postwar economic growth. Japan achieved its goal of catching up with and overtaking America. America no longer provided a model for Japan to emulate. In the 1960s Japanese students studying in America were astonished and totally shocked by faucets instantly providing hot water. In contrast, Japanese high school exchange students returning from America in the 1980s would say, 'What impressed me in America was that their standards of living are the same as in Japan.' Japan won the Japan–America controversy over business management and America became a synonym for 'second-class capitalism.' Was this situation ever imagined to happen?

For Japan or, more precisely, for Etō, America is the fateful 'other.' In succeeding years, Etō's obsession with America was repeatedly seen in his writings, including his comments on Ryū Murakami's *Kagirinaku tōmei ni chikai burū* (Almost transparent blue) published in 1976 (Murakami, R., 1976) and those on Yasuo Tanaka's *Nantonaku, kurisutaru* (Somewhat crystal) published in 1981 (Tanaka, 1981). Etō sensitively reacted to each turning point of the role played by America as a mode of life in the postwar history of Japan. It is easy to regard him as having an American complex, which was common in his generation.

However, what Etō saw in 'America' as a symbol is a 'father culture.' In *Hōyō kazoku* the protagonist confronts George about his wife's affair with this young man. The young man says, 'Responsibility? Who am I supposed to feel responsible for? I only feel responsible for my own parents and the State.' Both the protagonist and Etō are taken by surprise at the word 'State' coming out of the mouth of this young man who looks totally uneducated. He represents a cowboy who came from beyond the ocean, with the State, instead of God, as a transcendental value over him. In contrast, the patriarch in *Hōyō kazoku* reveals his lack of transcendent ethics, saying, 'If, for example, my wife has an affair with another man, then there are no grounds to declare her wrong. It's a mere discomfort to me. If so, then, this should mean that it's all right if there is some way to eliminate my discomfort.'

At this point we encounter the subject matter hidden behind the 'disintegration of motherhood:' the 'lack of father.' Japan was not originally a society based on the maternal principle and lacking transcendental ethics, as indicated in the following points made by

Etō: (i) the structure of Sōseki's novels was supported by 'Heaven' as a symbol of the 'Confucian transcendental, paternal principle,' and (ii) Sōseki's works produced after his return from London lacked 'Heaven' but he 'still had a sensibility to recognize the lack of transcendental perspectives as pain' (Etō, 1993: 148). According to Etō, the subject matter is a 'matter of how...a person who has buried his own "father" both internally and externally [would] be able to survive' (Etō, 1993: 152). Etō justifies his answer to this matter, saying, 'It was also "father" that Tokiko sought...' However, from this point onwards, the subject matter of *Seijuku to sōshitsu* begins to become oddly twisted. Etō lived in America for two years from 1962. The 'shadow of "America",' as named by Etō himself (Etō, 1993: 156), seems to remain behind his view.

This 'shadow of "America"' is commonly seen in postwar Japanese (male) intellectuals who experienced North America. It should not be regarded as a mere complex towards the winner. They discovered a 'father culture' in America and seem to be inclined to jump to the conclusion that they lost the war because they lacked this 'father.' With regard to Shunsuke, the patriarch of the Miwas, Etō points out his 'lack of ability to govern' as 'father' and asserts that what he 'should do' is to 'become "father"' – as if to say that everything will be all right if only Shunsuke becomes 'father.' However, was it really 'father' that Tokiko sought?

Half a century after Sōseki, the 'Third Generation of New Talent,' including Nobuo Kojima, lacked the 'sensibility to envision transcendental "Heaven" behind "father,"' in contrast to their sensitivity towards "mother"' (Etō, 1993: 152). Is this because the Confucian culture of the 'ruler' was replaced by the culture of ignorant agricultural people?

> The culture represented by Shunsuke and Tokiko is by far a lower social class than that represented by the young couple, Tsuda and his wife Onobu [of Sōseki's *Meian* (Light and darkness)]. The former culture is associated with a world where couples who often quarrel very noisily like residents in backstreet tenement houses might be planning to move to a house with Californian-style air conditioning (Etō, 1993: 73).

If you take the position of the dying 'ruler' who would lament the production of these 'upstarts' by 'modernization' as an 'increase of ignorant people,' you will see the creation of the 'conservatism' of Susumu Nishibe, a 'wannabe' Huizinga. This former young socialist, who had been enthusiastic for postwar democracy and reform, was another man 'converted' as a result of experiencing North America. A prodigy in modern economics, Nishibe had produced a brilliant work titled *Soshio ekonomikkusu* (Socioeconomics) (Nishibe, 1975) before he left Japan. He stayed in Western countries for two years, from 1976 to 1978. Based on his two-year experience, Nishibe wrote *Shinkirō no naka e* (Into a mirage) (Nishibe, 1979), a lyrical essay on his stay in these countries, the US and the UK. Subsequently, he emerged as an obstinate, cynical and conservative critic.

There are odd similarities between Nishibe's conversion and that of Etō. Similarly to Nishibe, Etō spent two years in North America, followed by the production of *Seijuku to sōshitsu*, which was produced very hurriedly as though he thought he had made a new discovery of the lack of father in Japanese culture. Subsequently, he produced a collection of gems of essays titled *Yoru no kōcha* (Tea in the evening) (Etō, 1972). After a break from the series of essays, Etō set out on a journey to trace his own roots in *Ichizoku saikai* (Family reunion) (Etō, 1973). In a word, he followed a path to the ruler.

Recovery of the 'ruler'

At this point, the subject matter that Etō had pursued consistently since *Natsume Sōseki* emerges. It is the familiar question of intellectuals that has repeatedly been asked since the Meiji era: 'How can Japan recover itself, after being completely uprooted by "modernity"?' In *Natsume Sōseki* Etō laments the loss of 'Heaven.' Masakazu Yamazaki, a contemporary of Etō, discusses the 'irritated patriarch' by finding a model in Ōgai Mori (Yamazaki, M., 1972). These two critics regard the struggle of Japanese intellectuals since the Meiji era as a history of the attempt and failure to become 'patriarch.'

Be it ruler or patriarch, why do male intellectuals always think that they can restore themselves by hastily becoming 'father?' I would dare to emphasize the term 'male intellectuals.' When man tries to become 'father' hastily, where is woman? Would Tokiko's problem be solved if only 'incompetent son' becomes 'reliable father?' When man seeks to become the ruler, should woman trust man and happily become the 'ruled?' This is similar to Freud's 'treatment' for 'hysterical women.' It would never be regarded as a solution by Etō, who so accurately discerned the mechanism by which modernity makes woman hate herself. The way the problem is posed by replacing the 'disintegration of motherhood' with the 'lack of father' seems to involve inversion or, alternatively, tricky evasion, of some kind of problem.

There is a common misunderstanding that when man became the ruler, woman also wanted to be the ruler, and this is one of the struggles of feminism. If this is true, that would mean that feminism has fallen into the trap set by modernity from the beginning. By definition, it is impossible that everybody becomes the ruler: if everybody becomes the ruler there will be no one left to be ruled. Although man might seek to become the ruler, woman no longer wants a ruler to rule her. When man becomes the ruler, he will look back and find no one to rule. This is the funny end of the fate of those men who want to become 'father' hastily. 'I don't think anyone asked you to be a "father",' Tokiko would say if she lived in the 1990s. At this point, man's tragic preparedness to take on the 'burden of the ruler' declines to a self-righteous comedy.

Nishibe's conservatism is full of irony because he is aware of the sarcasm that surrounds man who plays the role of father as he pleases, although he is aware that no one asked him to do so.

By taking Etō as an example, Norihiro Katō described the way in which those Japanese male intellectuals who, after undergoing a baptism of modernism, converted to conservatism, with their experience in North America as a turning point. He did this in his work *Amerika no kage* (The shadow of America) (Katō, 1985), which has a title borrowed from Etō's words. Born in postwar Japan, Katō is another man who has been to North America. But he is one of the few exceptions, including Shunsuke Trusumi, who did not convert to conservatism, unlike the case with many other intellectuals. For Katō, Etō's 'apostasy' must have been a matter of serious concern, which he could not treat as somebody else's problem in order to learn how to escape from this trap. Katō (1985) comments as follows:

> If, on one hand, he [i.e. Etō] had a firm belief in Japanese nature, or something that might be called a source of nationalism, then he could have come out as a modernist who advocated the 'protection of parliamentary democracy.' On the other hand, if he had believed in Japan's 'modernity' in its stability, then he would have been able to continue to write *Ichizoku saikai* and to be known as a conservative who deeply lamented what was being lost.

In reality, Etō became neither. In any case, becoming a conservative would have meant either isolating himself from the times in the ghetto of his own sense of beauty as was the case of Masakazu Yamataki, or, as was the case with Nishibe, living with an anachronistic paradox. Etō followed neither path, owing to his sensitivity to the times. After the publication of *Seijuku to sōshitsu*, Etō faithfully followed the confusion of the times. Yasuo Tanaka and Eimi Yamada, whom he valued as a writer, represent the sons and daughters of Shunsuke and Tokiko. These 'incompetent sons' no longer have the faintest intention to become 'father' but are being led by the nose by these 'irritating daughters,' who do not even try to hide their bad moods but easily leave their Japanese men. How would Etō view Japan in and after the 1970s, when the issue of maturity has vanished for both men and women?

Revisiting the 'disintegration of motherhood'

The 'disintegration of motherhood' as exposed by Etō still remains today, unreplaced by such dummy issues as the 'lack of father.' The absence of transcendental ethics did not result from the replacement of the 'paternal principle' with the 'maternal principle;' the latter principle does include a moment for transcendence. While Freud proposed the Oedipus complex, Japanese psychoanalysts who studied under Freud proposed, before the war, the Ajase complex, which is a story of 'suffering mother' instead of 'punishing father.' In contrast to the West-centric opinion on Japanese culture that a Japanese person grows up in a maternal society with his superego being hindered from forming, these Japanese psychoanalysts argued that transcendental norms can be formed by the existence of the 'suffering mother' who punishes herself for the failures of her own children. However, an even more frightening declaration was made by Tadao Satō, who discussed changes in women during the 1960s in his work *Katei no yomigaeri no tameni – Hōmu dorama ron* (For the re-birth of the home: Theorizing soap operas) (Satō, 1978). Satō's declaration was that the 'disintegration of motherhood' means the disintegration of this 'suffering mother.'

The expressions used by Etō, such as 'female self-hatred planted by modernity' and 'self-punishment,' suit the image of masochistic, self-punishing 'suffering mother.' However, what is in Tokiko's mind is a more direct desire. The way this desire made 'woman' overflow out of home in the 1970s is depicted in *Kishibe no arubamu* (The album on the shore) by Taichi Yamada (Yamada, 1977). When women no longer accept being tormented but begin to pursue their own desire shamelessly, modernity starts to disintegrate from the inside, easily and quietly like sand. When modernity no longer represents a goal to be achieved or suppression to be overcome, the effort of men to become the ruler will be something like an absurd one-man on-stage performance without an audience.

By referring to Junzō Shōno's 'Koyōte no uta (Song of the coyotes)' in his book *Yūbe no kumo* (Evening clouds) (Shōno, 1965), Etō points out that the loss of the sense of reality in the protagonist, who takes on the 'unhappiness of the ruler,' is associated with the destruction of nature as seen in the description, 'the hill on which his house stands is being cut away to construct a housing complex' (Etō, 1973). In his *Amerika no kage*, Norihiro Katō refers to *Namiutsu tochi* (The undulating earth) by Taeko Tomioka (Tomioka, 1983) out of context. Tomioka's novel begins in the middle of hilly land that is being cut away, again for the construction of a housing complex. For Katō, it was reasonable to discuss this novel in *Amerika no kage* because its subject matter symbolizes the 'disintegration of motherhood' and, moreover, the 'destruction of nature' assisted by women in person. As Katō says, when nature outside woman disintegrates, that inside her also has disintegrated. And, needless to say, nature in man, who encouraged and promoted the destruction, had broken down a long time ago. Etō's *Seijuku to sōshitsu* posed a painful question to me because he described woman not as a mere passive victim of this process but as an accomplice of man in the process.

The 'disintegration of motherhood' is an irreversible process of the history of civilization. 'Recovery of father' will not stop the 'disintegration of motherhood.' Wanted by no one, 'recovery of father' would only end up being a show of courage or an obvious, self-righteous ruse. Indeed, sons in the 1990s no longer have the faintest intention to become 'father,' whereas daughters have already killed 'suffering mother' by their own hand. Modernity, which attempted to confine women to neurosis, was naturally greeted by feminism with curses. However, according to *Danjoron* on gender by Kōichi Yamazaki (Yamazaki, K., 1993), women in the age of post-feminism:

> dare not take on the leading role in the sexual relationship between man and woman, despite the fact that women are ready to be a sexual subject equipped with the intention and ability. This is because they know very well that under the present circumstances, they will forever and ever be exploited by men who have given up being a sexual subject.

In this society, the issue of maturity that has been pursued since Sōseki seems to have vanished.

Would Etō say, with a bitter sense of disillusionment, that this was the consequence that both man and woman wanted from modernity – that Japanese people just got what they wanted?

Beyond 'modern family'

In the 1980s stories of disintegrated families began to appear in a number of works in comics and children's literature. As described by Shigesato Itoi in *Kazoku kaisan* (Family dissolution) (Itoi, 1986), family became an unstable entity that can be both formed and dissolved. No one feels this fragility of family more seriously than children who cannot live without a family. In Taku Tsumugi's comic work *Hotto rōdo* (Hot road) (Tsumugi, 1986–87), a sensitive girl whose boyfriend is a member of a motorcycle gang makes a request to her divorced mother, who belongs to the baby-boomer generation and whose only concern is her own love affairs: the girl says, 'Why don't you behave a bit more like a mother?' Divorces and broken families are also commonplace in children's literature. In *Ohikkoshi* (House-moving) by Tanaka Hiko (Hiko, 1990), the divorced husband and wife are both too busy with their own lives. In *Karendā* (Calendar) (Hiko, 1992), the girl protagonist has lost her parents and lives with an extended family consisting of her grandparents and a couple of lodgers who are accidentally found and brought home by her and thus are not her blood kin. With the fall of the modern family, the 'loss of father' and the 'disintegration of motherhood' are becoming common. If, as Hegel says, family is the basis of human ethics, it seems impossible to find the source of ethics in the modern family that has become so fragile. What, though, if Freud's theory, which finds the source of personality and ethics in family, was itself a product of 'modern family?'

The time when the 'world' was able to provide the basis of ethics is over, and 'family' has supposedly replaced the world to provide this basis. The life of this 'family myth' seems nearly to have expired, so are we able to work out another myth? Or, alternatively, will we become subject anomie, only to feel the approach of fanaticism and fundamentalism that might arise on the rebound from anomie?

9 Wives at 'Midlife Crisis' Stage

The title of Shigeo Saitō's work *Tsumatachi no shishūki* (Housewives' midlife autumnal period) (Saitō, 1982) coined an epoch-making term that characterizes the changes in Japanese family and woman during the 1980s, as was the case with Iku Hayashi's *Kateinai rikon* (in-house divorce) (Hayashi, 1985). With no increase in the divorce rate or the birth rate of illegitimate children, Japanese family used to boast outstanding stability as a system – before it began to collapse from the inside. The titles of the above two works expressed this collapse of Japanese family with such sharpness that they required no explanation.

'Tsumatachi no shishūki' was also the title of Part One of a series of articles titled *Nihon no kōfuku* (Japan's happiness), which was distributed as a long-term series by Kyodo News to various newspapers in 1982. What made Saitō's work an epoch-making event in Japanese journalism was the fact that his project caused the everyday lives of ordinary women to be treated as events worthy of being reported in the newspapers. This cannot be emphasized enough.

The first 'event' was that *women's* news items were published in city news pages of the newspapers. At that time, Saitō was a reporter of the city department. In conjunction with his colleagues, Saitō planned to report the '"secret of the strength" of corporate Japan' in (according to his words) the form 'not of financial articles for financial pages written by financial reporters but of financial articles for city news pages written by city news reporters' (Saitō, 1993). It was an unintended result that the series of articles started with 'Housewives' midlife autumnal period.' Let me quote his account:

> As we conducted more and more interviews, the initial plan gradually changed and the articles became less and less financial, pushing 'image of corporate Japan' far away...As is always the case with interviews, after many interviews we discovered a world that had been unknown to us before. With a fresh surprise and curiosity, we

conducted more interviews, until we found ourselves having strayed into a totally unexpected place. This is a more accurate explanation of the process (Saitō, 1984a: 61).

Until then, newspapers published articles on women generally in home life pages. As the kitchen was the place for women at home, so, in a newspaper, home life pages were the 'ghetto' for women. These pages were usually skipped by male readers. The very fact that articles on women moved from home life pages to city new pages was epoch-making in itself.

The 24 September issue of *Asahi Shimbun* ran a front-page story titled 'Divorce affirmed by one out of three women: A 40% increase in five years' (issued by the Osaka head office). The newspaper immediately faced criticism for confusing a minor event with major ones, with Den Kawakatsu, a contributor for article reviews, saying, 'I doubt Asahi's discernment.' This kind of social convention had to be fought off before the 'everyday lives of women and children' were recognized as events worthy of being reported. Saitō confesses that the significance of women's lives was a 'discovery' to himself, as well:

> I had never even imaged that the way women lived or were might affect the way men lived, the way businesses were or the way the entire society was as significantly as an international political event. Put simply, I had neglected 'women's issues' as their own problems (Saitō, 1984a: 61–2).

Second, in the 'event' that a woman did appear in a city news page, it was always because she had made some trouble that disturbed the public. Women who were interviewed by Saitō were neither celebrities nor criminals. Rather, these women apparently lived normal, or better than normal, happy lives. Saitō wrote stories about the moral decay and sense of helplessness in the minds of these apparently 'ordinary women.'

Under the social convention that a 'woman's trouble' meant 'trouble caused by the woman' (i.e. the woman was the troublemaker), if a woman was reported in an article, the focus tended to be on the 'problematic woman' instead of the 'woman's problem.' Women who got married, had children and became housewives were never regarded as problematic.

In order for ordinary women to become worthy of being reported, it was necessary to change the paradigm from 'women's problems' to 'women's studies.' The first book to appear in Japan with the words 'women's studies' in its title was *Joseigaku kotohajime* (An introduction to women's studies) by Hiroko Hara and Sumiko Iwao published in 1977 (Hara and Iwao, 1977). When women's studies emerged, some were suspicious of this new field of study because there had already been 'study of women's problems' as a discipline to study women. However, the subjects of 'study of women's problems' were, as the words suggest, 'problematic women,' such as former prostitutes, single mothers or working mothers, who were regarded as having problems because they had deviated, in some way, from the norms for the lives of ordinary women. In this sense, 'study of women's problems' was a sub-discipline of social pathology. 'Ordinary women' were rarely discussed in 'study of women's problems.'

In *Joseigaku kotohajime*, Hiroko Hara wrote 'Shufu kenkyū no susume (An invitation to housewives' studies).' The shift of viewpoint from 'problematic women' to 'ordinary women' and the change of the issue from questioning women to questioning the society that forces women to be 'ordinary' were not achieved until the emergence of women's studies. In response to Hara's proposal, works were produced in rapid succession in the field of women's studies, including Yoriko Meguro's *Shufu burūsu* (Housewife blues) (Meguro, 1980) and Masako Amano's *Daisanki no josei* (Women in the third stage, post-nurturing stage) (Amano, 1979). In 1982 I published *Shufu ronsō wo yomu* (Reviewing the housewife debate) (Ueno [ed.], 1982), which traced the postwar history of the process through which housewives were recognized as an issue. As the start of my career as a researcher in women's studies, this work was meant to respond to the problem posed by Hara. Saitō's work took the same line as this new trend. Moreover, he arrived at this discovery by feeling his way, relying only on his intuition as a journalist.

It was, indeed, novel that housewives were regarded as the subject of any research. In my work I compared housewives to a 'dark continent,' meaning a huge but invisible being. Housewives not only failed to be recognized as an issue by being overlooked as ordinary women, but once they were in a domestic life, they never appeared in any official statistics. In the case of employed women, their health status can be found through data from annual medical checkups conducted at their workplaces. In contrast, no statistical data were available on housewives, regardless of whether they might have suffered excessive fatigue or what kinds of illnesses they might have had.

Third, Saitō's work caused the everyday lives of ordinary women, such as their relationships with their husbands and children, to be treated as events worthy of being reported. In order for women and everyday life (which belong to the realm of private affairs) to be regarded as events worthy of being reported, the relevant paradigm shift had to take place accordingly. Private affairs tend to be particularly neglected in newspapers, which must give priority to public affairs. Through his research into corporate Japan, Saitō unexpectedly encountered *woman* behind his subject matter. As a matter of fact, when *woman* is recognized as an issue, it is often the case that this recognition results from research into some other matter that has been recognized as an issue in the realm of public affairs. Yasuko Minoura's excellent work *Kodomo no ibunka taiken* (Cross-cultural experiences of children) (Minoura, 1984) has one chapter in which mothers of the children are mentioned. When this book was published, the issue of education of Japanese school children who have returned from abroad had already received considerable media attention. Minoura, a researcher in education whose research topic was the adaptation of Japanese children residing in America to the local culture, found, behind these children, unusual circumstances surrounding their mothers, who were forced to stand alone as the wives of expatriate employees. In addition, these wives were feeling increasingly helpless in the directly imported Japanese-style marital relationship, where the husband works long hours and does not care about family. Minoura warned that before discussing children's maladaptation to a foreign culture, maladaptation of their mothers should be recognized as a serious problem. While husbands are cared for by their employers, no one cares about their wives. In later years businesses began to give consideration to the adaptation to the local culture of family members of employees, but only so that employees could work 'free from family cares.' However, what is made clear by Minoura's work and by relevant works including Hisako Cunningham's *Kaigai shijo kyōiku jijō* (Education of expatriate children) (Cunningham, 1988) is that children's adaptation to a foreign culture is deeply influenced by their parents' marital relationship, and that at the critical time when a couple lives abroad, existing problems in their marital relationship emerge and are expanded.

Recent research in social history has paid increasing attention to the history of the everyday lives of ordinary people based on criticism of the existing focus on the history of public political affairs or public incidents. History is not changed by specifically dated incidents. It is changed through slow but steady changes in the lifestyle and custom of nameless people at the grassroots level. At the same time, family history research has found that the separation of society into the public sphere and the private sphere was itself a product of modernity, and that the formation of the public sphere depends strongly on the private sphere. Saitō's work also independently arrived at this new discovery made by family history research.

Fourth, we must appreciate the fact that Saitō attempted to take up the issue of sex in marital relationships. In family research, the issue of sex was taboo for a long time. Saitō comments as follows:

> since the main topic is the husband and wife relationship, we cannot do without mentioning the issue of sex. For instance, whether or not sex is involved in a wife's dissatisfaction with or negative feeling towards her husband, or what place is given to sex by husband and wife between them – matters such as these must represent some of the important factors in discussing marital relationship (Saitō, 1984b: 25).

Researchers had long neglected this simple fact. With the increase of attention to private life in social history, research into the realm of sex finally came to be regarded as a proper subject of research. Along with the 'realm of women and children,' the 'realm of sex' had not only been disregarded as the most private and trivial matter but had been given a low priority in research. In order for sex to be regarded as an important subject of research, it had to be acknowledged that sex is at the core of male–female relationships and that sexual relationships are a product of society and culture. Publishing articles on sex in city news pages of a newspaper, instead of in sensational weekly tabloid journalism, was itself a risky attempt. In addition, Saitō had to draw out personal opinions from interviewees who were unwilling to speak on the matter. Considering that Saitō is a man and his interviewees were women, his behind-the-scenes efforts to come so close to his subjects should be recognized. It was generally considered indiscreet for a woman to mention anything about sex. It was only after the publication of *MOA ripōto* (The MORE report) (MORE Henshūbu [ed.], 1983), which is a Japanese version of the Hite Report published under the influence of women's liberation, that Japanese women began to talk about their own sex in their own words.

The fact that many of the wives interviewed by Saitō were forced to have sex with their husbands in a manner that might almost constitute 'domestic rape' is in sharp contrast to the fact that the wives in Iku Hayashi's *Kateinai rikon* almost unanimously say that they can live under the same roof with husbands they no longer love only because they have no sex with their husbands. 'I would have left him earlier if I had to have sex with him,' says one of the wives in *Kateinai rikon*. What emerges here is a tacitly accepted – never an openly accepted – lack of communication in the sexual relationships between these husbands and wives, where sex is merely compulsion of men's egoism on women. The wives in *Kateinai rikon* can maintain their empty relationships with their husbands only because they have no sexual relationships with them. Behind this phenomenon are the bleak realities of married women's sex lives as revealed in *Sei – tsumatachi no messēji* (Sex: Messages from wives) (Gurūpu Waifu, 1984), a report produced by the editorial office of *Waifu* (Wife), a housewives' magazine relying on contributions from readers. Japanese husbands and wives do not kiss or hold hands with each other and rarely have any physical contact with each other, but they do have intercourse.

Saitō's work treated the everyday lives of ordinary women, including their sexual lives, as events worthy of being reported in city news pages of newspapers. In doing so, his work made it clear that this subject matter was inseparably associated with a huge pathological phenomenon in Japanese society. In this regard, his work is of great significance. A mere journalist, Saitō arrived at this discovery on his own. His discovery, however, unexpectedly coincided with an upheaval in the world of intellect of the same period.

'Let them talk'

When interviewing his subjects, Saitō 'let them talk' from first to last. Most journalists translated their subjects' words into their own words, a practice that had mistakenly been regarded as objective. Saitō did not employ this method: 'In *Nihon no kōfuku*...a prerequisite for writing an article was to collect reports of lived experience directly from the persons involved in the event' (Saito, 1984b: 24).

Is this a *subjective* method? When a reality that has been believed to be *objective* is shaken and gives way to a strange reality that we have never seen before, we must have a new method and new words to describe the new reality. Where can we find the words to describe it? We have simply to go for the new reality. We can let the reality talk about itself. When the person facing a new reality attempts to describe the reality, her words will provide us with the new words we need to describe the new reality. All we need to do is to listen to her. The moment we arbitrarily interpret her words into an objective observation, the reality will be distorted. *Objectivity* is only another name for old stories describing old realities.

The method employed by Saitō was appropriate for detecting signs of a new reality at a time of paradigm shift in social science. A paradigm shift means a change in the way of understanding reality. Or, more precisely, it indicates that an unknown reality is emerging. The method is familiar to anthropologists, who are field workers. An anthropologist stands face to face with an unknown world and tries to draw out words from the native there. It is no surprise that at a time of paradigm shift sociology developed an ethnomethodology under the influence of the anthropological methodology.

Another characteristic of Saitō's method is that it is a thorough case study. The method is incompatible with a large-scale survey. Though it might look objective, a quantitative survey is actually a mere procedure to confine realities to a ready-made plot. On the other hand, qualitative research always faces a question of representativeness of cases. While Saitō's subjects all fall within the boundaries of ordinary women, each has something that makes her slightly out of the ordinary, such as alcoholism or divorce. But where in the world does a stereotype of 'ordinary woman' exist? Everyone faces her own reality that is slightly out of the ordinary. Conversely, a statistical average cannot find its match in reality. By thoroughly sticking to each case, Saitō actually uncovered a more universal image of society. This image successfully produced an expression suitable for a turning point in history by identifying an intersection between the personal history of the subjects and the social history of their time.

Around the same time as Saitō's work, new journalism made a sudden rise. New journalism made an issue of the boundary between fiction and nonfiction and questioned the definitions of objectivity and subjectivity. Saitō neither emphasized his personal opinion, as Kōtarō Sawaki did, nor did he make a fiction, as Katsutoshi Yamashita did. What Saitō did was to reconstruct realities strictly in accordance with 'their realities' as told by themselves. It is the most reliable, but painstaking, front-door strategy. Thus he created one distinct style of nonfiction.

The only potential drawback in Saitō's method is that it goes against the fact that there are always two parties involved in the realities of such marital relationships as described in *Tsumatachi no shishūki*. As is the case with Iku Hayashi's *Kateinai rikon*, listening to only one of the two parties involved is a one-sided way of reporting male–female relationships. By discussing sex, women's studies revealed a tremendous gap between man and woman in what sex – the most intimate of all activities – means to them in reality. The magnitude of the difference can be inferred from the difference between a rapist and a rape victim in what rape means to them in reality. When sex between husband and wife is close to rape, the two live different realities in the same bed. It is not a matter of which is right. This unclosable gap between husband and wife in the way they live a reality – in fact, they do not even share 'one reality' – speaks to us, more eloquently than anything else, of the horror of the realities. Can't we adopt a method like that used in Ryūnosuke Akutagawa's *Rashōmon* (which was followed by a film with the same title by a renowned director, Akira Kurosawa) and in Oscar Lewis's *The children of Sanchez* (Lewis, 1986)? It is a method that shows multiple realities just as they are – those pluralistic realities that remain inconsistent with each other, never to become consistent or reconciled. When the parties who seemingly shared a reality discovered that they were actually living different realities, both sexual love and the family myth began to disintegrate. What we need is a method to describe multiple realities.

Transformation of womanhood and family

What changes of the times did Saitō's work focus on?

The subject dealt with by Saitō was the wives of corporate employees. Not only that, their husbands worked for fairly large companies and held high posts and had high incomes. Thus, these wives belonged to a relatively wealthy class. Having gained a 'woman's happiness,' which consists of marriage and childbirth, to an outside observer they seemed to live in perfect comfort. Let us look back to the historical background of how 'housewives' midlife crisis' emerged as the price for material affluence.

The period of the economic growth during the 1960s was a historical turning point by which corporate employees came to account for a majority of Japanese workers. At the beginning of the 1960s the proportion of employees exceeded that of self-employed workers and their family workers. Until around 1950 Japan was an agrarian society in which peasant households accounted for nearly 40% of all households. The fact that men became corporate employees meant that women became housewives of employed husbands without jobs. In fact, the proportion of labor force participation of married women decreased consistently throughout the 1960s. Since the Meiji era, ordinary people's 'success' had always meant 'rising' from farmers' sons to employees to their wives, respectively. During the period of the economic growth, these sons and daughters fulfilled their dream of rising up the social ladder. Japan entered a period when 80% of people considered themselves as middle class.

From the end of the 1960s, however, the price for the economic growth emerged in the form of various counter culture movements. Among them, the women's liberation movement in 1970 represented an eruption of women's issues.

This movement, whose Japanese female supporters called themselves *ūmanribu* (an abbreviation of 'women's liberationist') in *katakana*, encountered many misunderstandings. Among them was an attack by the conservatives, who maintained that women's liberation was a mere imported thought representing an influence from American women. In 1963 Betty Friedan, the 'mother of women's liberation' in America and the first representative of the National Organization of Women, published *The feminine mystique* (Friedan, 1963; translated into Japanese as *Atarashii onna no sōzō* in 1977), now a classic of women's liberation. In this work, Friedan described how stifling the 'happiness' of suburban, middle-class wives was, and referred to the problem facing ordinary women as the 'unnamed problem.' While the women's liberation movement in Japan was supported mainly by young women in their twenties, older, married women gave them silent support. The Japanese women's liberation movement repeatedly questioned the pathology of the 'housewifely situation,' which was regarded as 'ordinary happiness' of 'ordinary women,' and, at the same time, questioned Japanese husbands who blithely and shamelessly made their wives unpaid workers called housewives. By the end of the 1960s, the unnamed problem described by Friedan in 1963 had already been shared commonly by Japanese women. This was a sufficient foundation for Japanese society to see the birth of the Japanese women's liberation movement in the 1970s.

Filicidal mother was a phenomenon that most clearly represented the stifling housewifely situation charged by women's liberationists of the time. There was a rash of cases where babies were abandoned in coin lockers, for which women were accused by the media of a 'loss of maternity.' Under the circumstances, Mitsu Tanaka, a spokesperson for women's liberationists, bravely announced that these 'filicidal mothers represent myself.' In the stifling housewifely situation, a housewife was forced to be isolated from society. The heavy burden of child rearing fell on a helpless, inexperienced woman. Moreover, her husband, absorbed in his work, paid no attention to her. These were the realities of a 'woman's happiness' that were awaiting those women who married and had children. Rather than blaming women who killed their children, women's liberationists accused society of driving them to kill their children, saying that anyone could become a filicidal mother under these horrible circumstances. The tragedy of filicide existed cheek by jowl with a 'housewife's happiness.'

The 'housewives' midlife crisis' dealt with by Saitō in the 1980s suggests what might happen to these filicidal mothers in ten or twenty years' time. While housewives remain in the same old stifling situation, they have become increasingly estranged from their husbands. Under the circumstances, their children, on whom these housewives' identities have been based, begin to become independent. Having lost sight of their targets, they chance to look at their husbands and find that they are left with their bleak relationships with these husbands. This has been termed *empty nest syndrome* by American family sociologists. In psychology, the same phenomenon is also called *burnout syndrome* or *housewife syndrome*. The term *housewife syndrome* really hits the mark. In this society, being a housewife is an 'illness' in itself. Around the end of the 1970s, alcohol-dependent housewives known as 'kitchen drinkers' began to be reported often as a problem. This problem was joined by a group of other problems, including depression and neurosis, that could not be dismissed only as menopausal symptoms. When you come to think of it, in the lifecycle where an average woman gets married at the age of twenty-five, has two children, and enrolls her last child in school before she is thirty-five, she has to face 'too early retirement.' It is too young an age to bury oneself alive. What the 'burnout' wives communicated through various mental and physical symptoms was simply that they did not want to go on and live the life of the dead.

Considering that the decade of the 1970s was called the 'women's era' and saw a greatly increased presence of women in the workplace, the existence of 'housewives in midlife crisis' looks odd. Do these wives represent women who missed out on the wave of the increase of working women and were left in the housewifely situation?

This paradox can be solved easily if we look at the real state of 'women's participation in the workplace.' While touted as 'radical women,' the increase of career women has been negligible throughout the past two decades. In reality, 'increased women's participation in the workplace' was nothing but mobilizing women as disposable labor in the field of high-technology and the service sector, which emerged anew as a result of changes in the industrial structure. When facing employed married women, housewives without a job were ashamed of themselves as if the had been incompetent. However, in the 1980s it was undeniably found that women who chose to work away from home did so because they had to, while those who chose not to do so did not have to.

In the era of 'increasing women's participation in the workplace,' wives who remain housewives when their children no longer keep them busy belong to a wealthy class. By focusing on the wives of employees of large companies, Saitō revealed a deep-rooted pathology facing these key workers who both support and enjoy the affluence of Japan. The pathology consisted of materialism that values appearance and honor; mammonism that tries to buy everything with money; consumerism that tries to satisfy all desires by spending money; and a disintegration of family that took place little by little under the influence of the above three factors. The price for affluence was charged not only on women. Considering that children are the most vulnerable of family members, it is no wonder that the same period saw the emergence of juvenile domestic violence and school-refusing children. Youngsters who survived adolescence and came to have values similar to those of their parents were called *shinjinrui* (the new breed) and were soon to be swallowed up by the waves of consumer society. This was how patients with 'brand disease,' as described in *Yutakasa no seishin byōri* (Psychopathology of affluence) by the psychiatrist Ken Ōhira (Ōhira, 1990), emerged. At this point, these people are only one step away from becoming 'Mr M.,' who cannot establish personal relationships with live others. ('M' is the initial of the last name of Tsutomu Miyazaki, the suspect in the 1988 serial girl abduction and murder case; 'Mr M.' became a synonym for young *otaku* [a Japanese slang word meaning geek or freak in relation to comics and video games].) Shigeo Saitō tirelessly continued his research into new pathologies of the times and produced another work titled *Hōshoku kyūmin* (The needy people who have too much) (Saitō, 1991). (For more details, please refer to this book.)

When I read Saitō's *Tsumatachi no shishūki*, there was just one point where I felt something was wrong. Housewife syndrome was first discovered at that time and received public attention due its pathology, which in some cases was so severe that the patients' families broke down. This situation was taken by the public as omnipresent, which was reflected in the fact that the term *shishūki* immediately became a vogue word. It was anticipated that 'housewives in midlife crisis' would continue to increase rapidly in number. However, this did not turn out to be the case.

While being carried away by the impact and reality of *Tsumatachi no shishūki*, I also felt intuitively that this phenomenon might not last a long time. There were grounds for my feeling. In 1983 the proportion of working married women exceeded 50% of all married women, making full-time housewives a minority. At the end of the 1980s, the proportion of two-income households exceeded 60% of all workers' households. These data showed a continued reduction in the number of men who had enough income of their own to support full-time housewives. As described above, full-time housewives belong to the privileged classes in which wives do not have to work away from the home. The full-time housewife as a social category was on the decrease on a long-term basis.

This was not all. There was another distinct factor that provided a basis for my feeling that 'housewives' midlife crisis' might be a temporary phenomenon. The wives interviewed by Saitō, who were in their forties to fifties at that time, married during the economic growth period. Together with their husbands, they belong to the generation that supported Japan's rapid economic growth under the slogan of 'catch up and overtake.' What I felt was that these wives were not only women but also Japanese people of that generation. In their seriousness and naive honesty, they shared the same values and the same way of life with their husbands, who worked selflessly for long hours. In other words, these wives represented the generation of Japanese women who were so serious that a loss of their goals might lead to their self-destruction.

In contrast, what I saw in the generation that followed were groups of women who were, unlike their immediate predecessors, neither serious nor naively honest. There have been few changes in the circumstances surrounding women, so what I found particularly suspicious was that despite the lack of improvement in the isolated situation in which wives were left to look after their children, reports of filicide cases ceased to be heard. What replaced these cases in media coverage were mothers who abandoned their children. The public was more forgiving than expected of these mothers. Some television idols, including Seiko Matsuda, kept working after childbirth, providing models that proved that 'neither marriage nor childbirth changes a woman.' This was the arrival of the era of *puttsun-mama* (wayward moms), who gave priority to their own convenience over child rearing.

If, despite the lack of substantial improvement in the circumstances surrounding women, filicide cases were no longer seen, then it must be because women had changed. What we saw was the emergence of a large number of women who were good at letting off steam – women who were unsteady but knew how to have fun and who, unlike Japanese people in the 1950s, did not regard playing as sinful. And the consumer society provided these women with limitless opportunities to let off steam.

In the latter half of the 1980s, *furin* (extramarital affair) became a vogue word. The same act was originally referred to as *kantsū* (adultery), followed by *furin*, which further changed in form from *kanji* to *katakana*, making the act look much less serious. Previously, *furin* partners were usually a married man and a single woman. Then, during this period, married women began to enter the *furin* market. An investigation conducted by *Waifu* revealed that one in six married women has had an extramarital affair; that they do not feel guilty about their affairs; and that, moreover, a wife's affair often does not constitute a good reason for the couple's divorce. Even a leading figure in sexology like Kiyoshi Ōshima says, 'Extramarital affairs are the secret of good marital relations.' While the divorce rate showed no noticeable increase, the disintegration of marriage and family proceeded gradually from the inside. This occurred through changes in women, who had very seriously shouldered the sole responsibility of maintaining the family.

'Housewives in midlife crisis' was a product of a turning point, born of an intersection between the era and the generation. History did not go in the direction where these women would emerge in large numbers.

Criticism of male-dominant, corporate-centred society

Saitō's original intention was to shed light, through women functioning as a photographic negative, on the pathology of the huge, male-dominant corporate society. Since then, Saitō has consistently used the same technique, which reveals facts about the majority from the viewpoint of the minority, or which reveals from severe pathology potential distortion of what is supposed to be 'normal.' 'Housewives in midlife crisis' were overly serious people who failed to take advantage of a historical turning point and, unable to deceive themselves, developed adjustment disorders.

As a sociologist keeping an eye on macro trends, I focus on another aspect of the times. What on earth is the majority doing – the fit people who managed to survive the same historical turning point by passing away the time each day without developing alcohol dependence or blaming themselves? Their being the 'fit' does not at all mean that they are 'normal.' Would the minority dealt with by Saitō show any problems facing the majority by dramatically magnifying those problems in their lives? However, what would be the way (if any) to describe potential decadence or abnormality in the fit, who are passing away the time each day? Saitō's work poses a new question to us.

Part V
The Paradox of Sexism

10 The Trap of Separate Surnames for Married Couples

Anthropology of separate surnames

There have been married couples with separate surnames since antiquity in Japan and many parts of the world, so it is rather odd to make an issue of the separate surname system now. The correct approach would be to reverse the angle of the inquiry and ask when married couples *stopped* using separate surnames in Japan.

The surname is a symbol to indicate the clan to which a husband and wife belong. It is logical that a husband and wife should use separate surnames in exogamous societies, since the same surname means endogamy, or consanguineous marriage. The use of separate surnames needs to be emphasized in such societies. The 'no marriage between persons having the same surname' rule in China and Korea represents the rule of clan exogamy. Under this rule, Mr Lee and Miss Lee are not permitted to marry: they are considered to have the same distant ancestor because of their surname, even if they are unrelated. Accordingly, couples are required to keep their respective surnames after marriage, as in the example of *Mao* Zedong and his wife, *Jiang* Qing.

In ancient Japan it is unlikely that a wife changed her surname to her husband's upon marriage. Moreover, it is doubtful that women had surnames at all. All that remains in historical records are such names as *Michitsuna-haha* (Michitsuna's mother) and *Michinaga-musume* (Michinaga's daughter), indicating the descent group to which they belong. In what Itsue Takamure called a matrilocal marriage (taking a son-in-law), the wife lived at her family home and used the surname of her own clan. Even during the periods of matrilocal marriages, powerful men such as emperors followed the patrilocal marriage system (taking a bride) and wives lived in their husbands' households. However, a wife would return to her parental home for such occasions as childbirth and generally maintained a very strong association with her descent group. She would keep the surname of her clan, as in the cases of *Fujiwara-musume* (daughter of the Fujiwara clan) and *Mononobe-musume* (daughter of the Mononobe clan).

A wife's surname is proof of her connection to her descent group. Japan has many commonalities with societies in the Oceanic region. In Polynesia women maintain their connections to their native clans through their relationships with their brothers, even after marrying into their husbands' clans. Since a bride-price is very high in this society, a wife would not move in to her husband's household even after childbirth until the price is paid in full in some cases. When the wife dies, it is her native clan that organizes her funeral, retrieves her body and buries it in the grave of her descent group. Because the husband and the wife belong to different clans, they are not buried in the same grave. A marriage is a long-term contract between the husband's kinship group and the wife's kinship group, and the contract ends upon the wife's death: the wife's clan never loses its rights and obligations to sisters who have married.

Where the wife maintains a strong tie with her parental home or descent group, she tends to have a high status in her marital household or in the husband's descent group. Her status is determined by the balance of power between her parental household and her matrimonial household. The wife often tries to exploit the power relations between her husband and brothers to further her own interests. In such circumstances the wife often runs back to her parental home when she has a problem, and the incidence of spousal violence against the wife (the husband battering his wife) is not often the case because of interventions from her own kin.

Now, the mystery of the transition to the system of husband and wife sharing the same surname can be solved easily: it severs the wife's tie with her parental household – this is the crux of the shared surname system.

There are two conditions for this:
1. A marriage is considered to be an irreversible transition of the wife's status, which occurs only once in her lifetime.
2. The husband chooses his wife from a kinship group whose status is lower than that of his own kinship group so that he is beyond the reach of its influence.

An old adage directs a man to 'choose your bride from the ashes in the kitchen hearth' – thus, hypergamy (marrying into a higher social group), or the Cinderella story, is born. The Cinderella complex entails two factors:
1. The woman breaks away from her descent group *completely*.
2. She assimilates into her husband's kinship group *completely*.

Even today, some women perceive marriage as a springboard to leave their own kinship groups. This is a reflection of a hypergamic attitude.

The husband establishes *complete* control over his wife (i.e. patriarchal system) in this paradigm of marriage. Interference by the wife's relatives must once have been a real nuisance to the husband. It appears that the 6,000-year history of the patriarchal system was dedicated to the efforts to stop matrilineal relatives from exerting influence. Parents tell a daughter the night before her wedding not to return home once she is married, no matter what happens. It is said that a dagger that the bride puts under her wedding kimono sash symbolizes a reminder that she is supposed to commit suicide by stabbing her throat if she has to leave her matrimonial home for any reason. In other words, once she is a married woman, she cannot return to her native home other than as a corpse. Further, in societies that value female virginity, a woman becomes a damaged article after the wedding night and this change is irreversible. All the discourses about marriage keep warning women that this transition is a once only, irreversible change. Since there is no such threatening discourse towards men, the relationship is clearly asymmetrical.

Thus, a husband is able to wield his power over his wife as he wishes. From enforcement of family tradition to infidelity, violence and desertion, he is 'entitled to do anything' to his wife with almost no regard for her personality in the relationship.

The mechanism of hypergamy

Once we realize that the shared surname system is inseparably bound to class society and the establishment of the patriarchal system within it, the psychology of women who willingly adopt their husband's surname seems nothing less than incomprehensible.

However, those who want to change their surnames also have a point or two to make. First, a marriage often means an *escape* from a detestable parental home. A desire to leave is reinforced by the Cinderella complex. Since the group into which a woman marries has a higher socioeconomic status than her own group under the rule of hypergamy, marriage is the chance of a lifetime for many daughters to escape their miserable circumstances.

Daughters are placed in the most vulnerable position in a family under 'father's authority' and are easily seduced by the idea of escaping and severing their ties with their parental family – until they realize that what is waiting for them is the 'husband's tyranny.'

In fact, I have heard many 'self-aware' women who willingly chose to change their surnames say, 'I wanted to change my surname because I didn't like my own family.' Since men do not see marriage as a chance to 'discard the family to which one was born,' this view of marriage is unique to women.

The shared surname system was established at the same time as hypergamy came into existence under the patriarchal system both in Japan and Europe, but aristocratic women who are proud of their own families often keep their maiden names (pre-marital surnames) as middle names after marriage, as in the case of Mary Wollstonecraft Shelley. Their children inherit their mother's middle name (namely, her maiden name) to indicate their origins both on the mother's side and the father's side. Consequently, descendants of distinguished families tend to have very long names, such as Harriet Beecham Stowe Winston Churchill, for example.

Women who are proud of their own families and do not wish to sever their ties do not give up their own family names. In fact, they retain the right of inheritance as a legitimate member of the family even after marriage, and it is passed on to their children. Women readily give up their own family names only when their families are so poor that they cannot offer anything or when they are deprived of their rights to inheritance and their families are of no benefit to them. And this mechanism as a whole creates the social environment in which women must rely on marriage to survive and in which marriage functions to force them to marry.

The patrilineal rule for a child's surname

From this angle, the mechanism that has created the environment in which 'women willingly give up their own surnames' must be patently clear. However, women who demand the right to have separate surnames for married couples today do not do so because they want to regain their ties with their own families – they are rebelling against the patriarchal view of marriage symbolized by the shared surname, and they do not wish to return to the ancient system of separate surnames tied to their clan of origin. Because one's surname always indicates the connection with one's descent group, parents can assert their authority over their daughters with unchanged surnames forever in societies where the parent–child relationship means rights and obligations such as property rights.

The separate surname system can also have oppressive effects under the patriarchal system. Some advocates of separate surnames think simplistically that the 'liberation of women is more advanced' in our Eastern Asian neighbors China and Korea, for example, where married couples maintain separate surnames. However, China and Korea are no less (and possibly more) patriarchal than Japan. In these societies, a woman who marries into a patriarchal group is saddled with a symbol of being an outsider to the group for life by being the only person in the group who has a different surname.

As long as a wife has a different surname in a patriarchal group, she carries the 'mark of another clan.' This is essentially the same for a nuclear family with only a couple and children. The surname of a child is a symbol indicating the kinship group to which he or she belongs, and affiliation of children has always been the cause of conflicting kinship structures. The advocates of separate surnames do not seem to be concerned about patrilinealism of a child's surname very much. I wonder if it is because they believe in biological bonds between mother and child and do not mind children having their father's surname to compensate for the shakiness of the bonds between father and child.

Rising number of families with separate surnames

There are signs that the number of separate-surname families is on the increase despite the continued prevalence of the patrilineal affiliation of children or, rather, because of it. This trend appears to come from the rising numbers of divorces and second and third marriages, not from some 'women seeking independence' who demand separate surnames for married couples. The increase in divorces is now unstoppable and single motherhood is no longer a barrier to remarriage. When a single mother remarries, she may adopt her new husband's surname but her children's surname does not change automatically. For her children to change their surname, they must make an adoption arrangement with their mother's new husband separately. Once the legal father–child relationship is established, it gives rise to rights and obligations, including the right to inheritance.

However, the parent–child relationship continues even after the divorce of parents. It is likely that more and more fathers in the future will refuse to give up their relationships with children who are taken by their estranged wives, including custody and access rights. On the other hand, there are new husbands who hesitate, or do not see the need, to adopt biologically unrelated children of their new wives because these children already have a father. When divorce rules become a little easier, divorce will no longer mean immediate deprivation of a biological father from his children.

Children may take their mother's maiden name upon divorce of their parents but their surname will be different from both parents' surnames if their mother remarries. If children retain their father's surname and their mother reverts to her maiden name and keeps it when she remarries, there will be three different surnames in one household. Belonging to a family will not mean the shared surname any more.

In societies such as the United States, where people divorce and remarry many times, it is common to find families with three or four different surnames in one household. Children from the first and second marriages have different surnames. If the mother remarries someone else and has more children, they will have different surnames.

This situation can be avoided if complete matrilinealism is adopted and all children from the same mother are given her surname. However, no one is demanding matrilineal affiliation of children – at least for children born in wedlock – even in the United States, which legally permits married couples to have separate surnames. Using a mother's surname in patrilineal society means carrying a stigma of being born out of wedlock. And, even if matrilinealism is adopted, the same problem will arise as an increasing number of fathers are given custody of their children.

If we try to maintain the 'shared surname for all family members' rule, children will be forced to change their surname every time their parents divorce and remarry. Because one's name forms part of one's identity, the only way to prevent such social confusion is to reject the preconceived idea that 'all family members share the same surname.' It is necessary to create an environment in which it is normal for a family to have more than one surname. In today's world, where marriage is no longer a once-in-a-lifetime, no-turning-back event, it is unrealistic to try to insist on one surname for one household.

What is the merit of legal marriage?

Is the call for the Civil Code reform for separate surnames for married couples meant to protect legal marriage and hence the family registration system?

Legal marriage creates rights and obligations between husband and wife. Between parents and children, however, rights and obligations exist even if parents are not legally married. Legal marriage therefore has no significance for protection of children's rights. Women insist on legal marriage when it protects their rights, or it benefits them in some ways. Under the current laws, legal marriage functions to benefit a wife if she has no financial resources (i.e. if she is a dependant).

If a wife has an income and does not qualify as a dependant, legal marriage has no benefit for her. In many jurisdictions outside Japan, adult men and women, except students and the disabled, do not qualify as dependants. Japanese laws protect the 'vested interests' of the status of a non-working wife and in turn encourage women to remain without jobs. If the tax deduction for a dependant spouse was totally abolished, what would happen to the percentage of full-time wives in Japan?

If legal marriage offers no benefit in terms of rights and obligations concerning income and property, its last merit would be to function as a proof of socially recognized husband–wife and parent–child relationships. However, why do people have to have their sexual relationships 'registered' or 'officially recognized?' And when discrimination between 'legitimate' and 'illegitimate' children disappears, legal marriage will become almost meaningless. The only thing left behind is the preconception that 'it would be hard on children if they didn't have the same surname.' It would be 'hard on children' because they would be 'picked on' if they didn't have the same surname. But what if this is simply a false belief? And does the problem lie on the side of society that picks on children just because they have different surnames? If these are the cases, reasons for *not allowing separate surnames* will mostly dissolve. The real problem is conformism of Japanese society, which anticipates the reaction of others and pre-emptively 'self-regulates.'

However, those who consider the recognized and registered 'family system' as the foundation of society and want to keep it that way will continue to distinguish marital sex and extramarital sex and to maintain discrimination between 'legitimate' and 'illegitimate' children.

The antagonist in the struggle for separate surnames for married couples is a persistent enemy called the patriarchal family system.

11 Old Age as Lived Experience

Cultural ideal and reality in senescence

When E. H. Erikson introduced the concept of *identity* into developmental psychology, the most serious *identity crises* in the developmental process were considered to lie mainly in adolescence (Erikson, [1963] 1973). Erikson began his career as a clinical researcher of adolescent psychology and used the keyword *identity* in his research. Initially, *developmental* tasks did not extend beyond adolescence for Erikson, and it was considered that the identity of an adult would generally stabilize after the crises of the 'storm and stress period' called adolescence.

Later, it was widely believed that the adult also had to encounter a series of developmental tasks throughout life. For example, marriage, childbirth, independence of children, and retirement are developmental tasks of life that may each demand reorganization of one's identity. At the time of identity reorganization, the existing identity loses its validity. If this task of reformation is accomplished well, it leads to *maturity*: if it fails, it leads to an identity crisis. Whether one succeeds or fails, the task of reorganizing one's identity is full of difficulties.

The view that all stages of life are part of an everlasting developmental process can be considered very American. This view of life is markedly different from, say, the view expressed in *The analects of Confucius*: 'at thirty, stood firm; at forty, freed from vacillation.' However, this statement from *The analects of Confucius* is the precept for life rather than the view of life – a type of cultural ideal of how life should be. Most people must feel that their *reality* in which they did not manage to stand firm at the age of thirty and were not freed from vacillation at forty is far from this *cultural ideal*.

There are two reasons why the view of adulthood as 'free from vacillation' gave way to the view of identity as constantly changing throughout one's life. One reason is that we now know more about the realities of adulthood psychology. The other reason is the failure of the cultural ideal about adulthood. The primary cause for this failure is longevity.

Around the time when Confucius wrote *The analects*, the average life span was probably shorter than fifty years. In Japan the average life span was forty-odd years for a very long time until it began to lengthen rapidly after the Second World War. As we can find in a song reportedly sang by Oda Nobunaga (a Medieval warrior) when facing death – 'man's life is only fifty years; compared with things under heaven, it is like a dream or illusion' – it is not hard to imagine that people commonly thought that 'man's life is only fifty years.' When Matsuo Bashō (a haiku poet in the Edo era) wrote at the opening of *Oku no hosomichi* – an account of his journey into the interior during which he was prepared to die – that he did not have many years left and this would be his last journey, he was only forty-five years old.

According to folk customs in various parts of Japan, the head of a family would retire at around the age of forty. The head of a family would hand over the headship to his successor when he turned forty and move into the world of public affairs, attending village meetings and parishioners' groups as the representative of his family, a move that represented the transition from the earthly affairs of carrying on the family business to the unearthly domain.

In this sense, the concept of 'freed from vacillation at forty' is the cultural ideal for senescence rather than that for adulthood. However, in today's world, where both adolescence and life span are prolonged, it is difficult to call the age of forty the entrance to senescence. The age of forty has a totally different meaning in the era of a fifty-year life span and an eighty-year life span.

Nevertheless, what if we regard 'freed from vacillation at forty' as the cultural ideal for senescence and convert it into the eighty-year life span? Is it possible to say 'freed from vacillation at sixty' or even at seventy? This cultural ideal literally indicates the *ideal* that there is an end point to growth and change at a certain stage of life and one *should* spend the rest of one's life peacefully after reaching this goal. This cultural ideal not only differs from psychological reality of senescence but also often suppresses the aged person's recognition of conflicts and difficulties that he or she faces in this reality and makes them invisible. What we need to do here is to perceive senescence as the time of identity reorganization, not as the period of psychological and social stability, and to adopt a dynamic approach to the reality of developmental tasks and difficulties during this period.

Identity crisis and its theoretical basis

Erikson's contribution to the field of adolescent psychology was truly great. He regarded adolescence as the period of identity crises that would emerge as a *gap* between *self identity* and *social identity*. Adolescence is a period of transition from *child identity* to *adult identity* for the individual. When the individual with 'child (self) identity' is required to have 'adult (social) identity,' a conflict arises between the two identities. Conversely, in some instances the individual is only given 'child (social) identity' when, in fact, he or she has 'adult (self) identity.'[1] According to Erikson's view, adolescence is the transition period when these two identities clash and adjust repeatedly to close this gap and finally reach the integration of 'adult self and social identity.'

All traditional societies distinguish between their *adult* and *child* constituent members.[2] Individuals are not usually given formal recognition as members of a group until they have undergone initiation (a coming-of-age ceremony), which is a rite of admission to the group. The rites in which one jumps over the boundary between the two categories are full of difficult tests in many societies. However, there is no *gap* between self identity and social identity before and after this jump. The child is a child and the adult is an adult; the individual must be either of them before and after initiation.

According to Erikson, this transition from child to adult is prolonged and established as one stage of life in modern society. This is the period of *adolescence*. Traditional societies had *child* and *adult* but no *adolescent*. *Adolescence* came into existence in the period of the modern era. This transition period can be considered as an awkward cat-and-mouse chase between self identity and social identity until the transition from 'child self and social identity' to 'adult self and social identity' is completed.

The reason for prolonged adolescence in modern society is the time gap between different aspects of *maturity*. Let us divide the maturity of an individual into four aspects: physiological maturity, mental maturity, social maturity and cultural maturity. In modern society, physiological maturity (age of first ejaculation and menstruation) tends to occur earlier due to better nutrition and a flood of sexual information, while social maturity (legal adult age and economic independence) and cultural maturity (marriage and childbirth) are occurring later than they used to in traditional society. Adolescence has come to last for over ten years because it starts earlier (at age twelve or thirteen) and ends later (between the ages of twenty-five and thirty). Erikson aptly named this unstable period when the individual is no longer a child but not yet an adult as a *moratorium* (probation period). Everyone goes through this period but it does not mean that it is easy to get through – just as a childbirth or a death are not easy events – even though everyone experiences it. Erikson used the term *moratorium syndrome* for clinical cases of adolescents who failed to integrate identities during this period of identity reorganization. In fact, a crisis in this life stage is associated with a higher incidence of depression, neurosis, schizophrenia and suicide than with any other life stage (Kasahara, 1977).

Identity crisis at the threshold of old age

I have discussed adolescence at some length in this section about aging precisely because everything about adolescence is directly applicable to senescence, as well. Developmental psychologists in the past regarded adolescence as the biggest developmental hurdle. They thought that there might be some crises after that, but they would not be as serious. However, they assumed that there were only two categories, childhood and adulthood, in a human life. What if adulthood is not the end stage of life and another category is waiting for us? This is the cultural category called *old person*.

The adult identity changes continually. There are several critical points in each stage during the process. The notion of *yakudoshi* (critical ages) must be the wisdom of traditional society in order to get through these critical points safely. However, the category itself changes after that. People suddenly realize one day that their social names have changed. When they are addressed as *grandfather* or *grandmother*, they can be shocked to find a large gap between their self identity and social identity.

We shall call the transition from the category of adult to the category of old person *senility*, in a similar manner to the use of the term *maturity*. And we shall call this transition period, which requires identity reorganization, *pre-senescence*. As with the task of maturity in adolescence, the same things can be said about the task of senility in pre-senescence. By way of analysis, senility progresses at the following four levels: physiological senility, mental senility, social senility and cultural senility.

As in the case of maturity, physiological senility is perhaps experienced earlier than the rest. As popularly claimed that the

signs of senility appear in 'the teeth, eyes and penis,' it is usually a
physical decline that announces the beginning of senility to people,
whether they like it or not. Physiological evidence suggests that the
cerebrum is complete by the age of four, after which the brain cells
continue to diminish, and that the human body begins to decline
after the peak age of eighteen. In this sense, there is no definite
sign, such as the first menstruation or ejaculation in physiological
maturity, to indicate the onset of physiological senility. Accordingly,
researchers these days simply call it *aging* instead of *senility*. In
any case, this much is known: first, the onset of physiological
senility is markedly delayed thanks to improved nutrition in modern
society; second, individual variability in physiological senility is
considerable. For example, if we view women's reproductive period
(from the first menstruation to the menopause) as the biological
maturity period, the female menopause is generally occurring later
than before and varies greatly from individual to individual, ranging
from the forties to the sixties.

Today, pre-senescence as an identity crisis is caused by a
gap between 'social = cultural senility' and the other levels of
senility.

The primary example of social senility must be the loss of social
= economic status as an adult, or age-limit retirement. The rate of
employment in Japanese society already exceeds 50% of the total
population, and 70% of all companies and 99% of large-sized
companies have some sort of age-limit retirement system (Labor
Ministry's 1976 survey). Most companies have had a retirement
age of fifty-five for many years. Some companies have moved to
extend the age limit in recent years in response to the aging society,
but the same survey found that only 30% of all companies had a
retirement age of sixty.[3]

Among internationally renowned Japanese labor practices, it
must look odd that the lifetime employment system is linked to
age-limit retirement at fifty-five. The compulsory retirement age
is sixty-five in the United States, sixty in Norway, and seventy in
Thailand, where life expectancy is shorter than in Japan.[4] People
can literally work to death in some Western countries. The legally
defined 'old age' starts at age sixty-five, which is consistent with
the commencement age for the old-age pension. In Japan the legal
definition of old age means little, but policy decision provides those
who lose their economic base at the age of fifty-five with *no* social
security for ten years (until the age of sixty-five they must solely

rely on their own efforts). Apart from this issue, how did the system of age-limit retirement at fifty-five come about?

It is presumed that this system was initially adopted by some businesses in the Meiji period and later spread to the rest of society. Since the average life span of Japanese people was in the forties in those days, the retirement age of fifty-five literally meant 'lifetime (to death)' employment. Considering the customary retirement age of around forty in traditional society, someone who worked to the age of fifty-five had worked long enough and deserved to retire. The problem with the present age-limit retirement system is that it has failed to keep up with the changing times and has remained the same, while the average life expectancy has rapidly risen to almost eighty since the Second World War.[5] Furthermore, due to different nutritional standards, the health condition of a fifty-five-year-old today is vastly different from that of a fifty-five-year-old half a century ago.

Workers are expelled from the category of economically in-depend-ent adult upon reaching the retirement age. Even if they are still economically independent, they lose the social identity of the gainfully employed. Saburō Shiroyama (1976), a novelist who portrayed post-retirement days in *Mainichi ga nichiyōbi* (Everyday is a Sunday), described age-limit retirement as a 'social death' and the day of retirement as a social 'funeral.' Post-retirement life is an 'afterlife' in a social sense, or extra days. Compared with the retirement practice in traditional societies, which allocated retirement to the world of 'public affairs' (pious) and pre-retirement activity to the world of 'private affairs' (secular) in an attempt to 'habitat-segregate (or social-partition)' (Imanishi, 1993) the social domain, the modern-day retirement is a more severe experience in which one is declared useless by society. Moreover, retirement shrinks not only one's economic scale but also one's area of activity and personal networks. This tendency is more marked for those who have been more devoted to their working lives – since the domain of their social activity and personal networks was so closely linked to their professional life, they lose employment and associated social relationships at the same time.

It is difficult to survive the 'social death.' As we can see in examples of primitive societies, the individual who was condemned to 'death' by witchcraft and whose death was acknowledged by the community would physiologically die by him or herself. Cases of people suddenly looking very old or becoming senile after age-limit retirement must have something to do with the shock from this 'social death.'

The cultural category of senility provides certain 'niches' (Umesao, 1991) for the 'extra life.' One of these is *kanreki* (the sixtieth birthday). The wearing of a red vest to celebrate the end of the sexagenary cycle on the sixtieth birthday was a cultural devise to permit one to regress to childhood at the completion of the life as a person, or to play freely in the so-called 'enchanted land.' In an era when the sixtieth and seventieth birthdays were celebrated as *kanreki* (literally 'returning to the birth') and *koki* respectively, only a small number of people reached these milestones and those who internalized this cultural ideal knew how to behave in the rest of their lives after sixty. However, this cultural ideal fails in an era when the average life span is eighty years and almost everyone lives beyond sixty. The remaining twenty years of life after sixty are too long to be called an 'extra life' and today's sixty-year-olds are simply too young in their path of life.

The main indicator of old age in the cultural category of senility is a change in family history. As in many traditional societies, men and women are not culturally regarded as grown-ups in Japan if they are single and merely economically independent. They need to be married (and have children in some cases) in order to be regarded as responsible members of their group. Just as *maturity* means a transition from the child category to the adult category in family history, *senility* means a transition from parent to grandparent. The maturity of children defines the senility of their parents. In more mundane terms, one's position in kinship terminology shifts to 'grandfather' or 'grandmother' as soon as his or her grandchild is born. Since Japanese kinship terminology is based on the 'child-centered usage' (Suzuki, T., 1973) from the viewpoint of the youngest member (grandchild in this case), children and their spouses begin using 'grandfather' or 'grandmother' instead of 'father' or 'mother' as soon as a grandchild is born.

Of course, when it was common for people to get married much earlier, many parents became grandparents in their forties. These days, the age of first-time grandparents is rising as the marriage age rises. However, the life-cycle model of the pre-war Japanese shows that parents in those days became grandparents in their forties, while their own youngest children were still at school, and they died before their youngest children became adults or before completely exiting the parent category. Now that people usually only have one or two children, the average life-cycle model shows that men are 57.7

years old and women are 55.1 years old when their youngest child marries (Prime Minister's Office, 1983). Social commentator Keiko Higuchi calls a child's wedding the 'parents' retirement ceremony.' Parents no longer need to be responsible for their children who have finally accomplished the task of reaching maturity, and, conversely, further interference in their lives will give rise to conflicts.

Quitting parenthood does not simply mean a change of kinship terminology. Children's marriages often involve the separation of the household and mean the loss of 'parental role' as a protector and overseer. Power relations with mature children change at the same time. Because both men and women lose their status and role as a parent in the family, the identity crisis arising from this change is as profound as that of age-limit retirement. It is even more so in the case of women who have been devoted to their role in the family.

People now have a very long life after exiting the parent category. And, unlike old people in traditional societies who had no other choice than looking after their granchildren, they are physiologically and socially very active. Designations such as grandfather and grandmother mean that the irreversible transition to the new category has been finalized, but today's young-looking grandparents feel uncomfortable when faced with this situation. The desperate measure they resort to is to create their family's own kinship terminology – for example, grandchildren call their grandmother 'big mother' and their mother 'little mother,' or 'mother' and 'mama' respectively. However, discrepancies between family designations and social designations only confuse grandchildren as they learn social kinship terminology.

What is more damaging to their identity than *intra*-family kinship designations is a transition from the 'uncle' and 'aunt' category to the 'grandfather' and 'grandmother' category when addressed by strangers *outside* their own families. This is called the fictitious use of kinship terminology. Many people remember the experience of being addressed as grandfather or grandmother by a total stranger for the first time with feelings of bewilderment, anger and sadness. The experience is accompanied by the painful self-recognition that their appearance has clearly shifted to the old person category and that there is a deep rupture between their social identity as the old person and their own self identity. The pre-senescence identity crisis is caused by the gap that is created when self identity lags behind the anteceding social identity. A conflict between these two identities gives rise to a crisis during pre-senescence that is similar to a crisis in adolescence. The growing incidence of suicide, depression, nervous breakdown and senile schizophrenia among the middle-aged and the elderly suggests that the task of identity reorganization is as difficult in pre-senescence as in adolescence (Kaneko and Shinpuku, 1972).

The negative self-image of the elderly

Pre-senescence can be described as a period of identity crisis that is analogous with adolescence but it does not end there. Pre-senescence presents another, even more difficult task. While pre-senescence is a product of modernity (just as adolescence is), pre-senescence is more difficult to survive than adolescence in modern society. The transition from child to adult generally accompanies a rise in status or a sense of power. While society encourages adolescent people to mature and perceives the transition in a positive light, the transition from adult to old person is completely opposite – it is accompanied by a fall in status and a scaling back of rights and freedom, which are perceived in a negative light. Naturally, identifying with a positive identity is easy, whereas identifying with a negative identity is difficult.

Katsuya Inoue (1978), of Tokyo Metropolitan Institute of Gerontology, has published a shocking report on the degree of self-denial that old people hold.

A Buddhist temple called Shimizuzan Kichidenji in Ikaruga, Nara Prefecture, is famous for attracting those who wish for a *pokkuri* (sudden, painless) death. Inoue interviewed old people who came to the temple to pray for a sudden death. He asked forty-three pilgrims (six men and thirty-seven women) with an average age of 70.3 years, 'Why did you come to the *pokkuri* temple?' Ninety-three per cent replied that they came because they did not want to become bedridden and to be a burden on others. The rest replied, 'I don't want to suffer from the pain of such diseases as cancer,' 'I feel so old and hopeless' and 'young people treat me as a nuisance.' Inoue noticed two elements in these replies: 'consideration for care-givers who will be inconvenienced' and 'sadness and indignation about being regarded as a nuisance.'

Inoue asked the pilgrims another question. In reply to his question, 'If your family does not treat you as a nuisance, even if you become bedridden, and truly wants you to live longer and takes really good care of you, will you still wish for a sudden death?' Eighty-two per cent replied, 'I will feel very grateful in that case but I will still wish to die a quick death.' Inoue considers that the psychology of these pilgrims, who reject the idea of becoming a 'bedridden old person,' even if the element of 'inconvenience to others' is removed, is underpinned by their sense of pride in actively rejecting the 'powerless self' who has to be looked after by others; it is also underpinned by their aggression on the reverse side of that coin.

He concludes, 'Their *pokkuri* wish is not a death wish. Although it takes the form of a death wish, it is essentially a wish for...a life filled with pride as a human being who tries to preserve quality of life by dying.' This interpretation enables us to understand that a *pokkuri* wish, which is seemingly inconsistent with one's wish for longevity, is not really inconsistent; rather, it is a reverse image of it. One's wish for longevity is not an attachment to life to 'want to live long even if I'm bedridden' but a desire to live a long life filled with human dignity.

Although longevity is often mentioned in conjunction with 'eternal youth,' a separate study by Inoue clearly demonstrates that 'eternal youth' is not simply a return to 'youth.' He asked a total of 105 people (thirty-one males and seventy-four females) over the age of seventy if they wished to be young again. Eighty per cent answered 'yes,' saying they wished to be young again 'very much' or 'if possible.' He asked what age they wished to be. Surprisingly, their answers concentrated on ages in their thirties and fifties.

When we mention youth, we think of ages in the tens and twenties, but few people picked these age brackets. People in their thirties can no longer be considered young, and those in their fifties are nearly old age. In the minds of the interviewees, however, 'thirties' conjures up the image of 'the peak period of life with a good balance between mental and physical powers,' and 'fifties' has the image of 'the peak of socioeconomic status.' Accordingly, we realize that the desire of old people to return to youth is not a simple desire for rejuvenation, but a desire to return to the periods when they were able to have a 'sense of power' in terms of mind, body and socioeconomic status.

In view of these criteria, it is difficult to deny that the present self of the old person is a powerless, constrained and miserable existence. Elderly people often have a very negative self-image because they look at themselves through the eyes of people in their thirties and fifties. Aiko Hada mentions a study by Helen Hacker (1951). Hacker pointed out that the self-image of a social minority was often the accepted assessment of its own group made by a social majority: Hada applied this principle to discrimination against women (Hada, 1976). Just as African-Americans internalize the image of a black person held by white people, for example, women as a social minority also internalize the image of a woman held by men – emotional, impulsive, immature and childish, less intelligent than men and so on – and build up a negative image of themselves. To women, 'becoming a woman' means acquiring this negative self identity, and hence becomes a conflicting and painful exercise. The fact that anorexia nervosa, a psychosomatic disorder that can be regarded as a type of 'maturity rejection disease,' is only found among girls and not boys suggests that the task of maturity appears to be experienced as a more acute crisis by adolescent females than adolescent males in a sexist society.

The mechanism of negative self-image formation by African-Americans and women also applies to old people as a social minority group. For example, surveys of people in their thirties and forties about the impressions formed from the term 'old people' generally return the following results – 'old people have no ability; getting old means degradation in value; burden on society; I don't want to get old…' However, old people return the same answers – in turn, as their self-image. In other words, old people still look at themselves through the eyes of people in their thirties and forties.

However, there is one big difference between the cases of black people in white society or women in men's society and old people in young people's society. While white people will never become black, nor men become women, most young people will eventually become old people. They will experience becoming what they, themselves, have attached a negative image to – this is the experience people go through during their pre-senescence. It is not difficult to imagine that such an experience should bring a sense of anger, despair or sadness.

Yasuo Arai (1978) introduces the five patterns of adjustment to aging devised by Suzanne Reichard, an American gerontologist: (1) Mature Group (carefree, forward-looking people), (2) Rocking Chair Group (passive, dependent people), (3) Armored Group (defensive people who are hostile towards youths), (4) Angry Group (depressive, closed people who blame others for their failures in life), and (5) Self-hater Group (pessimistic, lonely people who may even commit suicide).

These patterns are like catalogue samples and it is applicable to say that the Earl of Dorincourt, Cedric's stubborn grandfather in *Little Lord Fauntleroy*, falls into the category of Armored Man. As shown by common stereotypes of old people in fictional stories, these five patterns, except the first one, are negative or passive patterns of *maladjustment* to aging rather than adjustment to it. Even the first pattern does not mean anything more than indifference to the image of old people held by others; 'forward-looking,' in itself, is an attribute atypical of old people. In view of these patterns, it is not unreasonable for any person to conclude that a not-so-welcome future awaits them in their old age.

Since *adjustment* is better than *maladjustment* in one's old age, what are the conditions for adjustment?

Clark and Anderson (1967) nominate the conditions under which the aged can maintain a positive self-image in their senescence. They are (1) personal self-sufficiency (ability to satisfy one's own needs), (2) acceptance by others, (3) economic independence and health, (4) endurance to changing status and role, (5) endurance to changing self-image, and (6) sense of purpose and meaning in old age. Except for (4) and (5), these conditions are the same for any independent adult regardless of their age. These requirements are tantamount to an impossible paradox that tells you 'not to become an older person if you want to adapt well to old age.' Jun Katata, an anthropologist of comparative gerontology who introduced Clark and Anderson's model to Japan, criticizes it as follows:[6] 'The cause of maladjustment to post-retirement life lies in an attempt to maintain the value system developed in adolescence or prime of life even in old age' (Katata, 1979).

Cross-cultural comparison of old people

To conclude the discussion of the previous sections, I point out the following two requirements for achieving adjustment to aging: first, the accomplishment of the task of reorganizing identity in pre-senescence and, second, the transformation of the social identity of old person from a negative one to a positive one.

I wonder if there is any social condition under which the social identity of old person can become positive. Katata points out from the perspective of comparative cultures that the term 'old person' has become associated with a negative image since the age of modern industrial society. By reference to Cowgill's (1972) cross-cultural comparative study of old people's status, Katata formulates the common characteristics of society in which old people hold a relatively high status.

1. The status of old people in society is inversely proportional to the degree of modernization of that society.

2. The lower the percentage of the aged population, the higher the status of old people.
3. The status of old people in society is inversely proportional to the rate of social change.
4. Old people have a higher status in settled society and a lower status in moving society.
5. Old people have a higher status in societies without letters.
6. Old people have a higher status in extended families.
7. Rising individualism lowers the status of older people.
8. Old people have prestige where they have property ownership.

Based on the above cross-cultural comparison, it is possible to argue that agriculture-based traditional societies generally do not have 'old people problems.' Time is suspended in a cycle in such societies, which always look to the past to find examples for the present. Decision-making in these societies inevitably relies on precedents and therefore old people, who have the knowledge of precedents, have decision-making rights as the symbol of 'wisdom.' These are societies of gerontocracy.

Japan was traditionally a gerontocracy-type society. The link between status and age is clearly shown by official titles such as *toshiyori* (elder = senior official) and *rōjo* (elder woman = senior lady-in-waiting). Japan and the United States are at the opposite ends in their 'seniority orientation' and 'youth orientation.' American society values youth and newness because, first, new things are considered superior to old things in a society with rapid institutional and technological innovation, and, second, younger generations are closer to 'full American' in an immigrant society such as the United States. There, the first generation imitates the second generation and the second generation imitates the third generation, rather than children imitating their parents.[7] By contrast, a gerontocratic society values experience and the prevailing view is the older, the better. Youth orientation and seniority orientation extend to manners and customs. While in the United States it is desirable to maintain a young-looking, shapely body – proof of a person's usefulness – by working out, a slightly overweight, portly middle-aged body shape was a status symbol for a long time in Japan.

It is common knowledge that this gerontocratic-style Japanese society crumbled rapidly after the war. The word 'old,' which used to represent value, has now transformed into a negative symbol that can single-handedly inflict fatal damage. In this case, the difference between a youthful society and a gerontocratic society is, in fact, not the cultural difference between the United States and Japan but simply the difference between an industrialized society and a traditional society. Accordingly, it is possible to surmise that, just as Japan has transformed from a traditional agrarian society to an industrial society, Europe has been following the same historical steps. In fact, there is a strange coincidence between customs and manners of adult males in medieval Europe and early-modern Japan. An early-modern Japanese hairstyle called *chonmage* ranks with the Mongolian pigtail as one of the most bizarre hairstyles of the world, and involves shaving the hair off the front part of the head and making the remaining hair into a topknot. The style marks the coming-of-age and this custom can be interpreted as a symbolic act in which a young man imitates the bald head of an old man. If this hairstyle is considered to be a bizarre custom, the medieval European custom for adult men to wear wigs of white hair on official occasions is considered equally bizarre. This custom still remains as part of a judge's clothes and aptly demonstrates that white hair is a symbol of wisdom. In Japan, however, the age of *chonmage* gave way to the age of *Aderans* (Japan's leading brand of men's wigs) during the past century. A decline in the status of old people dramatically transformed the value of 'looking old' from positive to negative in the area of customs, as well.

Yet, a Japanese-style gerontocratic society does not simply mean a society in which old people have power. Japan still enjoys an international reputation as a society in which the elderly are treated well, but its lenient attitude towards old people entails a certain cultural contrivance. In comparing Japan and the United States in *The chrysanthemum and the sword*, Ruth Benedict ([1946] 1967) proposes something that can be called a life cycle curve (Figure 11.1), and points out that infants and the aged are afforded maximum freedom in Japan because infants and the aged are regarded as having the same figures as symbolized by *honkegaeri*, or *kanreki* (the sixtieth birthday, or returning to the birth). In the United States, since freedom is a right given according to the level of responsibility, those who have no capacity to take responsibility (infants and the old) are subject to restrictions and suffer lack of freedom. Conversely, in Japan infants and the aged, who have no responsibility, enjoy maximum freedom. Infants and the old are 'deities' who live in a place 'outside of the human world' and any behavior of the old is 'permissible if they are considered to be infants.' Therefore the post-retirement cultural ideal of the Japanese is a 'lovable old person' rather than a 'respectable old person.'

Figure 11.1: Freedom curves

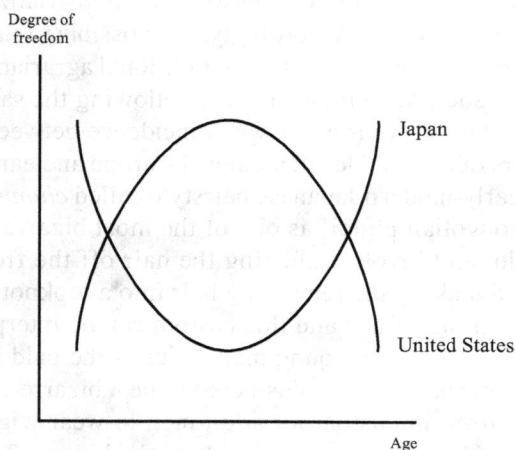

The category that the industrialized society of modern Japan has inherited from cultural traditions of gerontocratic society for the purpose of protecting the self identity of the aged is this 'sweet old person.' The industrialized society has removed 'dignity' from the cultural ideal of the aged and inherited 'childishness' alone. The cultural ideal of 'lovable old person' is mobilized as a cultural device to reconcile the self identity and social identity of old people.

For example, let us look at the following poem.[8]

Old people's wish
By Kaku Miyo (age sixty-one)

Old people want words
When we say something please respond
We may keep repeating because we forget
It may be annoying but please respond
Please don't get angry when we spill our food
Please don't scold when we wet ourselves
Because when we get old we become babies
...
Our bodies have shrunk too
Because we are gradually returning into babies

Katsuya Inoue (1978) views senility as a type of regression to infancy, which is a '*normal* state of aging' in people of advanced years. Like children, senile people only live in the present, not in the past or future. Although his view that senility is 'salvation given by God' to those facing imminent death is a valuable argument, it also seems to be 'very Japanese or too Japanese' – a view that is largely dependent on cultural manipulation in trying to come to terms with aging by identifying the old with infants.

Is aging really a regression to infancy? The cultural device to equate the aged with infants obscures the realities of aging. Senile people are not just old people regressing to their infancy. The movie *Hanaichimonme* portrayed the humiliation and sadness felt by an old man who was aware of his advancing senility. And not all old people become senile before death. When we understand more clearly how those who become senile are different from those who do not become senile, we will be able to consider the conditions for old age without senility.

Identifying the aged with infants appears to be an act of generosity, but, in fact, it deprives them of dignity in that it does not permit them any capacity for responsibility. In a society that rejects 'respectable old people' and only culturally accepts 'lovable old people' as a strategy to survive old age, life is paradoxically harder for old men than for old women. Since men are not used to being 'loved' because of the male values they have internalized over time, they are unable to switch their identity suddenly in old age. It is easier for women to identify with the cultural ideal of old age because they have been the passive figures who are 'loved' in male-dominated society. This can be one of the paradoxes generated by sexism.

The problem of old people and that of old age – in search of transformation of value

Our discussion so far can be summarized into the following three points:
1. Identity should be regarded as a continuous developmental process from maturity to senility.
2. As long as senility is interpreted as adaptation to a negative identity, the process of acceptance of old age is filled with difficulties and pain.
3. Senility means adaptation to a negative identity to the extent that the youth-based values supported by modern industrialized societies are internalized.

Until we understand these points, we may not understand why to-day's old people hate to be called 'old people' so much. That absurd proposal put forward by the government to call the early stages of old age *jitsunen* (fruitful or harvesting age) is understandable in this context. Of course, replacing the name without changing the substance is merely a maneuver. What is really needed here is the transformation of value to enable the acceptance of old age, including both aspects of vulnerability and dignity.

Tarō Hanamura argues that the issue of old people and the issue of old age should be distinguished, and it is the latter that requires an urgent discussion (Hanamura, 1980). The 'old people issue' treats old people as the *object* – something troublesome that needs care.[9] 'The issue of "old people" will preserve the system of culture that abhors and suppresses (and ignores if possible) human destiny called old age no matter how much their welfare is improved...' (Hanamura, 1980). In contrast, the issue of old age deals with the problems of old age that old people experience as the *subject*. According to Hanamura, even this old age issue 'does not go beyond the question of how to alleviate or prevent the miseries of that loathsome senescence' at this point in time. He considers that the real challenge of the 'old age issue' is this:

> The fundamental solution to the essence of the old age issue can only be found in facing the destiny of old age seriously and nurturing the so-called 'mature culture' that can attach human meaning and value to the reality called old age (Hanamura, 1980).

Half-hearted measures through such things as 'change of mind' or 'personal efforts' will only achieve limited results. What the old age issue is demanding is a re-examination of the whole value system of modern industrialized society, which can only give old age a negative identity.

12 The Possibility of Female Bonds

From *associational bonds* to *selective bonds*[1]

The world of *shaen* is undergoing an upheaval.

The term *shaen* (associational bond) originally meant *kes-shaen* (social/associational bond). It was aptly coined by Toshinao Yoneyama as a corresponding term for *gesellschaft*, as opposed to *gemeinschaft* (by F. Tönnies), and for *association*, as opposed to *community* (by R. M. MacIver). *Gesellschaft* and *association* are the concepts that have been created by sociologists in response to the dissolution of old restrictive and comprehensive blood and territorial bonds and the emergence of more artificial and partial interpersonal relationships in modern times.

Structurally, these sets of concepts are expected to be comprehensive classification systems that cover all spheres. Accordingly, *associational bonds* refer to all interpersonal relationships except blood and territorial bonds. However, now that the sphere of blood and territorial bonds has shrunk and the sphere of all other interpersonal relationships has expanded considerably, it has become difficult to fit them all into the concept of associational bonds. The concept of associational bonds is presently used as a 'residual category' to throw in all interpersonal relationships except blood and territorial bonds.

A move to subdivide the concept of associational bonds was initiated by urban sociologists. Eiichi Isomura (1975) proposed the idea of the *third space* at an early stage in his discussion of urban communication. C. H. Cooley divided interpersonal relationships into the *primary group* (relationships given at birth, such as family and neighborhood) and the *secondary group* (relationships formed later in life, such as at school and work). Isomura's *first space* and *second space* correspond to these respectively; in addition, he argued that urban areas had a completely new sphere that did not belong to the first space or the second space, and named it the third space.[2]

The third space theory was later used by researchers of urban communication in places such as shopping and entertainment quarters of

223

the city (Fujitake, 1973). While urban research by sociologists tends to be dragged back to conventional territorial bond concepts such as 'urban community,' people in the fields of architecture and urban engineering have come up with totally new concepts.

Teruhiko Mochizuki (1977), an urban engineer and the founder of *Machi-nology* (urbanology), created the category of *chien* (knowledge/intellectual bonds) to describe a type of interpersonal relationship that did not fall within the categories of blood, territorial or associational bonds. Mochizuki explains as follows.

> What requires consideration is the possible existence of an open system called urban community to replace the old closed system, and the discovery of media such as 'involvement' and 'connection' to replace 'blood bond' and 'territorial bond.' The medium is likely to contain such elements as necessity, selectivity and internal events of the individual rather than inevitable necessity imposed by external pressure inherent in a blood bond or a territorial bond, and perhaps should be called 'knowledge bond'[3] (Mochizuki, 1978: 124).

My concept of *selective bonds* was inspired by Mochizuki's concept of *knowledge bonds*.[4] The concept of knowledge bonds is also interchangeable with 'informational bonds,' 'symbolic bonds' or '(symbol-)mediated bonds,' but they do not clearly highlight the characteristic of interpersonal relationship in the third space, which is different from blood bonds, territorial bonds or associational bonds. Even a consanguineous group (such as a family) and a associational bond group (such as a corporation) are effected through the medium of information or symbolic mechanism in some aspect.

When we describe the third space as a selective bond, we can see a common thread that runs through the spheres of blood bonds, territorial bonds and associational bonds societies. They are all 'bonds we cannot choose.' The term 'associational bond' was originally created to describe secondary groups with the freedom of participation and withdrawal in contrast to more binding relationships such as blood and territorial bonds. However, the most typical associational bond in modern society, the *corporate bond*, is quite binding because people find it difficult to leave once they are in it. Of course, employees always have the 'freedom to leave' their employment but the 'freedom to get out' of associational bond society only means the 'freedom to starve' as far as the unpropertied common people are concerned. These days, even blood bonds have become a group that permits participation and withdrawal by marriage based on free will, but withdrawal is still not that easy. Parents and children do not have the freedom to choose one another. Territorial bonds have lost their binding force and people have the freedom to move in or out but they cannot choose their neighbors.

Compared with selective bonds, these conventional bonds more or less have the element of non-selectivity – one cannot get out of them or avoid them. In this sense, associational bonds are similar to blood and territorial bonds. The background element for my coinage of selective bonds is this observation that the sphere of free and pluralistic interpersonal relationship in which people can choose one another has been expanding.

The categorization of various human bonds into 'selective bonds' and 'non-selective bonds' has a grounding in pre-modern history. By a curious coincidence, Yoshihiko Amino (1978), an expert in medieval history, used the terms 'tied' and 'untied.' A tied society is a binding social relationship based on domiciliation. 'Untied' does not mean 'no ties' but refers to a marginalized form of interpersonal relationship that is outside a tied society. The untied relationship is a type of relationship that is the foundation of urban social relationships.[5]

This new interpersonal relationship created by urbanized society demands the formation of the fourth category that is separate from the concept of associational bonds and does not belong to any of the traditional concepts. These categories are summarized in Table 12.1.

The sphere of *selective bond* society

The concept of selective bond society was born from my attempt to conceptualize new interpersonal relationships in urbanized society but many researchers already share similar observations and discoveries. I describe some of the characteristics of selective bonds below.

First, it is a free and open relationship. Since a selective bond is an 'association by mutual selection,' participation and withdrawal are free and non-binding in principle. Unlike blood and territorial bonds, which are bound by *common residence*, or associational bonds, which are bound by *common occupation*, one is not placed at a disadvantage upon quitting.

Second, it is a mediated relationship. Since people are associated through the media, such as through certain information or symbols, they can maintain anonymity while taking part in communication, just as an audience does at a concert. With the addition of technological media such as telegraphic and electric transmission media,

Table 12.1: Types of human relationship

Yoneyama, T.	Blood bond	Territorial bond	Social bond	
Tönnies, F.	*Gemeinschaft*		*Gesellschaft*	
MacIver, R. M.	Community		Association	
Cooley, C. H.	Primary group		Secondary group	
Isomura, E.	First space		Second space	Third space
Mochizuki, T.	Blood bond	Territorial bond	Value bond	Knowledge bond
Ueno, C.	Blood bond (Non-selective bonds)	Territorial bond	Social bond	Selective bond (Selective bond)
Amino, Y.	Bondd			Unbondd

a relationship without any face-to-face contact can develop, such as among a late-night radio audience. Face-to-face meeting and sharing a physical space are no longer counted as prerequisites for the formation of a relationship.

Third, it has an element of the renunciation of hypersocialized roles. In bonded society based on blood, territorial or associational bonds, people behave in conformity with the standardized role expectations of their counterpart in bilateral relationships. Deviation from roles such as 'father' and 'manager' is regarded as abnormal. In an unbonded world, relinquishment of roles and transformation are possible. Role playing and performance are also possible in this space. For example, it is possible to freely create or control identities in an unbonded communitas at a pub (Turner, 1974).

The selective bond is a *residual category* in a set of all spheres that require standardized roles. While Talcott Parsons regarded the individual as 'a set of roles,' the modern individual can be regarded as nothing but the residual category that has spilled out of a set of all roles. In that case, selective bond society is the very infrastructure that provides individuals with identity as the individual.

Lastly, I mention the social function of the formation of this selective bond society. To use the words of Tadao Umesao (1981), selective bond society avoids competition in overcrowded society and guarantees the stability of identity through the creation of many 'social niches' that have nothing to do with real-world interest and profit. As industrial social values converge and status becomes scarce, 'habitat segregation' (Imanishi, 1993) through these niches will be seen increasingly as wisdom for peaceful co-existence in a society of corporate workers.[6]

However, the selective bond has weaknesses that stem from its very construction. Since participation and withdrawal are free and non-binding, it is unstable as a group and unlikely to provide stable identity.

The selective bond certainly provides a residual role category but it does not mean that it has little importance in human living. On the contrary, its relative importance in people's lives is increasing as blood, territorial and associational bonds become somewhat more selective today.

As an index to measure the relative importance of each type of human bond in our lives, it may be useful to consider which interpersonal relationships people would mobilize if faced with a life crisis. Take 'funeral assistance' for example. Death is an occasion on which people become most conservative with respect to formalities. Therefore, changes found at funerals can be regarded as the reflection of changes at the base level of social life. Faced with one of the biggest life crises, such as the death of an immediate family member, the surviving family members are usually too grief-stricken to carry out funeral arrangements. It has always been people other than the immediate family of the deceased who organize a funeral behind the scenes. In traditional societies they were relatives and neighbors. However, in today's society, where blood and matrimonial relatives live geographically far apart, 'relatives far off' may come to help but they are mere visitors who do not know their way around the place. And people do not have many brothers and sisters these days, so they have fewer relatives they can call on. Territorial bond society is long gone. Generally, people do not associate with their neighbors on friendly terms any more.

Instead of blood and territorial bonds, associational bonds were mobilized for funeral assistance. In Japanese-style industrialized society, where associational bond communities or corporate groups worked like village communities, the whole family became involved in the associational bond, and the 'corporate welfare' even took care of their post-retirement life and leisure. Company colleagues and subordinates were the first people who rushed to help with the funeral of an employee or his family member. The company's general affairs staff, wearing mourning bands, would act as a funeral committee in some cases. This state of corporate welfare was a clear indication that the blood and territorial bonds had been replaced by associational bonds.

The dominance of associational bonds lasted until the 1960s. Lately, there are signs that associational bonds are being replaced by selective bonds. 'Funeral assistance' means behind-the-scenes support such as attending to visitors throughout the funeral period, including a wake and a funeral. People from the associational bond group usually have no acquaintance with the family members and they do not know their way around the kitchen. In such cases, more day-to-day relationships formed through selective bonds come to the fore.

A woman in her fifties who has formed a selective bond network through a consumers' cooperative in Senri New Town commented:

> Actually, I saved up money from my extra job and bought a piece of land far away from here but I don't want to move now. I want to live here and have fun with my friends until I die. I'm telling my husband not to bother asking our relatives to help with my funeral when I die because all my friends will be here to help immediately.[7]

The selective bond was supposed to be an 'unreliable relationship' but it has become a strong trust relationship that even influences one's choice of residence in this case. The term *yoka* (leisure) literally means 'spare time' but the selective bond is not necessarily a mere 'spare interpersonal relationship' that appears in the leisure space.

The *pure model* and the *mixed model*

If we consider blood, territorial, social and selective bonds to be conceptual types, their typical empirical equivalents can be regarded as *pure models*. For example, groups based on hobbies or beliefs that are independent of either blood, territorial or associational bonds, such as a *haiku* poetry society or a bird watching society, can be considered a pure model of selective bonds.

Given the fact that selective bonds communities are established at the basic popular level of society and given greater importance in their lives in observed cases, it is clear that selective bonds are not exclusive of other types of relationship. Rather, it is where the selective bond overlaps with other relationships that we can find a *mixed model*, so to speak, of selective bonds.

The development of the mixed model of selective bonds is led by women, particularly urban housewives. Women had the need to create selective bond society.

The urban, nuclear family, wage-earning households that emerged as a result of industrialization were supported by the gender role assignment between 'husband as the breadwinner and wife as the homemaker.' Only men moved between the public sphere, which was workplace, and the private sphere, which was home. 'Separation of public and private' did not mean anything to women, who were left behind in the private sphere. The private sphere was a small nuclear family with one or two children. It was a narrow space where husband was the only other adult member in the family. While, for men, industrialization meant turning into salaried workers, to women it meant complete isolation as the housewife in the nuclear family. This isolation was more acute among the wives of relocated employees who were uprooted from their territorial community.

Many of the housewives' social groups that are growing in clusters in all parts of Japan are operated by the wives of relocated employees. They tend to be more active than local women. According to some data, public facilities for women, such as women's centres, are more frequently used by relocated women than local women.

Women's orientation to participate in the workplace has been consistently strong, even under the principle of 'separation of public and private,' but the door to the corporate world is firmly shut to women. Women are not only excluded from the public sphere of corporate society with associational bonds but also alienated from old blood and territorial bond networks. To escape from the 'loneliness of the housewife' (Friedan, 1963), women had to create social relationships that were not of the conventional blood, territorial or associational bonds – and they have been creating them. Women are one step ahead of men as far as the development of selective bond society. Since men are still deeply involved in associational bond society, they are provided with an adequately stable identity. Men do not feel the need to create social relationships that are different from any of the old types to replace the dissolved territorial and blood bonds as yet. Even though the stability of associational bond society is crumbling rapidly following the arrival of aging society and hollowing out of employment, they are not yet aware of the need to get out of there.

Housewives are involved in a broad range of activities (from consumers' cooperatives, joint purchasing of pesticide-free vegetables, children's libraries, collective childcare, community hall-based learning groups and cultural study groups to mothers' volleyball and choir groups) that are not quite the same as conventional 'community activities.' They are not based on territorial bond relationships that are imposed by coincidental 'proximity of residence' such as a parent–teacher association or a neighborhood association. For example, one housewife who is an active member of a consumers' cooperative in Senri New Town responded as follows when asked about the residents' association of her housing estate: 'Oh, the residents' association? I don't know much about it. I'm not living my life for my neighbors.'[8]

Community developers in the government and town-planning fields have envisioned row house-type territorial communities that are formed through joint use of the apartment floors and staircases but where the actual networks created by the residents are spatially extended to residents of different apartment complexes in the same housing estate. They are certainly within the limit of 'community,' which is within walking distance and allows face-to-face contact. However, people have very little contact with their immediate 'neighbors' in the same complex and floors, whereas they keep much more substantial contact with the people of the relationships they select by themselves. This is a 'territorial bond community' with an additional and more positive element.[9]

How are these 'medium range' territorial bonds, or rather, selective bonds, formed? There are a few characteristics to note.

First, these groups are formed through a medium. These women actively make use of community newspapers, advertisements, flyers and commercial newspapers. Rather than being sparked by face-to-face encounters, these groups develop through the media first and spawn direct contact at a later time in many cases.

Second, what is communicated through the media is a sense of common purpose, be it a hobby, lifestyle, values or ideology. For instance, there is a group initiated by a woman who went around the block and pasted up a bill on power poles advertizing her need for after-school care for school-age children. These women share the lifestyle of working mothers who continue to work in defiance of common sentiment to pity 'latchkey children' and they have the common experience of struggles with their husbands over the issue of gender role assignment. This group also drew some male members and they maintain strong bonds even after their children have grown out of childcare. There is an endless number of other examples, from groups involved in joint purchasing of non-pesticide vegetables and consumers' cooperative activities to children's library groups.

Third, these women actively utilize high technology in mutual communication within their networks in order to cover localities beyond the scale of the conventional territorial bond. As the means of transport changes from walking to a bicycle to a motorbike to a car, the size of the community expands considerably. It would be wrong to apply the traditional term 'territorial bond' to the networks that are formed under this condition. In this large residential area containing tens of thousands of people, these women select bonds with a dozen or so counterparts based on a set of values or feelings. Another trait is their effective use of the telephone as a means of communication. They maintain very close contact with one another. The news that a friend's cat has been run over by a car travels faster than the news that the next-door neighbor's father in the country has passed away. They often publish an internal magazine or a newsletter within the group. Thanks to the spread of word processors and photocopiers, anyone can easily publish printed materials. Supported by these types of communication, face-to-face contact is no longer always necessary. In one case, the group's monthly newsletter supports the network of a dozen or so members scattered around Kyoto City from Takatsuki (near Osaka) to Maizuru (a town facing the Japan sea). With personal computers coming into wider use and communication between computers becoming as easy as using a telephone, these women's networks are the first to benefit from advanced communication technologies.

The women's selective bond formed in this way has several characteristics.

First, it is generally a small group, with the membership ranging from several to just over a dozen people. An empirical study shows an average size of seven or eight members, fifteen or sixteen at most; this is consistent with the finding of a sociological survey about informal groups that this is the maximum group size that still allows mutually personal, face-to-face contact. The groups do not aspire to organizational growth or franchise operation. Once the group attains the optimal size, it usually stops trying to recruit new members and mutual relationships between members become stable. Groups do not have the 'bigger, the better' mindset that focuses on organization and expansion.

Second, it is a peer group of members of the same gender and the same age group. Women's life issues are segmented according to life stages and change year by year. Their lifestyle when their children are under the age of six is totally different from their lifestyle when their children are at school. New issues arise one after another as they and their parents age. Women form the 'school reunion' type networks with peer group members of similar age with similar

circumstances and similar life issues, and they move through
different issues stage by stage as they grow older together. They do
not actively seek to recruit new members from other generations.

Third, it has a stable membership but its boundary is unclear and
it lacks formal leadership and rules. This is a major difference from
the *associational* bonds formed by men. Men's selective bond groups
tend to be modeled after associational bond groups and have such
things as the formal 'rules of association' and a president.

Fourth, women's selective bonds are closely linked to their daily
living. They do not live in a space where blood, territorial and associational bonds are clearly and functionally separated from selective
bonds. They may create a selective bond within a territorial bond or
bring a selective bond into a territorial bond. Since many of the issues that trigger the formation of a selective bond involve parenting
(such as food and education), the selective bond tends to be drawn
into their daily living, including their children. In fact, housewives
from nuclear families must often bring their children to the group's
meetings and, in the process of looking after each other's children,
the details of each other's daily living become common knowledge
among members.

A positive reason for the mixed nature of the mixed model is found
in this 'daily living-based' pattern. Because women's selective bonds
are not completely separated from their blood or territorial bonds, it
assumes greater importance in their lives as a replacement for their
blood and territorial bonds. Women's selective bonds have replaced
blood and territorial bonds as the most reliable interpersonal relationships that are mobilized in daily life crises, including the aforementioned funeral assistance. One example of such a life crisis is when
a parent in a hometown falls critically ill and a woman needs to find
someone to look after her children so she can go back to help her parent. Instead of the relatives or neighbors who helped in the old days,
it is her 'friends from the group' or 'fellow members of the children's
library' who come forward to help these days. She might travel for
one hour by car or train to take her children to her friend's place.

Another life crisis is marital trouble. Every couple faces one or
more marital crises during a long period of marriage, and women
talk about their grievances with selective bond friends. Because most
women marry out of their own will these days, they are too proud
to confide their marital crises to their parents and siblings, and they
avoid discussing them with their old school mates to preserve their
vanity. They cannot tell their neighbors because they live too close.
A moderate distance that accompanies a selective bond is beneficial

here. In discussing personal problems while controlling the amount of information at a reasonable distance that limits the level of disclosure about their personal life, selective bond friends with no conflict of interest are most suitable.

From the individual interviewing of active key members of the women's networks I studied, another surprising finding emerged. Women who are active in one selective bond participate in other selective bonds and their interpersonal relationships with members of these groups seldom overlap. Let us look at a typical example. A woman in her fifties residing in Takatsuki City was the secretary-general of a local citizens' movement for semi-public election of members of the local education board, and her activist friend said her presence was so crucial that the movement would have been unviable without her. At the same time, she was a member of the Ancient Japanese Stone Art Society and attended a cultural course on Buddhist art. When the citizens' movement was actively collecting signatures for its petition at the peak of its campaign, she never asked her fellow members of the Buddhist art group for their signatures. They discovered her 'hidden face' as the leader of a citizens' movement only when a local newspaper featured her in its profile section. Those who knew her as a quiet and scholarly lover of Buddhist art were surprised to find her unexpected side as the shrewd secretary-general of a citizens' movement.

In her case, she divides multiple selective bonds into separate spheres and wears different hats for them, suggesting the pluralistic nature of the self, which cannot be measured by a single identity. In doing so, she avoids the risk of exposing her whole self to a single society at the same time. While one mistake can be fatal in a 'bonded' sphere based on inclusive role expectations, this kind of risk management of identity control becomes possible in segmented and arm's-length selective bond relationships. And such affiliation with plural intermediary groups has been considered the ideal model for the modern individual. Conversely, her husband has a dominant identity in the associational bond sphere as a professional. It is obvious which partner in this marriage is more individual.

Men's selective bonds tend to be more functionally differentiated after the pure model – a 'gentlemen's club' with no self-interest whatsoever. If not, it has some business strings attached – a mixed model involving associational bonds such as a cross-industrial exchange group. In either case, these bonds are unlikely to be reliable in the face of personal crises such as emergency baby sitting and marital trouble. How do men deal with personal life crises? They either refuse to ask anyone for help or completely rely on traditional blood bonds.[10] However, blood and territorial bonds are in their dismantling stage and no longer functional today, so women are one step ahead of men in the formation of alternative networks. Teruko Yoshitake (1982) calls these networks *female bonds*.

Masakazu Yamazaki points out the meaning of such small-sized selective groups to human life as follows:

> The change of which we are seeing some signs is, in short, the emer-gence of more flexible, small-scale organizations and the arrival of society that values interpersonal relationships with human faces more than abstract organizational systems. And only when more people begin to affiliate with such flexible groups and live their lives actually seeing the faces of their neighbors in the future, we will live in a society that is unmistakably different from an industrialization-era society. Over the period of 300 years of industrialization, we had the rigid and aggres-sive production organization on one hand, and the vague and faceless mass society on the other hand, and only rarely found more humane groups that were supposed to exist halfway between them. People could only enjoy stability and bemoan lack of freedom in the former, or enjoy freedom and endure uncertainty in the latter. It is possible to say that we now have a feeling that the time will come when we grow intermediate organizations and live in a 'mass society where we can see faces' of our neighbors, so to speak, or at least we recognize it as one possibility (Yamazaki, M., 1984: 94–5).

I have no objection to this observation about the 'change in mass society' except that the reference to 'neighbors' here requires more accurate and detailed categorization and is different from 'neigh-bors' in territorial bonds. In my own words, selective bond society can propose a new balance between the *mass* and the *individual* of modern society, which has been moving back and forth between excessive *mass society* on one end and excessive *atomized society* on the other.

Yamazaki continues as follows. 'These places of sociability are at the same time the places where people can express their interests to one another and confirm the correctness of their interests in tacit peer reviews' (Yamazaki, M., 1984: 95). In fact, selective bond society provides women with a place that sanctions their tastes, lifestyles, values and so on because 'when one gets dressed in the latest fashions, seeing a close friend and directly receiving a compliment for one's good taste offers greater joy than simply parading around the town'

(Yamazaki, M., 1984: 96). Selective bond society becomes a place of self-realization for women through acceptance by others, together with this sanction. They become 'individuals' for the first time in the company of 'other people with faces' who meet and appreciate one another as individuals with their own names, not as mothers or wives of someone, and regardless of their husbands' jobs or incomes. Overseas travel is one of the dreams of housewives in their forties and fifties. When they are asked with whom they would like to travel, their reply is not 'husband' or 'children' but 'friends of the same gender with mutual understandings.' In this sense, it can be said that women have already quit the roles of wife and mother and become fully individual, while men are still living in the roles of father, head of family and company employee in the traditional blood, territorial and associational bond societies. It is this selective bond society that offers women a space in which they can become individuals.[11]

Selective bond society can also offer a model for the new horizontal interpersonal relationship, which is different from the traditional vertical social relationship. The aforementioned housewife from Senri New Town commented, 'Men are living in a hierarchical society after all. In comparison, women do not live in a hierarchical society, so we can speak our minds freely.'

Indefinite membership boundaries, absence of rules and leadership, and horizontal peer group relationships – these characteristics of female bonds suggest the possibility of a more loosely structured and flexible horizontal society, which is different from the *ie* (family) model governed by the hierarchical social principle or the *mura* (village) model based on in/out exclusiveness.

The Japanese have internalized hierarchical social relationships; men have been confined in the vocational group called *company* and women in the blood bond group of patriarchal matrimonial *family* from which they could not escape. Selective bond society can maintain horizontal relationships because people are free to come and go as they wish. Although it is still unclear whether such an open bond can become an effective socializer (agent of socialization), Japanese society holds the potential to grow a new type of interpersonal relationship that does not follow the *ie* or *mura* model. The female bond has a lot to offer to selective bonds on this point as an advanced model.

In today's society, where the population is rapidly aging and the traditional blood, territorial and associational bonds are no longer functional, we have come to the stage where both men and women have no choice but to find their future in selective bonds.

13 Paradox of Sexism: Cross-cultural Adaptation and Gender Difference

Cross-cultural adaptation and gender difference

It is well known in the field of cultural anthropology that there are gender and age differences in cross-cultural adaptation. It is generally considered that, *all other conditions being equal*, women adapt faster than men and younger people adapt faster than older people. As demonstrated by the case of Imo, a female monkey on the island of Kōjima who learned a new cultural behavior of washing potatoes in sea water, new customs tend to be transmitted from the periphery of culture (that is, from women and children) to the center. In the case of Imo and other monkeys on Kōjima, this potato-washing behavior was transmitted from young monkeys to mother monkeys, and the last ones to adapt were the stubborn old male monkeys.

There have been relatively few studies of gender differences in overseas experiences of the Japanese. Hiroshi Inamura's (1980) series of studies on cross-cultural adaptation of the Japanese centered around businessmen, and Chie Nakane's *Tekiō no jōken* (Conditions for cultural adaptation) (1972), published prior to Inamura's work, was also mainly about businessmen and did not deal with women. A rapidly increasing number of studies on children returning from abroad mainly focus on variables such as the length of stay and age, but few studies treat gender as a significant variable.

There are a few likely reasons.

First, the introduction of gender as a variable is in itself a very new phenomenon in social science research. Under the influences of women's studies that were bolstered by women's liberation, gender difference has become a major theme in all areas of social science. Cross-cultural adaptation research is no exception.

Second, the study of gender differences is only meaningful when comparisons are made with *all other conditions being equal*. However, Japanese men and women have not traveled abroad *under equal conditions* to date. Men have traveled abroad mainly in the

236

capacity of company representative, government official, student or researcher, whereas women traveled as their wives or as the wives of foreigners. For the question of gender differences to become a focal point in overseas adaptation of businessmen, the number of businesswomen who travel abroad under the same conditions as men must increase considerably, but it is going to be some time before this happens. The issue of family in relation to overseas adaptation of businessmen was highlighted only after the problems of children returning from abroad were brought to public notice. Even then, the existence of women who went overseas as wives rarely attracted attention. As I have argued before, the 'housewife was a Dark Continent' in the history of discourse about housewife (Ueno (ed.), 1982), and the presence of wives who accompanied businessmen and students to foreign lands was treated as an accessory and invisible. The only exception was when the issue of wives was discussed in the context of a mother's influences on the cross-cultural adaptation process of children. Even in Yasuko Minoura's *Kodomo no ibunka taiken* (Cross-cultural experiences of children) (1984), which can be considered a classic study of repatriated children, Minoura admits that the wives of expatiate businessmen only became part of her study as a factor determining children's social environment. Her study did not explore the problems of women who were placed in peculiar circumstances as the wives of expatriate businessmen.

Third, the variable of gender difference is given relatively low priority in the study of repatriated children compared with children living in Japan. The core identity of repatriated children, regardless of their gender, is 'being a Japanese' while they are residing overseas and 'being an outsider' as a *henjapa* (odd Japanese) when they return to Japan. Gender identity tends to be relegated to second or third place in the order of priorities. The same thing has been found in ethnic minority studies. The women's liberation movement in the United States has historically had difficulty involving ethnic minority women because the core identity issue for them was ethnicity rather than gender. This is why American women with ethnic minority backgrounds may join forces with men from the same ethnic minority group but they may not think about linking up with white women.

Generally, gender comes into question as a variable only when the priority of other variables is lowered. It does not mean that gender is not an important variable. In fact, it means that gender is the *last variable* that is taken for granted so much that it attracts least attention.

A notable trend in research on gender differences in repatriated children (*returnees*) in recent years is that the imbalance in the male–female ratio increases with age due to the effects of ever intensifying competition for better universities in Japan. This phenomenon is common at local schools in all parts of the world and overseas Japanese schools are no exception. The number of male students decreases with age because their parents return their male children to Japan when they take an entrance examination to junior and senior high schools. For example, the intermediate class of the Japanese School in Bombay (Mumbai) had seven students in 1987, of which six were female and one was male; instead of advancing to the senior class, the male student was scheduled to leave to go to a boarding school in Japan.

According to Hisako Cunningham, who wrote *Kaigai shijo kyōiku jijō* (Education of expatriate children) (1988), Japanese male students who perform well at a local school tend to transfer to a Japanese school in the upper grades of an elementary school. On the other hand, male students with learning difficulties tend to remain at local schools. In other words, parents tend to dump their problem children at local schools. In contrast, better-performing female students tend to remain at local schools. Cunningham interprets this phenomenon as follows.

> [It is] interesting to see differences in education policy and expectations
> of Japanese parents for their sons and daughters. It appears to
> illuminate a pattern of their thinking in which they wish to prepare
> their sons so that they can function in Japanese organizations and to
> give their daughters overseas education as a bridal trousseau for the
> future (Cunningham, 1988: 31).

The differences in parental attitude towards sons and daughters stemmed from the defensive response of parents to a widespread awareness of difficulties associated with the re-adaptation process of returnees.

The earlier overseas workers had a naive belief about children's education. First, they were optimistic about children's adaptation to a foreign culture and re-adaptation to their original culture following their repatriation. Second, they were extremely optimistic about the future of these children with international backgrounds. Third, they were corporate and intellectual elites themselves, and were also extremely optimistic about the heredity of their status and capabilities. Some data suggest that parents with higher education expect their children to have even higher education. While these elite parents took it for granted that their children would have high academic qualifications, they failed to realize that competition in school entrance examinations had become so fierce in the space of one generation that students required specialized training.

This optimism brought disastrous results for the first generation of repatriated children. The first postwar corporate workers who were posted overseas were corporate elites but their children were not necessarily recruited into the same business elite class. As competition in entrance examinations intensified and students were differentiated by their standard deviation values in the school education system, corporations came to place greater emphasis on academic qualifications, which made nepotistic employment difficult. The best they could do for their children, who were left to themselves according to their parents' naive beliefs, was to use their connections to get them hired as the local bilingual staff. Corporations valued domestically educated personnel with a strong sense of group loyalty more highly than returnees with an ambiguous sense of belonging.

Parents' optimism quickly dissipated as a result. Parents began to choose to have their sons study at a local Japanese school or to send them back to Japan as a defensive measure. Japanese parents think that boys basically have no other choice but to live in Japanese society and they are fully aware of the fact that Japanese society will never welcome noncommittal outsiders of a group into the elite classes.

In relation to the study of gender differences in cross-cultural experiences, new gender studies from a linguistic anthropological angle have appeared in recent years. For example, the Japanese language has gender-assigned personal pronouns. It also has gender-specific speech style at the vernacular level. The first page of the Japanese language textbook used by the first grade of a Japanese continuation school in New York starts with the following phrase: *boku to watashi* ([male] I and [female or neutral] I). It does not make sense when it is translated into English. It means that children who go to a local school and a Japanese continuation school are constantly jumping over a cultural gap between the world of gender-assigned pronouns and the world of non-gender-assigned pronouns. Conflict in their awareness of gender roles caused by this jump has become a new research theme for linguistic anthropology influenced by women's studies.

According to a linguistic anthropological study of American–Japanese bilingual women on the West Coast of the United States, they exhibited more positive attitudes in English and more passive and restrained attitudes in Japanese when answering the same question in these two languages. This result serves as an example that thinking patterns are dictated by the language used.

As I mentioned at the beginning, it is necessary to control other variables in order to study gender differences in overseas experiences under equal conditions. I have also stated that the sample size is too small to achieve this. Still, when we look at Japanese students studying at universities in the United States, we find that female students generally learn the language faster and perform better than male students. This tendency has been supported by a survey of postwar Fulbright students.

There are several theories for this.

The first theory is that women are generally more diligent and better suited to repetitive learning tasks such as language learning than men. This is based on gender stereotypes and sounds like a self-fulfilling prophecy.

Second, women have less pride in their own culture and take a more positive attitude in cross-cultural adaptation than men. In other words, women are less loyal to their own culture than men. This theory is also highly biased and difficult to prove.

Third, under the resource distribution structure that favors men, women generally have fewer opportunities to study abroad than men. Those who manage to study abroad under this condition are a privileged minority among women. Even in today's society where overseas study is no longer only for the elite, the average academic standard of female overseas students tends to be higher than that of male overseas students. This explanation is sufficiently convincing in view of the ratios of overseas students to the population by gender and age group.

Fourth, women are conditioned to be less afraid of mistakes at the entry level in language learning due to gender socialization, and therefore improve faster. By contrast, men have too much pride or dignity to make rudimentary mistakes. Similar observations have been made by teachers who teach Japanese to foreigners. When teaching the Japanese language to Chinese researchers, they have found that men may learn at a slower pace due to resistance or anger stemming from their pride and dignity, and their wives may learn faster in some cases.

The fifth theory states that Japanese women can be more active in the world of English-speaking culture, which is not gender specific nor age specific, than when they use the Japanese language. This is supported by the abovementioned linguistic anthropological study.

Sixth, under the gender role expectations for active males and passive females, women tend to have many opportunities to be spoken to even if they do not initiate conversations, whereas men feel the pressure to initiate conversations and therefore get fewer opportunities to practice their language skills.

It is likely that more than one factor is involved.

Cross-cultural experience is a sort of limit situation that turns both men and women into a kind of powerless minority. In such a critical situation, it is, paradoxically, women with *structural inferiority* (Turner, 1974) in society who have an advantage over men. This paradox is commonly found in other limit situations such as ethnic minority employment and family living in an economic recession (Elder, 1974). In these situations, it is difficult for men to find full-time jobs, while it is easier for women to find jobs for 'pin money.' Consequently, a reversal of roles in which the wife earns a daily wage to support the family while the husband is unemployed may occur among ethnic minorities and during an economic recession.

Since overseas students have less social resources than business-men, they tend to find themselves in a limit situation more often. Here is an actual case of a Japanese student and his wife. She followed her husband to the United States but she learned the language faster than he did and had a chance to find a part-time job, enabling her to earn more income than her husband. Once subservient to her husband, the experience of living in the English-speaking environment made her more assertive. As a result, their previous power relationship reversed during their stay, and they divorced three years after their arrival in the United States.

How about gender differences in cases of company-sponsored students and workers with a guaranteed distribution of social resources? Unfortunately, we must wait a while until we have more female samples under equal conditions before finding an answer to this question.

Wives of expatriate employees

The most numerous cases of female overseas experience comprise the wives who accompany their husbands to overseas posts. Yasuko Minoura became interested in cross-cultural experiences of children while taking a postgraduate course in anthropology at the University of California, Los Angeles, and conducted interview surveys of eighty families of Japanese expatriate workers in Los

Angeles from 1976 to 1981. The survey result was published in 1984 and is now regarded as a classic in this field (Minoura, 1984). She approached the subject from the angle of children's cross-cultural experiences but ended up looking at the situations of the Japanese wives behind these children. Her work reveals another aspect of gender differences in cross-cultural adaptation.

In cases of expatriate families, it is the wife rather than the husband who has more difficulty adapting to the foreign environment according to Minoura's report. This is contrary to the case I mentioned in the previous section. This is because husband and wife are not experiencing an expatriate life *under equal conditions*.

First, because of the gender role assignment between 'husband as a breadwinner and wife as a homemaker,' the wife generally has fewer opportunities to be exposed to a foreign culture than her husband, who participates in a workplace.

Second, the wife tends to stay at home or within the Japanese expatriate community due to a lack of information and a language barrier, while the husband tends to be given more preparatory training prior to his overseas posting.

Third, many of the expatriate couples are hypergamic, and the wife generally has lower education and language skills than her husband.

Fourth, many of the wives are dependent and family-oriented, even in Japan, and they are not willing to go into local communities while residing overseas partly because their sojourns are only for limited periods.

Fifth, if the wife tries to become involved in community activity or employment, she tends to come under tangible and intangible forms of pressure from her Japanese community or her husband's employer.

Corporations are keen to address the issue of cross-cultural adaptation and stress of businessmen, and many studies have been conducted for that purpose; however, they make little mention of the families. Problems of repatriated children have been in the news but the issue of cross-cultural adaptation of wives draws little attention. However, the number of reports and non-fiction stories about the feelings of entrapment and the struggles experienced by the wives of expatriate businessmen has been increasing lately, including *Tsumatachi no kaigai chūzai* (Overseas posting from a wife's point of view) by Hiroko Mutō (1985) and *Madamu shōsha* (Trading company wives) by Etsuko Taniguchi (1985).

Overseas posting can be a type of critical situation for wives as well. There have been various cases of trouble, such as husbands sending their families back to Japan due to overwhelming pressure from their triple-handicapped wives (who can't answer the telephone, can't speak and can't drive), husbands cutting their overseas assignments short due to their wives' depression or nervous breakdowns, or couples divorcing due to marital discord during or after their overseas posting.

The peculiarities of a Japanese community consisting of the families of Japanese expatriate businessmen have also been reported. The pecking order is linked to the husband's status and length of stay in the foreign country; women who actively pursue exchanges with local communities are ostracized; and there are ambivalent attitudes of dependency and contempt towards Japanese permanent residents such as Japanese descendants and the Japanese wives of local men. No matter how large and dispersed their living space is, they still live in a small Japanese-speaking community. Compared with *shataku-zuma* (company flat wives) in Japan, they live in an even more isolated 'information-starved zone' in a sense. Corporations' attitudes towards the families of their overseas employees reinforce the isolation of their wives from local communities. Corporations say that they restrict the wives' community activity and employment because they pay enough salary, including an overseas allowance, so that the employees and families can maintain the prestige of their employers. We can clearly see the logic of family corporatism rather than corporate familism by which corporations hire the services not only of the husband but of the whole family (Kinoshita, 1983).

Recently, corporations have begun to recognize the importance of the role of the wife in the life of an expatriate employee. The role of an active and sociable wife with language skills is considered important. Some corporations give preparatory training to the whole family or provide counseling about schooling of repatriated children. Other companies conduct life skills seminars for men to rectify the shortcomings of those husbands who are excellent businessmen but 'reliant on their wives for everything outside of work.'

Through counseling of children with learning disabilities, Cunningham reports in *Kaigai shijo kyōiku jijō* that she discovered a distortion in the *Japanese-style family* in the background. The distortion in the Japanese-style family is, according to her, a pathological manifestation of maternal society. One problem is the absence of the father at home due to long working hours and the gender role assignment; another problem is the resulting closeness of the mother and her children and their isolation that is promoted by a language barrier and other reasons. The inherent distortion of the Japanese-style family that may not surface in Japan tends to come to light in a limit situation at overseas posts. Pre-existing friction between husband and wife and between parents and children surface in this process. While overseas postings have united some families, many couples have been driven to the brink of divorce. Whether positive or negative, the experience of overseas posting is a family crisis. A mother's anxiety is communicated to her children. Cunningham has dealt with clinical cases of anxious children suffering from various maladjustment disorders.

She points out some common attitudes among the fathers of these children with learning disabilities.

First, they respond to their children's trouble by showing an attitude of indifference or by ignoring it. They do not go to see teachers or counselors, even when they are asked to.

Next, they go beyond indifference and into a state of denial and make the situation worse rather than better. For example, when a child with a language adaptation problem is advised to repeat the same grade or transfer to a Japanese school, it is predominantly the father who rejects such a proposal. A father may deny the reality and try to impose his own values or expectations, thinking, 'Why should my child repeat the grade while all other children are moving up,' or, 'There is no way my child cannot succeed; I want him to grow strong and powerful.'

Third, to make matters worse, his denial sometimes turns into an attack on his wife and child, who may be driven into the corner by his rebuke. For example, he may punish his wife for his child's trouble by hitting her or shouting at her, or shift the blame onto her by saying, 'My family line has never had an abnormal child.' The troubled mother and child who are in need of support are driven to isolation by the father, who is closest of all people to them. At this point, the mother and her child are only one step away from a double suicide. In such cases, Japanese fathers are not only neglecting their role as father but actively abandoning their children. Cunningham's report on clinical cases contains many such disastrous examples.

Cunningham also points out the predominance of boys among children with learning disabilities and two possible reasons for this. First, Japanese families place much greater expectations and pressure on sons than daughters. Second, mothers tend to become closer to sons and spoil them as a result.

Gender differences in developmental disorders in puberty have been decreasing in recent years. In the past, it was said that truancy and domestic violence were more common among boys, while eating disorders were peculiar to girls, and these gender differences in pathology were explained by excessive expectations and pressure on boys and the internalization of inferiority and rejection of maturity by girls. However, psychopathologists are reporting that such gender differences in developmental disorders are decreasing lately. There is no male–female difference in the incidence of refusal to attend school any more, and juvenile domestic violence has been reported in girls as well as boys. Even eating disorders are seen in boys. Now that most children are either the eldest son or the eldest daughter or even an only child, parental expectations and pressure on children and the tendency for the closer mother–child relationship are perhaps no longer gender specific. There is the possibility that this trend will also be found among repatriated children.

Repatriated children

We already have ample research on the effects of overseas experiences on children's socialization and identity formation. The general understanding is that younger children adapt to foreign cultures more rapidly and thoroughly, and have serious trouble re-adapting to Japanese culture when they are repatriated. The turning point is said to be the age of eight. Ryōko Nakatsu (1976), an expert in bilingual education, argues that children should not start learning a foreign language until they establish their identity in their native tongue during the language formation period at around the age of three or four.

How about gender identity and gender socialization? Masako Kuroki (1986) conducted a comparative survey of Japanese residents and Japanese Americans in the Bay Area on the West Coast about their views of gender roles (see Tables 13.1 and 13.2).

Of the gender role norms in Table 13.2, the levels of agreement to the second proposition, which asks about the relative importance between individualistic norms and familistic norms ('It is okay to give priority to personal desires over family obligations'), are very interesting. The result is rather unexpected in that Japanese residents without permanent residency agreed to this proposition most, followed in order by the Japanese residents with permanent residency, the third-generation Japanese Americans, the first-generation Japanese Americans and the second-generation Japanese Americans.

Table 13.1: Breakdown of each subject group

	Japanese		Japanese American		
	Group A (non-resident)	Group B (permanent resident)	Group C (first generation)	Group D (second generation)	Group E (third generation)
Average age	29	37	84	60	30
Years of US residency	4	13	61	56	28
Years of schooling	15	16	10	16	17
% of women	30	53	84	52	53
Primary language[a]	15	23.5	0	95.2	100

Notes:

All figures are the average values of each group.

a: Primary language = % of people who feel more comfortable using English in daily living

The result suggests that, first, the second-generation Japanese Americans show a higher level of conformity to traditional gender norms than the first-generation Japanese Americans; second, Japanese Americans have more traditional Japanese values than Japanese residents; and third, short-term residents have a stronger un-Japanese, individualistic tendency than permanent residents.

Kuroki cites the following five reasons for these findings.

1. Japanese Americans and permanent residents are ethnic minority groups in the United States and therefore have a stronger sense of loyalty to their ethnic identity and a stronger sense of belonging to the Japanese community.
2. The first-generation Japanese Americans and the second-generation Japanese Americans are at different life stages. The former are able to be more individualistic because they are older and relieved from family obligations, while the latter are still at the life stage of greater family obligations.
3. New immigrants who were born in Japan are much younger than the first-generation Japanese Americans who immigrated before the Second World War and they have already experienced changes in Japanese society in terms of declining family values.
4. Japanese residents left Japan for more positive reasons compared with Japanese Americans.
5. Short-term residents are generally students, academics and businesspeople who have higher academic qualifications.

Table 13.2: Norms regarding the roles of wife and husband in a marriage and 'family' ideology

	Japanese		Japanese American		
	Group A (non-resident)	Group B (permanent resident)	Group C (first generation)	Group D (second generation)	Group E (third generation)
1. Wife's work is as important as husband's work.					
	1.59 (3)	1.46 (2)	1.93 (4)	1.95 (5)	1.40 (1)
2. It is okay to give priority to personal desires over family obligations.					
	2.21 (1)	2.25 (2)	3.00 (4)	3.10 (5)	2.85 (3)
3. It is okay for parents to leave children with a babysitter and go out for pleasure.					
	2.57 (2)	2.00 (1)	2.92 (4)	2.75 (3)	2.94 (5)
4. I would rather rely on my family than strangers when I need help.					
	2.40 (4)	1.80 (1)	2.00 (3)	1.85 (2)	2.50 (5)
5. I should do what I think is right even if it is against my parents' wishes.					
	1.83 (1)	2.08 (3)	1.91 (2)	2.38 (5)	2.33 (4)

Note 1: Figures are the average values. Numbers in brackets show rankings in order of agreement to each statement.

Note 2: (1) Strongly agree; (2) Agree; (3) Disagree; (4) Strongly disagree; (5) Not sure. The average values were calculated excluding 'not sure.'

Source: Kuroki (1986).

Generally speaking, the nature of overseas experience depends largely on whether it is voluntary or involuntary. It is possible to say that the first-generation Japanese Americans and short-term residents who voluntarily go abroad have relatively low loyalty to their own culture, whereas those who live overseas involuntarily, such as the second-generation Japanese Americans and the children of expatriate businessmen, feel a stronger sense of loyalty to traditional values due to their identity problems.

Regarding gender differences in loyalty to one's own culture, it appears that women generally have lower loyalty to their own culture than men. This is also evidenced by the state of interracial marriages of Japanese Americans. The rate of interracial marriages among Japanese Americans has been very high in recent years but there is a considerable gender difference. Women have a high rate of exogamy and men have a high rate of endogamy within the same ethnic group. And they both show a clear interracial hypergamic tendency. Women tend to marry white men, including Jews, and men tend to marry Asian women such as Korean Americans or Chinese Americans. It is difficult to refute the claim that 'the Japanese are racists' based on this trend in interracial marriages.

The gender difference in interracial marriage reflects the male-dominant patriarchal system. First, women are destined to 'marry out' to their husbands' family lines under patriarchy and, second, women marry up into a higher class under male chauvinism. Women leave their own culture when they marry into a foreign culture. They adapt quickly, perhaps because they have to when they are thrown into a new environment. Women's relatively low loyalty to their own culture and quick cross-cultural adaptation are consequences and not causes. The gender differences in cross-cultural adaptation may be regarded as the paradox of a patriarchal conspiracy to raise daughters 'to be easily assimilated to the way of any other family traditions.'

This paradox has merits and demerits. One of the demerits is the appearance of the so-called *bairingyaru* (bilingual girls), who have failed to develop an ethnic identity under a fine-sounding slogan of 'raising a daughter as an internationally minded person.' As I mentioned above, parents have different expectations for sons and daughters and do not worry too much about the future of daughters. Parents tend to keep their daughters at local schools for a longer period because they want to dote on them as if they were their pets. This has produced a new breed of Japanese called the *henjapa* (odd Japanese), who are ethnically 100% Japanese with native Japanese parents but whose language and behavior are rather foreign. The July 1987 issue of *Akurosu* (Across) magazine featured the *ritānī-chan* (little returnees) boom and defined a returnee as 'a Japanese with a high foreigner level in the blood' (Akurosu, 1987: 54–77). The *banana* is a derogatory term for the Japanese – yellow outside and white inside – but a returnee is not pretending to be a foreigner; she has a completely *foreign mind*. These odd Japanese people with 'a high foreigner level in the blood' who have failed to adapt to Japanese society or to develop an identity as a Japanese have managed to enjoy popularity as a type of new passing fad because they are female; they would have been simply shunned if they were male. The *bairingyaru* is a girl, not a boy. These bilingual girls are being hired as DJs at domestic English-language radio stations such as FEN and as newscasters and international reporters on television, and are becoming new cultural heroines of their generation. No matter how bright their world seems, however, full membership of

Japanese society is unavailable to these women who are being used as disposable marginal workers in the mass media.

These women, who are not required to have loyalty to their own culture 'because they are women,' are conversely those who are *abandoned* by their own culture. Gender differences also cast a dark shadow on the issue of repatriated children as abandoned people.

Conclusion

I would like to point out two issues in conclusion.

One is the issue of cross-cultural adaptation and the family. The family has been regarded as the base unit for cross-cultural adaptation until now. Based on her study of returnees and their families from China, Young-hae Chon raises an objection to this hypothesis about the process of adaptation to Japanese culture. She presents a clear-cut fact that the family never works as a unit in overseas adaptation (Chon, 1988).

A family is a group containing gender and age differences. Chon points out that adaptation is, after all, an internal process of each individual; such processes may happen to interact with one another within a family unit to create group dynamics, but the family never becomes a coherent higher unit – in other words, adaptation of the father does not lead to adaptation of the whole family. Adaptation of parents does not guarantee adaptation of children and adaptation of the husband does not guarantee adaptation of the wife or vice versa. It is an individual task for individual members of the family and any gaps and distortions between them will create new family dynamics. It may unify the family in some cases and it may magnify the existing discord and lead to various crises in other cases. The mythical image of a father grappling with the power of nature to protect his family, as in Laura Ingalls Wilder's *Little house on the prairie*, crumbles away here. The family is not a higher-level shelter to protect individuals and mediate their adaptation; the individual is the unit for adaptation. In that case, what is required is a more active investigation into the significance of gender and age differences as variables in the process of cross-cultural adaptation. Also, more in-depth studies are needed on the subject of dynamics in the multicultural family that has greater adaptation gaps between its members.

The second issue is assimilationism and post-repatriation re-adaptation. There are two sides to cross-cultural adaptation:

adaptation to foreign cultures and re-adaptation to one's own culture. Here we find the issue of a hierarchy of different cultures. Assimilationism works only in relation to superior cultures. Accordingly, overseas experiences of the Japanese are totally different between those who go into a European or American culture, which is considered superior, and those who go into an Asian or African culture, which is considered inferior. In third-world countries, Japanese expatriates rarely send their children to local schools and they live within Japanese colonies as a matter of course. Since Westerners believed in their cultural superiority over everyone else, they persisted in colonialism and maintained their way of life wherever they went. Thanks to economic prosperity, the Japanese are attaining the level of the former European/American colonialists.

The history of repatriated children can be divided into three periods. The first period was dominated by a total noninterventionist attitude and optimism. In reaction, *gaikoku-hagashi* (peeling off the foreignness) and forced re-adaptation upon return became widespread in the second period. In the third period, the number of returnees increased sufficiently to begin forming privileged ghettos that looked like foreign enclaves inside Japan. More parents are now sending their returnee children to domestic American and international schools in order to protect them from the pressure of *gaikoku-hagashi* and re-adaptation. Some returnees who have failed to re-adapt are returning to foreign lands. On the other hand, some universities are giving them preferential treatment, such as special admission quotas, as part of *countermeasures* for returnee problems; in some quarters returnees are feted as a privileged class of people with a special resource called bilingualism. International schools and American schools are virtually foreign enclaves in Japan but they are now becoming ghettos for Japanese children who are ethnically 100% Japanese but use English in their daily living. Some Japanese parents are wanting to send their children to these schools even though they are not returnees. This reversal appears to be triggered by the perception that being a Japanese-foreigner in Japan without 'peeling off the foreignness' has a positive value. However, considering that this trend is again stronger among girls than boys, it is doubtful that Japanese society is seriously hoping to utilize human resources with 'overseas experiences' as I mentioned earlier.

And this situation only applies to returnees from culturally superior countries. Returnees from culturally inferior countries did not need to try to assimilate into local cultures because they lived in Japanese colonies and hence they are not subjected to re-adaptation pressure to 'peel off the foreignness.' European and American colonists did not suffer serious returnee problems because they simply moved about their cultural enclaves in their colonies all over the world.

The history of returnees now appears to be entering the fourth period, which can be called the colonialist period. It is ironic that this tendency is increasing in both the culturally superior and inferior countries as Japan is becoming more and more *internationalized*. Now that non-elite workers of medium to small companies go abroad on transfer and the population of overseas Japanese has reached a critical mass that forms ethnic communities in many parts of the world, paradoxically it has become possible for them to live completely within the bounds of their ghettos, such as in the Japanese quarters. There will be more and more Japanese people with overseas experiences who return home after residing in a foreign country where they only spoke the Japanese language, just as Europeans and Americans did in the past. The expected rise in the number of Japanese whose overseas experiences are not really overseas experiences is perhaps the paradox of internationalization of the Japanese.

Notes

Foreword

1 Etsuko Yamashita (1991), *"Josei no jidai" to iu shinwa: Ueno Chizuko wa onna o sukueru ka* [The myth of "the era of women": Can Chizuko Ueno save women?]': Seikyūsha; Takashi Uehara (1992), *Ueno Chizuko nanka kowaku nai* [Who's afraid of Chizuko Ueno?]: Mainichi Shinbunsha; Yōko Haruka (2000), *Tōdai de Ueno Chizuko ni kenka o manabu* [Learning how to fight from Ueno Chizuko at the University of Tokyo]: Chikuma Shobō.

2 'Kōzō shugi no ninshiki moderu: Lévi-Strauss no baai [The epistemological model of structuralism: The case of Lévi-Strauss],' *Shakaigaku hyōron* 26, no. 2 (1975): 2-17. These structuralist essays were later collected as *Kōzō shugi no bōken* [Adventures in structuralism]: Keisō Shobō (1985).

3 *Shihonsei to kaji rōdō: Marukusu shugi feminizumu no mondai kōsei* [Capitalism and domestic labor: The problematique of Marxist feminism]: Kaimeisha (1985); *Kafuchōsei to shihonsei: Marukusu shugi feminizumu no chihei* [Patriarchy and capitalism: The horizon of Marxist feminism]: Iwanami Shoten (1990).

4 *Sekushii gyaru no dai kenkyū: onna no yomikata, yomarekata, yomasekata* [The great study of sexy gals: How to read women, how women are read, how to make women readable]: Kōbunsha (1982); *Sukâto no shita no gekijō: hito wa dōshite panti ni kodawaru no ka* [The theater under the skirt: Why people care so much about panties]: Kawade Shobō Shinsha (1989).

5 Ueno made this statement in her afterword to *Onna asobi* [Women's play]: Gakuyō Shobō (1988).

6 Minako Saitō discusses these and other aspects of Ueno's popularity in *Bundan aidoru ron* [A study of idols of the literary establishment]: Iwanami Shoten (2002).

7 Sandra Buckley (1997), *Broken Silence: Voices of the Japanese Feminism* (Berkeley: University of California Press). Chapter 5 of *The Modern Family in Japan* briefly reprises some of these debates.

8 'In the feminine guise: A trap of reverse orientalism' and 'Collapse of "Japanese mothers",' in Richard F. Calichman (ed.), *Contemporary Japanese Thought,* New York: Columbia University Press (2005).

9 *Nationalism and Gender,* Melbourne: Trans Pacific Press (2004). Originally published as *Nashonarizumu to jendā*: Seidosha (1998).

10 *Danryū bungaku ron* [Discussing men's literature]: Chikuma Shobō (1992).

11 *Ueno Chizuko ga bungaku o shakaigaku suru* [Ueno Chizuko sociologizes literature]: Asahi Shinbunsha (2000).

12 *Ohitorisama no rōgo* [Old age for the single person]: Hōken (2007).

13 Yōko Haruka's aforementioned book vividly conveys Ueno's charismatic presence as a teacher at the University of Tokyo. My own first encounter with Ueno's work came while I was an undergraduate in Japan, reading her booklet *Capitalism and Housework* (1985) for a course taught by Yumiko Ehara, another prominent feminist sociologist. Ueno's proposal to 'take back the means of reproduction' as a feminist solution to the oppression of women struck me then as a hip and non-sentimental way to talk about motherhood. It was a perspective and tone that appealed to many – both female and male readers were attracted to these qualities in Ueno's writing.

14 See her edited volume *Kyanpasu sei sabetsu jijō: sutoppu za akahara* [The situation of sexual discrimination on campus: Stop academic harassment]: Sanseidō (1997).

15 See *Tōjisha shuken* [Sovereignty of those who are concerned]: Iwanami Shoten (2003), which Ueno co-wrote with Shōji Nakanishi, an activist for the rights of the disabled.

16 See the Japanese government's website *www.gender.go.jp*

17 *Radikaru ni katareba...: Ueno Chizuko taidân shū* [Radically speaking...: Dialogues with Chizuko Ueno]: Heibonsha (2001).

18 Chizuko Ueno *et al.* (2006), *Bakkurasshu!: naze jendā furī wa tatakareta no ka?* [Backlash! Why gender free was bashed]: Sōfūsha.

19 'Famirī aidentiti no yukue,' originally published in *Kazoku no shakaishi* [The social history of the family], vol. 1 of *Henbō suru kazoku* [The changing family]: Iwanami Shoten (1991).

20 'Josei no henbō to kazoku,' originally published in Sōichi Endō, Toshiyuki Mitsuyoshi, and Minoru Nakata (eds.), *Gendai Nihon no kōzō hendō: 1970nen ikō* [Structural transformation of contemporary Japan: After 1970]: Sekai Shisōsha (1991).

21 'Nihon gata kindai kazoku no seiritsu.' This chapter was not previously published elsewhere and was written for this collection.

22 'Kazoku no kindai,' originally published as 'Nihon gata kindai kazoku no tanjō [The birth of the Japanese model of the modern family]' in Shinzō Ogi, Isao Kumakura, and Chizuko Ueno (eds.), *Fūzoku, sei* [Customs, sexuality], vol. 23 of *Nihon kindai shisō taikei* [Compendium of modern Japanese thought]: Iwanami Shoten (1990).

23 'Joseishi to kindai,' originally published as 'Joseishi to kindai: feminizumu wa dō toraete kitaka [Women's history and modernity: How feminism has appraised it]' in Tamito Yoshida (ed.), *Gendai no shikumi: shakaigaku no riron de toku* [Contemporary structures: Decoding through sociological theories], Shinyōsha (1991).

24 '"Umesao kateigaku" no tenkai,' originally published as 'Umesao "katei" gaku to bunmei shi teki nihirizumu' [Umesao's "home" science and his nihilism from the perspective of the history of civilizations],' in *Josei to bunmei* [Women and civilizations], vol. 9 of *Umesao Tadao chosakushū* [Collected works of Umesao Tadao]: Chūōkōronsha, 1991.

25 Chizuko Ueno (ed.) (1982), *Shufu ronsō o yomu: zen kiroku* [Reading the housewife debates: Complete records] (2 vols.): Keisō Shobō.

26 'Gijutsu kakushin to kaji rōdō,' originally published in *Kazoku no fōkuroa* [Family folklore], vol. 4 of *Henbō suru kazoku* [The changing family]: Iwanami Shoten (1991).

27 '"Haha" no sengo shi,' originally published as 'Kaisetsu *Seijuku to sōshitsu kara sanjū nen* [Commentary: Thirty years since *Maturity and Loss*]' in *Seijuku to sōshitsu: 'haha' no hōkai* [Maturity and loss: The disintegration of 'motherhood'] by Jun Etō (1967; Kōdansha, 1993).

28 '"Posuto shishūki" no tsuma tachi,' originally published as 'Hihyō: "futsū no onna" ga jiken ni natta' [Critique: "Ordinary women" become news], in *Saitō Shigeo no ruporutâju Nihon no jōkei 1: tsuma tachi no shishūki* [Shigeo Saitō's reportage of Japanese scenes 1: Midlife crisis stage of wives]: Iwanai Shoten (1993).

29 'Fūfu bessei no wana,' originally published as 'Fūfu bessei no jinruigaku [The anthropology of separate surnames for married couples],' *Gendai no esupuri* [Contemporary esprit], no. 261, special issue 'Fūfu bessei jidai o ikiru [Living in the era of separate surnames for married couples]:' Shibundō (1989).

30 'Ikirareta keiken toshite no rōgo,' originally published as 'Rōjin mondai to rōgo mondai no rakusa [The disparity between the old people issue and the old age issue],' in *Oi no paradaimu* [Paradigm of aging], vol. 2 of *Oi no hakken* [Discovering old age]: Iwanami Shoten (1986).

31 '"Onna en" no kanōsei,' originally published as 'Eraberu en, erabenai en' [Ties that can be chosen, ties that cannot be chosen], in Yasuyuki Kurita (ed.), *Gendai Nihon ni okeru dentō to hen'yō 3: Nihonjin no ningen kankei* [Tradition and transformation in contemporary Japan 3: Japanese human relations]: Domesu Shuppan (1987).

32 'Sei sabetsu no gyakusetsu: ibunka tekiō to seisa,' originally published in Shūzo Koyama (ed.), *Nihonjin ni totte no gaikoku* [What foreign countries mean for the Japanese]: Domesu Shuppan (1991).

Chapter 1

1 This chapter is based on my research project titled *Family identity* sponsored by Odakyū Gakkai (Odakyū Society) in fiscal 1990. Other collaborators of the research include Teiko Mukōda, Yoshiko Yamada, Mikiko Ōshima, Mihoko Yamamoto, Motoko Takahashi, Ayako Mori, Rika Miyai, Kazuko Zura and Toshiki Tsujinaka. I would like to express my gratitude to the Odakyū Gakkai and my collaborators. All data in this chapter were originally generated by the *Family identity* research project, with the exception of secondary sources that have been explicitly referenced.

2 These days the abbreviation CI is in some cases used to refer to *community identity*. This also reflects the increased mobility of residents and the resulting change of local communities into associational groups whose members can join or leave their community at any time.

3 For instance, the duolocal marriage practiced during the Heian era was associated with patrilineal descent and matrilocal residence. A child did not live with his or her father but, according to the principle of patrilineal descent, was considered to belong to the father's family rather than the mother's family with which the child actually lived. Cultural anthropological studies on kinship have found that although a matrilineal descent/patrilocal residence system is theoretically possible, such a system has not been observed in reality (Lévi-Strauss, [1947] 1968).

4 'Arutsuhaimā-byō rikon riyū ni (Alzheimer's disease recognized as justification for divorce),' *Yomiuri Shimbun*, evening edition, 17 September 1990.

5 A survey has revealed that parents of disabled children are more likely to divorce and that there are substantial gender differences between fathers and mothers in the way they deal with their disabled children (Yōda, 1986).

6 The increase of cases of matrilocal residence might be a result of the increase of households with no son, which, in turn, has resulted from the declining number of births. On the other hand, the trend in the change of family name by marriage shows that over 95% of married couples have chosen to use the husband's family name, indicating that the cases of matrilocal residence shown in the data do not represent cases of the conventional adoption of a daughter's husband by her parents as a son-in-law so as to enable her to succeed to her own family's name.

7 A separate survey conducted by the same author's team has found that married couples over forty years of age are more likely than younger couples to sleep in separate bedrooms and that those who do so tend to have sex less often.

8 The custom of levirate marriage, in which the widow would marry her deceased husband's unmarried younger brother, remained inveterate and continued beyond the end of the war. Both the widow and her brother-in-law were sacrificed for the family's continued existence. Tragic, unamusing comedies in which the eldest son was officially reported to have been killed in war but who actually survived and returned to his wife – who had already married his younger brother – were ubiquitous all over the country immediately after Japan's defeat in the war.

9 Under Japanese law, remarriage does not automatically create a parent–child relationship between one party and the other's children from his or her previous marriage. To become a stepparent of the new partner's children, one must enter into an adoption arrangement with the children separately from the marriage.

10 Girls' comics have repeatedly portrayed fateful pairs, such as Gilbert and Serge in *Kaze to ki no uta* (The poem of wind and trees) by Keiko Takemiya (1977–84), Mari Takatō and Shingo In'nami in *Mari to Shingo* (Mari and Shingo) by Toshie Kihara (1979–84), and Minato and Hotaru in *Jurietto no tamago* (Juliet's egg) by Yoshino Sakumi (1988–89). These pairs are prohibited from having sex with each other by the fact that they are of the same gender in pairs of non-blood-related people or by a blood relation in pairs of both genders, creating a balance between similarity and distance (Ueno, 1989b).

Chapter 2

1 The text of this chapter was initially published in 1991.

2 'Younger women are more housewife-oriented – Survey by Lady's Forum reveals high proportion of young women wishing to become housewives,' *Asahi Shimbun*, Evening Edition, 23 May 1989.

3 Masako Amano has conducted a detailed survey on the workers' collectives of consumer cooperatives. According to this survey, members of these

workers' collectives are, again, women who have higher levels of education and belong to higher economic classes than average women (Amano, 1988).

Chapter 3

1 Satō argues that individualism can be nurtured only within the scope of family rights asserted against public authority. In this sense, his argument agrees with that of Kojita, to be described later. However, Satō calls our attention to the historical process in which Japanese nationalism first broke up families into separate individuals before freshly reorganizing *ie*. There is a discontinuity between Japanese familism and its premodern counterpart.

2 This is in agreement with Kanji Itō's view that the life span of 'pseudo-family state ideology' was the half century 'from the late Meiji era to Japan's defeat in the war' (Itō, M., 1982: 42). 'The *ie* system, which had taken root in Japanese society since early-modern times, was forced to change with this series of postwar changes. As a result, pseudo-family state ideology lost the support from the *ie* system and had no choice but to collapse. In this sense, Japan's defeat in the war as a historical fact was a key factor behind the collapse of pseudo-family state ideology which had played a leading role for nearly half a century since the late Meiji era...' (Itō M., 1982: 207).

3 The first Japanese national census was conducted in 1920. No reliable demographic data are available before this date. The national census as a complete count survey of the Japanese people itself reflects the trend of the times, when records of the family registers are no longer reliable due to rapid population migration.

4 In the succession of Okinawan *tōtōmē* (the equivalent of family Buddhist altars and memorial tablets in the Japanese mainland), exclusive male inheritance is practiced. Women, including direct descendants of the patriarch, are forced by their relatives to waive their right to inherit family property (for the reason that it is costly to maintain the religious services for *tōtōmē*). This exclusive male priority system, which gives priority to collateral men over direct female descendants, is of Chinese origin. In Okinawa equal inheritance among all children regardless of gender, as guaranteed by the postwar civil code, has little effect at the common law level. There have been only two lawsuits after the war in which women sought the right of inheritance on the grounds of the law. In both cases the female plaintiffs won, but in one case the plaintiff was forced to move to the mainland because of social sanctions against her (Horiba, 1990; *Ryūkyū Shinpō Sha* [Ryūkyū Shinpō Newspaper], 1980).

5 'Descendant worship' can replace 'ancestor worship' in providing a foundation for the superindividual 'perpetuity of family.' Ayako Mori, who conducted investigative research on women and tombs, points out that some people's practice of making an advance payment to a temple or shrine to have services performed in perpetuity for the repose of their souls is an indication of descendant worship. Those who make this kind of donation in advance before their death do not make their tombs personal. Instead, they make the tomb the family grave and expect that the tomb

will be joined by their children (and also that their children will thank them for having the tomb available for them).

6 Lévi-Strauss termed the former the *mechanical model* and the latter the *statistical model* (Lévi-Strauss, 1958).

7 According to the 'homogamy/heterogamy index by husband's and wife's education' (Inoue and Ehara, 1991: 11), which can be regarded as representing today's class system, the homogamy index is highest for married couples whose husband and wife are both university graduates, followed by those whose husband and wife are both junior high school graduates. In addition, there is generally a strong tendency for female hypergamy, which has made it exceptional that a wife has higher education than her husband. Even the data for 1987 (*Dai kyū-ji shussanryoku chōsa* [The ninth Japanese national fertility survey], Institute of Population Problems, Ministry of Health and Welfare), when love marriage had gained an advantage over arranged marriage, seem to indicate a strong tendency for class endogamy.

8 In this regard, it is questionable to treat cultural representations, such as films and literary works, as folkloric materials. This is because artistic expressions are normative to varying degrees. It is also intriguing that the images of autonomous patriarchs mentioned by Satō as examples all occur in such geographical settings as southern France or Italy, where the medieval tradition of extended family strongly remains. It is likely that the images of patriarchs depicted in these settings are idealized, dying images.

9 The Meiji era saw a rapid increase in parent–child suicides, which can be regarded as a result of the isolation of families from the community. The increased exclusiveness of families from kin other than lineal relatives resulted in parents being no longer able to think that they could leave their children in the care of relatives after committing suicide. Instead, these parents chose to take their children with them, resulting in the increase of parent–child suicides.

10 The deflationary fiscal policy implemented in the 1880s by Finance Minister Masayoshi Matsukata, who attempted to curb the inflationary trend caused by the expenditure of the Seinan internal war after the Meiji Restoration.

11 The fact that these three authors write the word *ie* in katakana instead of kanji (as people normally do) in the original Japanese text indicates their intention to use the word to refer to the ideology instead of the entity. Their use of katakana in writing the word *ie* also intends to discuss *ie* as a folk category in the context of comparative history of civilization.

12 Nakane's argument is originally based on the model proposed by F. L. K. Hsu in *Clan, cast and club* (Hsu, 1963). Hsu regards family as the smallest unit of social structure and attempts to model all other social structures as extending in concentric circles from family, based on which 'vertical' personal relations and 'horizontal' personal relations are dominant in each of the other social structures. However, it is questionable to regard Hsu's model as 'universal.' First, groups at different levels, such as family, village, company and nation, cannot always be regarded as extending in concentric circles based on the same principle (i.e. even if the family or company has a *herrschaft*-like (hierarchical) nature, the village or union

may have a *genossenschaft*-like (egalitarian) nature). Second, Hsu's family model itself is a 'modern' thing in that it is under the influence of Freud.

Chapter 4

1 See, for examples, Ariès, [1960] 1973 and Badinter, 1981. For a definition of the modern family, see Ochiai, 1989.
2 In locations where husband and wife by custom eat separately, eating together constitutes a violation of a taboo in that it causes a confusion of categories (Noma, 1961).
3 An edited reprint in Japanese was published in 1961 with Kōshin Noma as editor.
4 Unlike the courtesans, the *jiwon'na* referred to here would have had connections through locality and blood lineage and were nonprofessional women who would have been targets for marriage.
5 Even having said this, as a conclusion the author takes an exceedingly compromising stance, listing the respective evils of free marriage and of arranged marriage, saying that 'accordingly, I myself the writer hope that the right mode of marriage for our present society will allow a compromise between freedom and intervention from family so that we can enjoy that which is beneficial and avoid that which is evil.'
6 For more about *Irogoto no shikata*, see 'Shinsen zōkaki ron (New version: Anatomical studies on genital organs)' in Ogi, Kumakura and Ueno, 1990.
7 Most of this is recorded in Tonozaki (ed.), 1971. While Ueki argues that a man should show love and respect to the woman who is rightfully his wife, in Ueki's real life there was perfect compatibility between his nightly entertainment and love for his wife. Some researchers in women's history have criticized him for this lack of consistency between his words and deeds, but this criticism does not quite seem to be on target. Given the social environment in those days, where there were massive class differences, for Ueki women who belonged to the same class who could become his wife were in a completely different category to the women he would have mixed with on his visit to a brothel. So the logic here is that it was only natural that Ueki would take a different posture to these two different classes of women.
8 Chūbu Katei Keieigaku Kenkyūkai (The Chūbu Society of Home Economics) (ed.), 1972, Chapter 9, 'Joshi kyōiku (Girls' education),' pp. 373–432. This work consists of the following chapters: Introduction, Characteristics of and family life in Meiji era; Chapter 1, Family relations; Chapter 2, Household economy; Chapter 3, Clothing life; Chapter 4, Dietary life; Chapter 5, Dwelling life; Chapter 6, Health life; Chapter 7, Home culture; Chapter 8, Home education; Chapter 9, Girls' education; Chapter 10, Women's issues; and Chapter 11, Social welfare.
Although I owe much to this challenging work that advocates *kateigaku* (home studies), it differs from my view in several respects. Points I am dissatisfied with include: the authors have not freed themselves from the tendency to discuss 'household economy' in the context of national economy rather than as household economy per se in the literal sense of the word; the attractive concept of 'home culture' mainly covers material

culture only; the chapter on 'Health life' includes sections relating to sex, and mentions venereal disease and childbirth/childrearing, but no mention is made of new sexual information such as *zōkaki ron* (anatomical studies on genital organs); and, above all, there is no independent section on sex life in any of the eleven chapters.

9 An immortal book written in 1931 when Yanagita was fifty-six years old. A paperback edition is available from Kōdansha (1976).

10 Compared to Western wives, it is remarkable that Japanese wives had control over the household management, particularly household economy. In Western countries, it was the husband and not his wife who had control over the household management. Japanese wives' control over the household economy and their resulting higher position in the household seem to derive from the housewives' authority in farming households. See Ueno, Chizuko, 'The position of Japanese women reconsidered,' *Current Anthropology*, Vol. 28, No. 4, 1987.

11 The period from the end of the Meiji era to the Taishō era saw the successive emergence of new, unprecedented types of employment for female workers (e.g. typist, secretary, telephone operator, female clerk and journalist).

12 There still is a deeply rooted idea among middle- and upper-class women today that having an occupation is lowly and that working for money is contemptible. This is a result of the combination of (1) the tendency for women to marry into a better family than their own, and (2) samurai class values.

13 A voluminous work comprising a total of four volumes (Murakami, 1969–72).

14 For the double meanings of the labor welfare legislation, see Ueno, 1990a.

Chapter 5

1 This paper is based on the transcript for the author's lecture entitled 'Sekai no naka no nihon II-7: Josei ni miru kindai to datsu-kindai (Japan in the world II-7: Modernity and postmodernity seen in women)' and given at the International Research Center for Japanese Studies on March 17, 1989.

Chapter 6

1 Anthropologists often break through gender boundaries in the field as outsiders. Even in highly gender-segregated societies, male researchers are allowed to enter the 'women's domain' and female researchers can enter the 'men's domain' as 'honorary men.'

2 Umesao does not forget to point out that a housewife's rights are 'a surprisingly limited sovereignty' and the division of labor between husband and wife is 'a vertical division and not a horizontal division.'

3 The dispute over gender difference between minimalists and maximalists became a major battle line in feminism during the 1980s. If we had set aside the issue of essential gender difference and instead asked 'in what way gender difference manifests itself (in history),' we could have avoided this unproductive dispute (Sullerot and Thibault (eds.) 1983).

4 Women's studies researcher Yoshiko Kanai called them *katsudō sengyō shufu* (full-time activist housewives) instead of *kaji sengyō shufu* (full-time

housekeeping housewives). See Ueno and Dentsu Nettowāku Kenkyūkai (1988) about *joen* (women's grassroots networking activity).
5 See Ueno (1990a) for a discussion of women's unpaid labor.

Chapter 7

1 The folk vocabulary of Japan has *ietoji* and *ienushi* (both meaning 'the head of a house') and there are *hausfrau* and *housewife* in European languages.
2 Unfortunately, empirical studies of the history of domestic labor are few so far and are only slowly appearing in the English-speaking sphere under the influences of women's studies. There are some historical studies of the housewife (e.g. Matthews, 1987), in addition to the aforementioned study by Oakley. For a discussion on the politics of domestic labor, see Delphy (1984), Mallos (1980) and others.
3 Strasser cites an example of a laundry detergent advertisement (Tide) in 1980. It is the scene in which Mrs Claudia Fortson compares the whiteness of washed items and exclaims, 'I BEAT MY MOTHER-IN-LAW' (Strasser, 1982: 271). It suggests that technical innovation is having an impact on the power relations between the wife and the mother-in-law.
4 Interviews conducted in my study of the postwar history of underwear have confirmed that the average frequency of underwear change among the Japanese increased from 'two to three times a week' to 'once a day' in the 1960s and that this shift occurred across almost all age groups (Ueno, 1989a).
5 Tadao Umesao (1959), 'Tsuma muyō-ron (Superfluous wife theory),' *Fujin kōron* (Women's review), September edition. Reprinted in Ueno (ed.), 1982a: 203.
6 A survey has revealed that there are more non-employed housewives than employed housewives among the users of domestic labor services.
7 See Meguro (1987) for *individualization* and Kumon, Murakami and Satō (1979) for *individuation*.
8 These observations were made in a survey called *Kurieitibu mizu chōsa* (Creative Ms. survey) (unpublished) which I conducted jointly with Atelier F.
9 This refers to the situation in which 'land-sharks' attempted to force landowners to sell land in order to resell it at a huge profit.
10 See Ueno (1990a) for a discussion on the link between women's entry into the workplace and opportunity cost.

Chapter 8

1 The second wave of feminism, which started with the women's liberation movement in the 1970s, is widely misunderstood as an 'ideology to expand women's rights' that was upheld by 'women who wanted to be like men.' It was actually an 'ideology for liberation of women' and criticized modern industrialized society, which is based on the masculine principle and in which women refused to assimilate themselves because they 'do not want to be like men.'

Chapter 11

1 Individuals in adolescence are unsettled by conflicting identities when they are sometimes told that they are already adults and, at other times, that they are still children.

2 Usually, only the adult members who have completed initiation are put in the folk category that signifies '(hu)man.' Children are considered pre-human in folkloric vocabulary. In many cases, children who have died before reaching adulthood do not receive burial or are buried differently from adults.

3 There is a gap between retirement at age sixty and the commencement of the aged pension, so there is no security during this gap period.

4 The compulsory retirement age is linked to the commencement age of the pension in both the United States and Norway.

5 Because the lifetime employment system is linked to the seniority-based wage system, the age-limit retirement system has a function to define the upper limit of the seniority pay scale for Japanese companies. It is difficult for them to extend the retirement age even by one year because they have to raise the upper limit and pay higher wages to older employees accordingly. Some companies that are unable to protect the seniority-based system from the pressure of an aging workforce are gradually switching to the performance-based or skill-based systems, but the breakdown of seniority-based pay may threaten the very nature of Japanese corporations, which fosters a sense of belonging and loyalty. Companies are caught in a dilemma of being unable to give up the seniority-based pay system while being unable to raise the retirement age. Recently companies introduced a re-employment system with a renewed contract with employees reaching the retirement age so that they could be kept at low wages and at low positions as a device for virtual postponing of the retirement age.

6 Katata (1979) advocates cross-cultural studies of the aged, which he calls gerontologic anthropology.

7 Language use is a type of *politics*. In immigrant communities in the United States, younger generations speak perfect American English and children laugh at their parents for their poor command of English or for foreign accents.

8 Quoted from the *Onnatachi no uta* (Women's poems) concert held in November 1974.

9 Yoshiya Soeda (1981) proposes 'to call the discourse that views old age as both the subject and object of society the geriatric generation theory, as distinct from discourses on the old age issue and the old age security issue.' Here, I follow the distinction between 'old people' as the object and 'old age' as the subject as proposed by Hanamura.

Chapter 12

1 On the subject of the selective bonds formed by women, or the so-called female bonds, I conducted an interview survey of twenty-three groups and five key persons based on a preliminary study of 335 groups in the Kansai region in 1987 with the collaboration of Atelier F. and Dentsu Nettowāku Kenkyūkai. The survey result was published in Ueno and

Dentsu Nettowāku Kenkyūkai (1988). The revised new and additional version of *Joen ga yononaka wo kaeru* with supplementary chapters on 'twenty years after *joen*' was published in 2008 by Iwanami Shōten. This chapter is a revised version of my article previously published as 'Eraberu en, erabenai en (Selective tie, nonselective tie)' in Kurita, Yasuyuki (ed.) (1987), *Nihonjin no ningen kankei (Interpersonal relationships of the Japanese)*: Domesu Shuppan.

2   The 'space' in the third space is a social 'space' in which social communication is established, and does not necessarily mean a physical space. However, Isomura himself tended to give physicality to the concept of 'space' and applied it to spatial segmentation such as urban zoning. As a result, he ended up including the commercial center, such as a shopping area, and the central business district in the third space without differentiating them (Isomura, 1975). People such as Akira Fujitake (1973) and Hiroshi Zaino (1978) looked at communication in urban space from a functional perspective and moved on to the discourse on the 'amusement quarter.'

3   Mochizuki later replaced *chien* (associational bond) with *chien* (value bond), which enabled all the four bonds in the same pronunciation: *chien*.

> The most primitive community tie in the past was the 'blood bond'...it spread to local social units such as villages and hamlets. This is 'territorial bond' society...some refer to contemporary society as the age of 'associational bonds.' Associational means 'company' and 'corporate' here but, in defence of my 'chien theory,' I would like to call this 'chien (value bond)' society because people are associated based on the 'worth' or 'value' of each individual. However, this 'value bond society' may be approaching the end of its life. We are noticing some signs of a society of free people who do not wish to affiliate with companies or associations. My hypothesis is that we are going to see the birth of a society based on 'knowledge bonds' that is formed through 'recognized' information and extremely easy to form and dissolve (Mochizuki, 1985: 81–2).

4   Mochizuki's *knowledge bonds* or *value bonds* and Yasuyuki Kurita's *jō(hō) en* (informational bonds) are similar to my selective bonds. And Keiko Higuchi has coined the term *shien* (intentional bond). However, I do not use these terms because, first, *chien* is aurally indistinguishable from 'territorial bonds' and, second, both *chien* and *jōen* can be interpreted narrowly as representing 'knowledge, information or intention' and excluding others. I do not use *jōhōen*, either, because 'mediation by information' is not inherent to selective bonds for the reason discussed below.

5   I have previously discussed communication in the urban central space, particularly commercial activity, centered around the key concept set of 'tied' and 'untied' (Ueno, 1980).

6   Regarding 'niche creation' as a survival strategy in corporate workers' society, the 'corporate novelist', Taichi Sakaiya and the advisor to the Long-Term Credit Bank of Japan, HiroshiTakeuchi, have made similar proposals to Umesao's.

7   This is a comment made by a female community leader involved in a consumers' cooperative activity as part of the interview survey of Senri

residents conducted by the Urban Life Research Institute (director: Yukiko Shinozaki) on 26 August 1983.

8 The same source as Note 6.

9 *Mimizu no Gakkō* (School of Earthworms) was originally founded by Sachiko Takahashi as a territorial bond group for neighbors who used the same staircase in an apartment complex. It later became an 'alternative school' to let some fresh air into control-oriented school education and attracted like-minded people from a wider area (Takahashi, 1984). The starting point of her movement is the image of a pre-modern row-house community but, paradoxically, such *an sich* communities (communities-in-themselves) are not pre-existent in contemporary society and they have to be intentionally and selectively created. I called them *oban-yado* (housewives' abodes) in the same sense as *idobata kaigi* (backstairs gossip sessions) (Ueno, 1985a, 1985c).

10 This difference clearly shows up in the way crises are dealt with by the divorced single mother family and the divorced single father family. The single mother tends to develop a support network and receives support relatively easily, whereas the single father has no one to talk to, finds life hard to cope with, and gives up his children to a child welfare center or his own mother in the country, ending in separation of father and children in many cases (Kasuga, 1985).

11 Sociologically speaking, since the modern individual is a residual category of a person after all roles are stripped away, it must be logical to expect that the place of social relationships that allows the individual to exist is surplus to all 'tied' relationships based on standardized role expectation and role taking, or, in other words, a residual time-space called 'spare time.'

Bibliography

Akurosu (1987), FM Yokohama – Daiyon yamanote ni bairingaru bunka ga kaikasuru (FM Yokohama: A bilingual culture is flourishing in the fourth quarter uptown), *Akurosu* (Across) No. 160: Parco Shuppan.

Amano, Masako (1979), *Daisanki no josei* (Women in the third stage): Gakubunsha.

Amano, Masako (1988), '"Ju"dō kara "nō"dō eno jikken – Wākāzu korekutibu no jikken (From "passive" labor to "active" labor: A workers collective experiment), in Yoshiyuki Satō (ed.), *Joseitachi no seikatsu nettowāku* (Women's life networks): Bunshindō.

Amino, Yoshihiko (1978), *Muen, kugai, raku* (Untied, public, free zone): Heib-onsha.

Anderson, Michael (1980), *Approaches to the History of the Western Family 1500–1914*: Macmillan.

Anderson, Michael (1988), *Kazoku no kōzō, kinō, kanjō – Kazokushi kenkyū no shin tenkai* (The structure, function and emotion of the family: A new development in the study of the history of family), translated from Anderson (1980) by Masaaki Kitamoto: Kaimeisha.

Aoki, Yayoi (1983), 'Seisabetsu no konkyo wo saguru – Nihon ni okeru kindaika to jukyō ideorogī ni tsuite no oboegaki (Exploring the root of gender discrimination: A note on modernization and Confucian ideology in Japan)' in Tetsushi Yamamoto (ed.), *Keizai sekkusu to jendā* (Economic sex and gender), Shirīzu puragu wo nuku (Unplugging series) 1: Shinhyōron.

Aoki, Yayoi (ed.) (1983), *Feminizumu no uchū* (The universe of feminism), Shirīzu puragu wo nuku (Unplugging series) 3: Shinhyōron.

Aoki, Yayoi (1986), *Feminizumu to ekorojī* (Feminism and ecology): Shinhyōron.

Arai, Yasuo (1978), 'Rōjin no shinri (Psychology of the aged)', *Kōreika shakai to rōjin mondai* (Aging society and its problems), Jurisuto zōkan sōgo tokushū (Jurist special edition) 12: Yūhikaku.

Ariès, Philippe ([1960] 1973), *L'enfant et la Vie Familiale sous l'Ancien Régime*: Plon, Editions du Seuil.

Ariès, Philippe (1980), *'Kodomo' no tanjō – Anshan rejīmu-ki no kodomo to kazoku seikatsu* (The birth of 'child': Children and family life in the *ancien régime*) translated by from Ariès ([1960] 1973) Mitsunobu and Emiko Sugiyama: Misuzu Shobō.

Badinter, Elisabeth (1981), *Purasu rabu* (Plus love), translated by Shō Suzuki: Sanrio.

Beauvoir, Simone de (1953), *Daini no sei* (The second sex), translated by Ryōichi Ikushima: Shinchōsha.

Bebel, August (1958), *Bēberu fujin ron* (Bebel's theory of women) I & II, translated by Tsutomu Itō & Yasuo Tsuchiya: Ōtsuki Shoten.

Beechy, Veronika (1987), *Unequal Work*: Verso.

Benedict, Ruth (1946), *The Chrysanthemum and the Sword: The Patterns of Japanese Culture*: Houghton Mifflin, Co.

Benedict, Ruth (1967), *Kiku to katana* (The chrysanthemum and the sword), translated by from Benedict (1946) Matsuji Hasegawa: Shakai Shisōsha.

Bourdieu, Pierre (1979), *La Distinction: Critique social du judgement*: Editions de Minuit.

Bourdieu, Pierre (1990), *Distankusion* (Distinction) I & II, translated from Bordieu (1979) by Yōjirō Ishii: Fujiwara Shoten.

Chon, Young-hae (1988), 'Aru "chūgoku kikokusha" ni okeru kazoku – Tekiō katei ni shōjita kazoku no kattō (The family in the cases of "returnees from China": Family conflicts during their adaptation process)', *Kaihō shakaigaku kenkyū* (Journal for liberating sociology) 2: Akashi Shoten.

Chūbu Katei Keieigaku Kenkyūkai (Chūbu Society of Home Economics) (ed.) (1972), *Meijiki katei seikatsu no kenkyū* (A study of home life in the Meiji era): Domesu Shuppan.

Clark, M and B. G. Anderson (1967), *Culture and Aging: An Anthropological Study of Older Americans*: Charles C. Thomas.

Cowan, Ruth Schwartz (1983), *More Work for Mother: The Ironies of Household Technology from the Open Hearth to the Microwave*: Basic Books.

Cowgill, D. (1972), 'A theory of aging in cross-cultural perspective', in D. Cowgill & L. D. Holmes (ed.), *Aging and Modernization*: Meredith Co.

Cunningham, Hisako (1988), *Kaigai shijo kyōiku jijō* (Education of expatriate children): Shinchōsha.

Davidson, Caroline (1982), *A Woman's Work is Never Done: A History of Housework in the British Isles 1650–1950*: Chatto & Windus.

Delphy, Christine (1984), *Close to Home: A Materialist Analysis of Women's Oppression*: The University of Massachusetts Press.

Donzelot, Jacques (1991), *Kazoku ni kainyūsuru shakai – Kindai kazoku to kokka no ronri* (Public intervention in the family: The logic of the modern family and the state) translated from the French original entitled *La police des familles* by Akira Unami: Shinyōsha.

Duden, Barbara and Claudia von Werlhof (1986), *Kaji rōdō to shihonshugi* (Domestic labor and capitalism), translated and edited by Masato Maruyama: Iwanami Shoten.

Eagleton, Terry (1982), *The Rape of Clarissa*: Basil Blackwell.

Eagleton, Terry (1987), *Kurarissa no ryōjoku* (The rape of Clarissa), translated from Eagleton (1982) by Yōichi Ōhashi: Iwanami Shoten.

Ehara, Yumiko (1983), 'Midareta furiko – Ribu undō no kiseki (The erratic pendulum: Trajectory of the women's liberation movement)' in Ehara (1985).

Ehara, Yumiko (1985), *Josei kaihō toiu shisō* (The philosophy of women's liberation): Keisō Shobō.

Elder, Glen H. (1974), *Children of the Great Depression: Social Change in Life Experience*: The University of Chicago Press.

Elder, Glen H. (1986), *Daikyōkō no kodomotachi* (Children of the great depression), translated from Elder (1974) by Honda, Itō *et al.*: Akashi Shoten.

Emori, Itsuo (1992), 'Kafuchōsei no rekishiteki hatten keitai – Fuken wo chūshin tosuru ichi kōsatsu (The history of the development of patriarchy:

An inquiry centering on husband's rights)' in Nagahara *et al.* (eds.) (1992).

Engels, Friedrich (1965), *Kazoku, shiyū zaisan, kokka no kigen* (The origin of the family, private property and the state), translated by Shirō Tohara: Iwanami Shoten.

Erikson, E. H. (1963), *Identity: Youth and Crisis*: W. W. Norton & Co.

Erikson, E. H. (1973), *Aidentiti – Seinen to kiki* (Identity: Youth and crisis), translated from Erikson (1963) by Nobutada Iwase: Kanazawa Bunko.

Etō, Jun (1956), *Natsume Sōseki* (Sōseki Natsume): Tokyo Raifusha.

Etō, Jun (1972), *Yoru no kōcha* (Tea in the evening): Hokuyōsha.

Etō, Jun (1973), *Ichizoku saikai* (Family reunion): Kōdansha.

Etō, Jun (1993), *Seijuku to sōshitsu – 'Haha' no hōkai* (Maturity and loss: The disintegration of 'motherhood'): Kōdansha Bungei Bunko. Initially published in 1967 and 1988 by Kawade Shobō.

Etō, Jun and Shigehiko Hasumi ([1985] 1988), *Ōrudo fasshon – Futsū no kaiwa* (Old fashion: An ordinary conversation): Chūō Kōronsha.

Friedan, Betty (1963), *The Feminine Mystique*: Dell Publishing.

Friedan, Betty (1977), *Zōho Atarashii josei no sōzō* (The creation of new women, the enlarged edition), translated from Friedan (1963) by Fumiko Miura: Daiwa Shobō.

Fujieda, Mioko (1985), 'Ūmanribu (Women's liberation)', *Asahi jānaru* (Asahi Journal), 22 February issue. Also (1985) in *Onna no sengo-shi* (Women's postwar history) III: Asahi Shimbunsha.

Fujin Kyōiku Kenkyūkai (ed.) (1987, 1988, 1989), *Tōkei ni miru josei no genjō* (The present conditions of women according to statistics): Kakiuchi Shuppan.

Fujitake, Akira (1973), 'Toshi kūkan no komyunikēshon (Communication in the urban space)' in Susumu Kurasawa (ed.), *Toshi shakaigaku* (Urban sociology), Shakaigaku kōza (Sociology series) Vol. 5: Tokyo Daigaku Shuppankai.

Fukutake, Tadashi *et al.* (eds.) (1958), *Shakaigaku jiten* (The sociology dictionary): Yūhikaku.

Gavron, Hannah (1966), *The Captive Wife: Conflict of Housebound Mothers*: Routledge and Kegan Paul.

Gavron, Hannah (1970), *Tsuma wa torawareteiruka* (The captive wife), translated by Takako Onoe: Iwanami Shoten.

Gurūpu Waifu (1984), *Sei – Tsumatachi no messēji* (Sex: Messages from wives): Gurūpu Waifu.

Hacker, Helen (1951), 'Women as a minority group,' *Social Forces*, 30: 60-69

Hada, Aiko (1976), 'Shakaigaku to seibetsu yakuwari bungyō ron (Sociology and theory on gender role assignment)', *Fujin mondai konwakai kaihō 25: Tokushū, seibetsu yakuwari bungyō shisō wo megutte* (Discussion report on women's issues 25: About the idea of gender role assignment): Fujin Mondai Konwakai.

Hakuhōdō Seikatsu Sōgō Kenkyūjo (Hakuhōdō Institute of Life Style) (ed.) (1989), *90-nendai kazoku* (Families in the 1990s): Hakuhōdō.

Hanamura, Tarō (1980), '"Rōjuku" bunka e mukete (Toward an "old and mature" culture)', *Bessatsu takarajima 18 Gendai shisō no kīwādo*

(Treasure island special edition 18, keywords in contemporary philosophy): JICC Shuppankyoku.

Hara, Hiroko and Sumiko Iwao (1977), *Joseigaku kotohajime* (An introduction to women's studies): Kōdansha.

Hardyment, Christina (1988), *From Mangle to Microwave: The Mechanization of Household Work*: Polity Press.

Hasegawa, Kōichi (1989), 'Kenkyū nōto Kafuchōsei toha nanika (Research notes: What is patriarchy?)' in Yumiko Ehara (ed.), *Jendā no shakaigaku – Onnatachi/Otokotachi no sekai* (A sociology of gender: Women's world/ men's world): Shinyōsha.

Hasegawa, Michiko (1984), '"Danjo koyō byōdōhō" wa bunka no seitaikei wo hakai suru (A "gender equal employment law" will destroy our cultural ecosystem)', *Chūō Kōron* (Central Review), May issue: Chūō Kōronsha.

Hasegawa, Michiko (1986), *Karagokoro – Nihon seishin no gyakusetsu* (Chinese mind – A paradox of the Japanese spirit): Chūō Kōronsha.

Hayashi, Iku (1985), *Kateinai rikon* (In-house divorce): Chikuma Shobō.

Heiwa Keizai Keikaku Kaigi (1987), *Kokumin no keizai hakusho 1987* (The people's economic white paper 1987): Nihon Hyōronsha.

Hijiya-Kirschnereit, Irmela (1992), *Shishōsetsu – Jiko bakuro no gishiki* (Autobiographical novels: Rituals of self-revelation), translated by Ken'ichi Mishima: Heibonsha.

Hirano, Ken (1971), '"Hōyō kazoku" no atarashisa (The novelty of "Embracing Family")', *Kojima Nobuo zenshū daigokan geppō* (The complete works of Nobuo Kojima Vol. 5 monthly newsletter): Kōdansha.

Hobsbaum, E. and T. Ranger (eds.) (1983), *The Invention of Tradition*: Cambridge University Press.

Hobsbaum, E. and T. Ranger (1992), *Tsukurareta dentō* (The invention of tradition), translated from Hobsbaum and Ranger (1983) by Keiji Maekawa *et al.*: Kinokuniya Shoten.

Honda, Shūgo (1965), 'Bungei jihyō (jō) (Comments on current literature (I))', *Tokyo Shimbun*, 28 June evening edition.

Honda, Shūgo, K. Yamamoto and T. Fukunaga (1965), 'Sōsaku gappyō (A joint review of creative works)', *Gunzō*, August issue: Kōdansha.

Horiba, Kiyoko (1990), *Inaguyananabachi (Women have seven sins)*: Domesu Shuppan.

Hsu, F. L. K. (1963), *Clan, Caste, and Club*: Van Nostrand.

Hsu, F. L. K. (1971), *Hikaku bunmei shakai ron – Kuran, kasuto, kurabu, iemoto* (A comparative civilization and social study: Clan, caste, club, *iemoto*), translated from Hsu (1963) by Keiichi Sakuta & Eshun Hamaguchi: Baifūkan.

Illich, Ivan (1971), *Deschooling Society*: Marion Boyars Publishers.

Illich, Ivan (1976), *Limits to Medicine: Medical Nemesis; The Expropriation to Health*: Marion Boyars Publishers.

Illich, Ivan (1977), *Datsu gakkō no shakai* (Deschooling society), translated from Illich (1971) by Hiroshi Azuma & Shūzō Ozawa, Shakai kagaku sōsho (Social science series): Tokyo Sōgensha.

Illich, Ivan (1979), *Datsu byōin shakai – Iryō no genkai* (Dehospitalizing society: Limits to medicine), translated from Illich (1976) by Tsuguo Kaneko: Shōbunsha.

Illich, Ivan (1981), *Shadow Work*: Marion Boyars Publishers.

Illich, Ivan (1982a), *Gender*: Marion Boyars Publishers.

Illich, Ivan (1982b), *Shadō wāku – Seikatsu no arikata wo tou* (Shadow work: Questioning the way we live) translated from Illich (1981) by Yoshirō Tamanoi & Akira Kurihara, Iwanami gendai sensho (Iwanami contemporary selection) and (1990), Dōjidai raiburarī (Contemporary library): Iwanami Shoten.

Illich, Ivan (1984), *Jendā* (Gender), translated from Illich (1982) by Yoshirō Tamanoi, Iwanami gendai sensho (Iwanami contemporary selection): Iwanami Shoten.

Imai, Kenichi (1984), *Jōhō nettowāku shakai* (Information network society): Iwanami Shoten.

Imanishi, Kinji (1993) *Seibutsu shakai no ronri* (The logic of living beings), Imanishi Kinji zenshū (Complete works of Kinji Imanishi), Vol. 4: Kōdansha.

Inamura, Hiroshi (1980), *Nihonjin no kaigai futekiō* (Overseas maladaptation of the Japanese), NHK Books: Nihon Hōsō Bunka Kyōkai.

Inoue, Katsuya (1978), 'Pokkuri shinkō no haikei (The background of a sudden death wish)', *Kōreika shakai to rōjin mondai* (Aging society and its problems), Jurisuto zōkan sōgō tokushū (Jurist special edition) 12: Yūhikaku.

Inoue, Kiyoshi (1948), *Nihon josei-shi* (A history of Japanese women): San'ichi Shobō.

Inoue, Teruko and Yumiko Ehara (eds.) (1991), *Josei no dētabukku – Sei, karada kara seiji sanka made* (Women's data book: From sex and body to political participation): Yūhikaku.

Inoue, Tetsujirō (1891), *Chokugo engi* (The commentary on the Imperial Edict) I & II.

Inoue, Tetsujirō (1908), *Rinri to kyōiku* (Ethics and education): Kōdōkan.

Irigaray, Luce (1977), *Ce sexe qui n'en est pas un*: Editions de Minuit.

Irigaray, Luce (1987), *Hitotsu dewanai onna no sei* (Women's sex is not one), translated from Irigarray (1977) by Naoko Tanasawa *et al.*: Keisō Shobō.

Isomura, Eiichi *et al.* (eds.) (1975), *Ningen to toshi kankyō 1* (Human being and the urban environment 1): Kajima Shuppankai.

Itoi, Shigesato (1986), *Kazoku kaisan* (Family dissolution): Shinchōsha. Also (1989): Shinchō Bunko.

Itō, Kanji (1982), *Kazoku kokka-kan no jinruigaku* (An anthropology of the pseudo-family state ideology): Minerva Shobō.

Itō, Sei (1965), 'Sakka no shōmei (Proof of authorship)', *Chūō kōron* (Central review), November issue: Chūō Kōronsha.

Itō, Sei, S. Yasuoka, and J. Etō (1965), 'Bungaku no katei to genjitsu no katei (The family in literature and the family in reality)', *Gunzō*, October issue: Kōdansha.

Josei-shi Sōgō Kenkyūkai (The Research Society for Women's History) (ed.) (1990), *Nihon josei seikatsu-shi* (The social history of Japanese women), Vol. 4 'Kindai (Modern times)': Tokyo Daigaku Shuppankai.

Kamata, Hiroshi (1992), '"Kafuchōsei" no riron (The theory of patriarchy)' in Nagahara *et al.* (eds.) (1992).

Kamishima, Jirō (1961), *Kindai Nihon no seishin kōzō* (The mental structure of modern Japan): Iwanami Shoten.

Kaneko, Jirō and Hisatake Shinpuku (eds.) (1972), *Rōjin no seishin igaku to shinrigaku* (Geriatric psychiatry and psychology), Kōza Nihon no rōjin (The Japanese elderly series) 1: Kakiuchi Shuppan.

Kano, Masanao (1983), *Senzen 'ie' no shisō* (The prewar ideology of *ie*): Sōbunsha.

Kano, Masanao (1989), *Fujin, josei, onna* (Lady, female, woman): Iwanami Shoten.

Kanō, Mikiyo (1987), *Onnatachi no 'jūgo'* (Women behind the front line): Chikuma Shobō.

Kasahara, Yomishi (1977), *Seinenki* (Adolescence): Chūō Kōronsha.

Kasuga, Kisuyo (1985), 'Dansei ni okeru sōho nigenteki ryōsei kankei no mujun – Fushi katei no "koritsu" to "kodoku" (Contradictions in mutually complementary dual gender relationships in men: isolation and loneliness of single father families)', *Iwakuni tanki daigaku kiyō* (The journal of Iwakuni Junior College), No. 14: Iwakuni Tanki Daigaku.

Kasuga, Kisuyo (1989), *Fushi katei wo ikiru* (Life of a single father family): Keisō Shobō.

Katata, Jun (1979), 'Chūnen to rōnen (Middle age and old age)' in Tsuneo Ayabe (ed.), *Ningen no isshō – Bunka jinruigakuteki tankyū* (A human life: A cultural anthropological inquiry): Akademia Shuppankai.

Katō, Norihiro (1985), *Amerika no kage* (The shadow of America): Kawaide Shobō Shinsha.

Kawakami, Tetsutarō (1966), 'Bungakushō sakuhin sonota – Bungaku jihyō (Award winning works and others: Comments on current literature) (8)', *Shinchō* (New current), January issue: Shindrōsha.

Keizai Kikakuchō Kokumin Seikatsukyoku (Economic Planning Agency Social Policy Bureau) (ed.) (1987), *Atarashii josei no ikikata wo motomete* (In search of a new way of life for women): Ōkurashō Insastukyoku.

Kihara, Toshie (1979–1984), *Mari to Shingo* (Mari and Shingo) 1–13: Hakusensha.

Kinoshita, Ritsuko (1983), *Ōkoku no tsumatachi – Kigyō jōkamachi nite* (Wives of the corporate kingdom: In a company town): Komichi Shobō.

Kojima, Nobuo (1965), *Hōyō kazoku* (Embracing family): Kōdansha.

Kojita, Yasunao (1993), 'Shohyō joseishi sōgō kenkyūkai hen "Nihon josei seikatsu-shi" daiyonkan "kindai" (A book review: Joseishi Sōgō Kenkyūkai (ed.) "The social history of Japanese women" Vol. 4 "Modern times")', *Nihonshi kenkyū* (A study of Japanese history), 336.

Kokusai Josei Gakkai (International Society for Women's Studies) (ed.) (1978), *Kokusai Josei Gakkai 1978 Tokyo kaigi hōkokusho* (Report on the 1978 International Society for Women's Studies Conference in Tokyo).

Komashaku, Kimi (1982), *Majoteki bungakuron* (A witch-like theory of literature): Sanichi Shobō.

Komatsu, Makiko (1987), *Josei keieisha no jidai* (The age of female entrepreneurs): Minerva Shobō.

Koyama, Shizuko (1991), *Ryōsai kenbo toiu kihan* (The norms of a good wife and wise mother): Keisō Shobō.

Kumon, Shunpei, Y. Murakami and S. Satō (1979), *Bunmei to shite no ie shakai* (The *ie* society as a civilization): Chūō Kōronsha.

Kuroki, Masako (1986), 'Nichibei no bunka hikaku kara miru nikkeiamerikajin no sei yakuwari (Gender roles of Japanese-Americans based on a cultural comparison between Japan and the U. S.)' in *Joseigaku Nenpō* (Women's studies annual report), No. 7: Nihon Joseigaku Kenkyūkai

Kurosawa, Takashi (1987), *Kenchikuka no kyūjitsu – Mono no mukō ni hito ga mieru* (An architect's holiday: Seeing people behind objects): Maruzen.

Laslett, Peter and Richard Wall (eds.) (1972), *Household and Family in Past Times*: Cambridge University Press.

Le Play, F. (1855), *Les Ouvriers Européens*.

Leacock, E. (1981), *Myths of Male Dominance: Collected Articles*: Monthly Review Press.

Lewis, Oscar (1986), *Sanchesu no kodomotachi* (The children of Sanchez), translated by Toshihiko Shibata & Akio Namekata: Misuzu Shobō.

Lévi-Strauss, Claude (1958), *Anthropologie Structurale*: Librairie Plon.

Lévi-Strauss, Claude ([1947] 1968), *Les Structures Élémentaires de la Parenté*: Mouton.

Lévi-Strauss, Claude (1972), *Kōzō jinruigaku* (Structural anthropology), translated from Lévi-Strauss (1958) by Ikuo Arakawa & Keizō Ikimatsu: Misuzu Shobō.

Lévi-Strauss, Claude (1977–1978), *Shinzoku no kihon kōzō* (The elemental structures of kinship) I & II, translated from Lévi-Strauss ([1947] 1968) by Tōichi Mabuchi & Setsuo Tajima: Banchō Shobō.

Malos, Ellen (ed.) (1980), *The Politics of Housework*: Allison & Busky.

Matthews, Glenna (1987), Just a Housewife: The Rise and Fall of Domesticity in America: Oxford University Press.

Meguro, Yoriko (1980), *Shufu burūsu* (Housewife blues): Chikuma Shobō.

Meguro, Yoriko (1987), *Kojinkasuru kazoku* (Individualization of the family): Keisō Shobō.

Millett, Kate (1970), *Sexual Politics*: Doubleday. Also (1977): Virago.

Millet, Kate (1977), *Sei no seijigaku* (Sexual politics), translated from Millett (1970) by Mioko Fujieda *et al.*: Jiyū Kokuminsha. Also (1985): Domesu Shuppan.

Minoura, Yasuko (1984), *Kodomo no ibunka taiken* (Cross-cultural experi-ences of children): Shisakusha.

Mita, Munesuke (ed.) (1988), *Shakaigaku jiten* (The encyclopedia of sociology): Kōbundō.

Mitchell, Juliet (1975), *Psychoanalysis and Feminism*: Kern Associates.

Mitchell, Juliet (1977), *Seishin bunseki to onna no kaihō* (Psychoanalysis and women's liberation), translated from Mitchell (1975) by Hiroshi Ueda: Gōdō Shuppan.

Mitterauer, Michael and Reinhard Sieder (1977), *Vom Patriarchat zur Partnerschaft: zum Structurwandel der Familie*: C. H. Beckschen Verlag.

Miterauer, Michael and Reinhard Sieder (1993), *Yōroppa kazoku shakai-shi – Kafuchōsei kara pātonā kankei e* (A social history of the European family: From patriarchy to partnership), translated from Mitterauer and Sieder (1977) by Yūji Wakao & Noriko Wakao: Nagoya Daigaku Shuppankai.

Mizuta, Tamae (1973), *Josei kaihō shisō no ayumi* (Tracing the philosophies of women's liberation): Iwanami Shoten.

Mochizuki, Teruhiko (1977), *Machinorojī – Machi no bunkagaku* (*Machi-nology*: The study of town culture): Sōseiki.

Mochizuki, Teruhiko (1978), *Toshi wa mikai dearu* (Cities are uncivilized): Sōseiki.

Mochizuki, Teruhiko (1985), *Chiiki sōzō to sangyo bunka seisaku* (Local community creation and industrial and cultural policies): Gyōsei.

MORE Henshūbu (ed.) (1983), *Moa ripōto* (The MORE report): Shūeisha.

Mori, Ayako (Group Nogiku) (1987), 'Onna to haka Yureru ie ishiki (Women and the grave: Uncertainty about a sense of *ie*)', *Joseigaku nenpō* (Women's studies annual report) 8: Nihon Joseigaku Kenkyūkai.

Morioka, Kiyomi *et al.* (eds.) (1993), *Shin shakaigaku jiten* (New dictionary of sociology): Yūhikaku.

Murakami, Junichi (1985), *Doitsu shiminhō-shi* (A history of German civil law): Tokyo Daigaku Shuppankai.

Murakami, Nobuhiko (1969–1972), *Meiji josei-shi* (A history of women in the Meiji era), Vols. 1–4: Rironsha.

Murakami, Nobuhiko (1980), *Kindai-shi no onna* (Women in modern history): Daiwa Shobō.

Murakami, Ryū (1976), *Kagirinaku tōmei ni chikai burū* (Almost transparent blue): Kōdansha.

Muta, Kazue (1990a), 'Nihon kindaika to kazoku – Meijiki "kazoku kokka kan" saikō (Modernization of Japan and the family: Reconsidering the Meiji-era "view of the family and the state")' in Kiyotada Tsutsui (ed.), *'Kindai Nihon' no rekishi shakaigaku* (Historical sociology of 'modern Japan'): Bokutakusha.

Muta, Kazue (1990b), 'Meijiki sōgō zasshi ni miru katei zou – "Katei" no tōjō to sono paradokkusu (The image of the family in intellectual magazines of the Meiji era: The emergence of "home" and its paradox)', *Shakaigaku hyōron* (Japanese sociological review), Vol. 41, No. 1: Nihon Shakai Gakkai.

Mutō, Hiroko (1985), *Tsumatachi no kaigai chūzai* (Overseas posting from the wife's point of view): Bungei Shunjūsha.

Nagahara, Keiji *et al.* and Hikaku Kazoku-shi Gakkai (eds.) (1992), *Ie to kafuchōsei* (*Ie* and patriarchy): Waseda University Press.

Nakane, Chie (1967), *Tate shakai no ningen kankei* (Personal relations in a vertical society): Kōdansha.

Nakane, Chie (1972), *Tekiō no jōken* (Conditions for cultural adaptation): Kōdansha.

Nakatsu, Ryōko (1976), *Ibunka no hazama de* (Between different cultures): Mainichi Shimbunsha.

Nishibe, Susumu (1975), *Soshio ekonomikkusu* (Socioeconomics): Chūō Kōronsha.

Nishibe, Susumu (1979), *Shinkirō no naka e* (Into a mirage): Nihon Hyōronsha.

Nishikawa, Yūko (1985), 'Hitotsu no keifu – Hiratsuka Raichō, Takamure Itsue, Ishimuta Reiko (A genealogy of feminists – Raichō Hiratsuka, Itsue Takamure, Reiko Ishimuta)' in Haruko Wakita (ed.), *Bosei wo tou – Rekishiteki hensen* (The question of motherhood: Historical changes) (II): Jinbun Shoin.

Nishikawa, Yūko (1991), 'Kindai kokka to kazoku moderu (The modern state and the family model)' in Rin'itsu Kawakami (ed.), *Yusutitia 2, tokushū 'kazoku, shakai, kokka* (Justitia 2: 'family, society, state'): Minerva Shobō.

Nishikawa, Yūko (1993), 'Hikaku-shi no kanōsei to mondaiten (Possibilities and problems of comparative history)', *Joseishigaku* (The annals of women's history) 3: Josei-shi Sōgō Kenkyūkai.

Nishikawa, Yūko (2000), *Kindai kokka to kazoku model* (The modern state and the family model): Yoshikawa Kōbunkan.

Noma, Kōshin (ed.) (1961), *Kanpon shikidō ōkagami* (The great mirror of the erotic way): Yūzan Bunko.

Oakley, Anne (1974), *Woman's Work: The Housewife Past and Present*: Vintage Books.

Oakley, Anne (1986), *Shufu no tanjō* (The birth of the housewife), translated from Oakley (1974) by Meika Okajima: Sanseidō.

Ochiai, Emiko (1987), '"Kindai" to feminizumu – Rekishi shakaigaku-teki kōsatsu ("Modernity" and feminism: A historical and sociological discussion), *Joseigaku nenpō* (Women's studies annual report): Nihon Joseigaku Kenkyūkai. Also in Ochiai (1989).

Ochiai, Emiko (1989), *Kindai kazoku to feminizumu* (Modern family and feminism): Keisō Shobō.

Ōgi, Shinzō, Kumakura, I. and Ueno, C. (annotation) (1990), *Fūzoku Sei* (Customs and manners: Sex), Nihon kindai shisō taikei (An anthology of Japanese modern philosophies) 23: Iwanami Shoten.

Ōhira, Ken (1990), *Yutakasa no seishin byōri* (Psychopathology of affluence): Iwanami Shoten.

Ōkonogi, Keigo (1978), *Moratoriamu ningen no jidai* (The age of the moratorium man): Chūō Kōronsha.

Reichard, Suzanne, Florine Livson and Paul G. Petersen (1980), *Aging and Personality: A Study of Eighty-Seven Older Men*: Ayer Publishing.

Richardson, Samuel (1741), *Pamela, or, Virtue Rewarded*: Basil Blackwell.

Ryūkyū Shimpōsha (ed.) (1980), *Tōtōmē kō – Onna ga tsuide naze warui* (A discussion about the ancestral memorial tablet: Why are women not allowed to inherit it?): Ryūkyū Shimbunsha.

Rōdōshō Fujin Kyoku (Ministry of Labor Women's Bureau) (ed.) (1989), *Fujin rōdō no jitsujō heisei gannenban* (The present conditions of women's labor, the 1989 edition): Ōkurasho Insatsukyoku.

Saitō, Shigeo (1982), *Tsumatachi no shishūki* (Housewives' midlife autumnal period): Kyōdō Tsūshinsha. Re-published (1993) in *Saitō Shigeo ruporutāju Nihon no jōkei 1 tsumatachi no shishunki* (Shigeo Saitō reportage on Japanese emotional landscapes 1: Housewives' midlife autumnal period): Iwanami Shoten.

Saitō, Shigeo (1984a), 'Jidai no jōkyō wo misueru (Staring at the current of the times)', *Shimbun kenkyū* (Press studies), October issue.

Saitō, Shigeo (1984b), 'Kigyō shakai toiu shuyaku no kao (The face of the leading actor called corporate society)', *Shimbun kenkyū* (Press studies), October issue.

Saitō, Shigeo (1991), *Hōshoku kyūmin* (The needy people who have too much): Kyōdō Tsūshinsha.

Satō, Tadao (1978), *Katei no yomigaeri no tameni: Hōmu dorama ron* (For the re-birth of the home: Theorizing soap operas): Chikuma Shobō.

Sakuta, Keiichi ([1967] 1981), *Haji no bunka saikō* (Reconsidering shame culture): Chikuma Shobō.

Schwartz, Pepper and Philip Blumstein (1985a), *American Couples*: Pocket Books.

Schwartz, Pepper and Phillip Blumstein (1985b), *Amerikan kappuruzu*

(American couples) I & II, translated from Schwartz and Blumstein (1985a) by Minami Hiroshi *et al*.: Hakusuisha.

Sechiyama, Kaku (1990), 'Kafuchōsei wo megutte (About patriarchy)' in Yumiko Ehara (ed.), *Feminisumu ronsō* (The feminism controversy): Keisō Shobō.

Segal, L. (1987), *Is the Future Female? Troubled Thoughts on Contemporary Feminism*: Harper & Row.

Segal, L. (1989), *Mirai wa onna no monoka* (Is the future female?), translated from Segal (1987) by Motoko Oda: Keisō Shobō.

Seiyama, Kazuo (1993), '"Kaku kazoku-ka" no nihonteki imi (Japanese meaning of the "trend toward the nuclear family")' in Atsushi Naoi *et al*. (eds.), *Nihon shakai no shin chōryū* (New currents in Japanese society): Tokyo Daigaku Shuppankai.

Sekine, Eiji (1993), *'Tasha' no shōkyo* (Elimination of 'others'): Keisō Shobō.

Shiroyama, Saburō (1976), *Mainichi ga nichiyōbi* (Everyday is a Sunday): Shinchōsha.

Shorter, Edward (1975), *The Making of the Modern Family*: Basic Books.

Shorter, Edward (1987), *Kindai kazoku no keisei* (The making of the modern family), translated from Shorter (1975) by Toshihiro Tanaka: Shōwadō.

Shōno, Junzō (1965), *Yūbe no kumo* (Evening clouds): Kōdansha.

Soeda, Yoshiya (1981), 'Rōnen shakaigaku no kadai to hōhō (The issues and approaches of geronto-sociology)' in Soeda (ed.), *Kōza rōnen shakaigaku I rōnen sedai ron* (Lectures in geronto-sociology I: Geriatric generation theory): Kakiuchi Shuppan.

Sokoloff, Natalie (1980), Between Money and Love: The Dialectics of Women's Home and Market Work: Praeger Publishers.

Sokoloff, Natalie (1987), *Okane to aijō no aida* (Between money and love), translated from Sokoloff (1980) by Yumiko Ehara: Keisō Shobō.

Sōrifu (The Prime Minister's Office) (ed.) (1983), *Fujin no genjō to shisaku – Kokunai kōdō keikaku daisankai hōkokusho* (The present condition and policy implementation for women: The third report on the domestic action plan): Gyōsei.

Stendhal, (2002), *The Red and the Black*, translated by Roger Gard: Penguin.

Stone, Lawrence (1977), *The Family, Sex, and Marriage in England, 1500– 1800*: Penguin Books. Also (1979), Abridged and Revised Edition: Pelican Books.

Stone, Lawrence (1991), *Kazoku, sei, kekkon no shakai-shi – 1500–1800 no Igirisu* (A social history of the family, sex and marriage in England, 1500– 1800), translated from Stone (1977) by Masaaki Kitamoto: Keisō Shobō.

Strasser, Susan (1982), *Never Done: A History of American Housework*: Pantheon Books.

Sullerot, Evelyne and Odette Thibault (eds.) (1983), *Josei towa nanika* (What is the woman?) I & II, translated by Yuko Nishikawa *et al*.: Jinbun Shoin.

Sumiya, Kazuhiko (1992), 'Owarini – "Kafuchōsei" ron no tenbō (In closing: A review of the theory on "patriarchy") ' in Nagahara *et al*. (eds.), *op cit*.

Suzuki, Takao (1973), *Kotoba to bunka* (Language and culture): Iwanami Shoten.

Suzuki, Yūko (1986), *Feminizumu to sensō* (Feminism and war): Marujusha.

Takahashi, Sachiko (1984), *Mimizu no gakkō* (School of earthworms): Shisō no Kagakusha.

Takamure, Itsue (1954–1958), *Josei no rekishi* (A history of women), Takamure Itsue zenshū (The complete works of Itsue Takamure) Vols 4 & 5: Rironsha.

Takatori, Masao and Mineo Hashimoto (1968), *Shūkyō izen* (Before religion): Nihon Hōsō Shuppan Kyōkai.

Takemiya, Keiko (1977–1984), *Kaze to ki no uta* (The poem of the wind and the trees) 1–17: Shōgakukan.

Tanaka, Hiko (1990), *Ohikkoshi* (House-moving): Fukutake Shoten.

Tanaka, Hiko (1992), *Karendā* (Calendar): Fukutake Shoten.

Tanaka, Yasuo (1981), *Nantonaku kurisutaru* (Somewhat crystal): Kawaide Shobō.

Taniguchi, Etsuko (1985), *Madamu shōsha* (Trading company wives): Gakuseisha.

Tomioka, Taeko (1983), *Namiutsu tochi* (The undulating land): Kōdansha.

Tonozaki, Mitsuhiro (ed.) (1971), *Ueki Emori katei kaikaku, fujin kaihō ron* (Emori Ueki: Family reform and women's liberation): Hōsei University Press.

Toyonaka-shi Josei Mondai Suishin Honbu (Toyonaka City Division for Promotion of Women's Interest) (ed.) (1989), *Shimin no kurashi no ishiki ni kansuru chōsa hōkokusho – Dansei no nichijō seikatsu to jiritsu wo megutte* (Survey report on the citizens' attitude toward life: About men's daily living and independence).

Tsubouchi, Reiko (1992), *Nihon no kazoku "ie" no renzoku to furenzoku* (The Japanese family: Continuity and discontinuity of the ie): Akademia Shppan.

Tsumugi, Taku (1986–87), *Hotto rōdo* (Hot road) 1–4: Shūeisha.

Turner, Victor W. (1974), *The Ritual Process: Structure and Anti-structure*: Penguin.

Tuttle, Lisa (1986), Encyclopedia of Feminism: Longman.

Tuttle, Lisa (1991), *Feminizumu jiten* (The encyclopedia of feminism), translated from Tuttle (1986) by Kazuko Watanabe *et al.*: Akashi Shoten.

Ueno, Chizuko (1980), 'Hyakkaten no kigōgaku (Semiotics of the department store)', *Kōkoku* (Advertizing), Nov–Dec issue: Hakuhōdō.

Ueno, Chizuko (1982a), 'Shufu no sengōshi (The post-war history of housewives)' in Chizuko Ueno (ed.) (1982) I.

Ueno, Chizuko (1982b), 'Shufu ronsō wo kaisetsusuru (The commentary on the housewife debate)' in Chizuko Ueno (ed.) (1982) II.

Ueno, Chizuko (ed.) (1982), *Shufu ronsō wo yomu, zen kiroku* (A review of the housewife debate: A complete record) I & II: Keisō Shobō.

Ueno, Chizuko (1984), 'Matsuri to kyōdōtai (Festival and community)' in Shun Inoue (ed.), *Chiiki bunka no shakaigaku* (A sociology of local culture): Sekai Shisōsha.

Ueno, Chizuko (1985a), 'Oban-yado (housewives' abodes),' Kyōdō tōgi, shin sesō tanken, daiikkai 'onna kodomo bunka' (A discussion: An exploration of new social trends, No. 1 'women's and children's culture'), *Asahi Shimbun*, Osaka evening edition, 15 June.

Ueno, Chizuko (1985b), 'Onna wa sekai wo sukueru ka – Iriichi "jendā" ron tettei hihan (Can women save the world?: A thorough criticism of Illich's theory on 'gender') in Ueno (1986).

Ueno, Chizuko (1985c), *"Watashi" sagashi gēmu – Yokubō shimin shakai ron* (A game of self-discovery: Theorizing a society of private citizens driven by consumer desire): Chikuma Shobō.

Ueno, Chizuko (1985d), *Shihonsei to kajirōdō* (Capitalism and domestic labor): Kaimeisha.

Ueno, Chizuko (1986), *Onna wa sekai wo sukueruka* (Can women save the world?): Keisōshobō.

Ueno, Chizuko (1989a), *Sukāto no shita no gekijō* (A theater beneath the skirt): Kawade Shobō Shinsho.

Ueno, Chizuko (1989b), *Jendāresu wārudo no ai no jikken* (An experimental love in the genderless world), Kikan toshi (City quarterly), No. 2: Toshi Mondai Kenkyūjo.

Ueno, Chizuko (1989c), 'Nihon no onna no nijūnen (Twenty years of Japanese women)', *Joseigaku nenpō* (Women's studies annual report), No. 10: Nihon Joseigaku Kenkyūkai.

Ueno, Chizuko (1989d), 'Oyabanare shinai musumetachi ga tasseisuru "danjo byōdō" ("Gender equality" achieved by daughters who are still dependent on their parents)', *Chūō kōron* (Central review), May issue: Chūō Kōronsha.

Ueno, Chizuko (1990a), *Kafuchōsei to shihonsei* (Patriarchy and capitalism): Iwanami Shoten.

Ueno, Chizuko (1990b), 'Ren-ai no shakaishi (A social history of romantic love)' in Chizuko Ueno (ed.), *Nyū feminizumu revyū 1: Ren-ai tekunorojī* (New feminism review 1: Technology of love): Gakuyō Shobō.

Ueno, Chizuko (2008), *Joen woikita onna taski* (Women who have lived female bonds): Iwanami Shoten.

Ueno, Chizuko and Dentsū Nettowāku Kenkyūkai (1988), *'Joen' ga yono-naka wo kaeru* ('Women's bonds' can change the world): Nihon Keizai Shimbunsha.

Umesao, Tadao (1981), *Watashi no ikigai-ron – Jinsei ni mokuteki ga aruka* (My view on the meaning of life: Is there a purpose of life?): Kōdansha.

Umesao, Tadao (1991), *Umesao Tadao chosakushū* (The collected works of Tadao Umesao), Vol. 9: Chūō Kōronsha.

Weber, Max (1921–1922), *Wirkungen des Patriarchalismus und Feudalismus, in Wirtschaft und Gesellschaft.*

Weber, Max (1957), *Kasansei to hōkensei* (Patrimonialism and feudalism), translated from Weber (1921–22) by Akira Hamashima: Misuzu Shobō.

Werlhof, C. von. (1983), *Die Frauen und die Peripherie: Der Blinder Fleck in der Kritik der politischen Ökonomie: Arbeitspapiere Nr. 28*: Universität Bielefeld.

Yamada, Taichi (1977), *Kishibe no arubamu* (Album on the shore): Tokyo Shimbun Shuppankyoku.

Yamashita, Etsuko (1988a), *Takamure Itsue ron* (A study on Itsue Takamure): Kawade Shobō Shinsha.

Yamashita, Etsuko (1988b), *Nihon josei kaihō shisō no kigen* (The origin of Japanese women's liberation philosophy): Kaimeisha.

Yamazaki, Kōichi (1993), *Danjoron* (On men and women): Kinokuniya Shoten.

Yamazaki, Masakazu (1972), *Ōgai Tatakau kachō* (Ōgai: A fighting patriarch): Kawaide Shobō Shinsha.

Yamazaki, Masakazu (1984), *Yawarakai kojinshugi no tanjō* (The birth of soft individualism): Chūō Kōronsha.

Yanagida, Kunio (1931), *Meiji taishō-shi sesō hen (Meiji taishō-shi daiyonkan)* (The social history of the Meiji–Taishō era: The history of the Meiji-Taishō era, Vol. 4): Asahi Shimbunsha. Also (1976), *Meiji taishō-shi sesō hen I & II*: Kōdansha.

Yasuoka, Shōtarō (1959), *Umibe no kōkei* (A view by the sea): Kōdansha.

Yoshihiro, Kiyoko (1989), *Sukuranburu kazoku* (Scrambled families): Sanseidō.

Yoshimoto, Banana (1988), *Kicchin* (Kitchen): Fukutake Shoten.

Yoshino, Sakumi (1988–1989), *Jurietto no tamago* (Juliet's egg), 1–5: Shūeisha.

Yoshitake, Teruko (1982), 'Ketsuen kara chien, joen e (From blood bonds to territorial bonds, female bonds) in Yōko Satō *et al.*, *Tomobataraki, rikon, tomodachi* (Working couples, divorce, friends): Kyōiku Shiryō Shuppankai.

Yoshiyuki, Junnosuke (1966), *Hoshi to tsuki to wa ten no ana* (Stars and the moon are holes in the heavens): Kōdansha.

Yōda, Hiroe (1986), 'Tomadoi to kōgi – Shōgaiji juyō katei ni miru oyatachi (Bewilderment and protest: Parents in the process of acceptance of disabled children)', *Kaihō shakaigaku kenkyū* (Review for liberating sociology) 1.

Yuzawa, Yasuhiko (1987), *Zusetsu gendai Nihon no kazoku mondai* (Illustrated data of the family problems of modern Japan), NHK Books: Nihon Hōsō Kyōkai.

Zaino, Hiroshi (1978), *Kaiwai – Nihon no toshi kūkan* (The busy quarter: Japan's urban space): Kajima Shuppankai.

Index